RED ALERT!

D1569432

Studies in the
Postmodern Theory of Education

Joe L. Kincheloe and Shirley R. Steinberg
General Editors

Vol. 87

PETER LANG
New York • Washington, D.C./Baltimore • Boston • Bern
Frankfurt am Main • Berlin • Brussels • Vienna • Canterbury

Stuart J. Foster

RED ALERT!

Educators Confront the Red Scare in American Public Schools, 1947–1954

With a Foreword by
O. L. Davis, Jr.

PETER LANG
New York • Washington, D.C./Baltimore • Boston • Bern
Frankfurt am Main • Berlin • Brussels • Vienna • Canterbury

Library of Congress Cataloging-in-Publication Data

Foster, Stuart J.
Red alert!: educators confront the Red Scare
in American public schools, 1947–1954 / Stuart J. Foster;
with a foreword by O. L. Davis, Jr.
p. cm. — (Counterpoints; vol. 87)
Includes bibliographical references (p.   ).
1. Academic freedom—United States—History—1945–1953. 2. National
Education Association of the United States—History—1945–1953. 3. Anti-
communist movements—United States—History—1945–1953. 4. Education and
state—United States—History—1945–1953. 5. Public schools—United States—
History—1945–1953. I. Title. II. Series: Counterpoints (New York, N.Y.); vol. 87.
LC72.2.F67   371.1'04—dc21   98-009782
ISBN 0-8204-4050-7
ISSN 1058-1634

Die Deutsche Bibliothek-CIP-Einheitsaufnahme

Foster, Stuart J.:
Red alert!: educators confront the red scare
in American public schools, 1947–1954 / Stuart J. Foster;
with a foreword by O. L. Davis, Jr.
–New York; Washington, D.C./Baltimore; Boston; Bern;
Frankfurt am Main; Berlin; Brussels; Vienna; Canterbury: Lang.
(Counterpoints; Vol. 87)
ISBN 0-8204-4050-7

Cover design by Lisa Dillon

The paper in this book meets the guidelines for permanence and durability
of the Committee on Production Guidelines for Book Longevity
of the Council of Library Resources.

Printed in the United States of America

To my three beautiful "girls"
Jackie, Natalie, and Francesca

Acknowledgments

The journey to complete this book began while I was in graduate school at the University of Texas at Austin. In support of my endeavors Dr. O . L. Davis, Jr. (Professor, Curriculum and Instruction) and Dr. Don E. Carleton (Director, Center for American History) were especially influential. The decision to focus on the intriguing years of the "red scare" era largely was inspired by Dr. Carleton. His willingness to share with me his extensive knowledge of this compelling historical period and his cheerful and sagacious advice proved invaluable to this work. Without question, however, the personal encouragement and professional support of Professor O. L. Davis, Jr. proved most vital to this book. From beginning to end O. L. offered me thoughtful guidance, astute commentary, and the benefit of his vast knowledge. I am truly privileged to know him and to consider him a mentor and a friend.

Other individuals also assisted me on my journey. In particular I owe a debt of gratitude to colleagues in the Department of Social Science Education at the University of Georgia, to Sylvia Hutchinson (former Associate Dean), and to Professor Roy A. Lowe (Head of the Education Department at the University of Wales, Swansea). Special thanks are also due to Kristi Leonard (Instructional Services Coordinator). Her ability to prepare the text and the index for publication helped to preserve my sanity at a time when I thought the book would never be completed! My initial archival research both in Virginia and at the National Education Association Headquarters in Washington D.C. also was greatly assisted by the friendliness of Olivia Aguilar-Gattis, the helpful support of the NEA, and the generosity of Bob and Cindi Jenkins who made me welcome at their home during my stay in the nation's capital.

Finally, I wish to express my deep and love and appreciation to the Foster family in England (Maureen, Geoff, and Barry) and to the Foster family in the United States (Jackie, Natalie, and Francesca) for their unceasing love and encouragement. In particular I owe a boundless debt of gratitude to my wife Jackie who has always offered me, and our two girls, deep understanding, good humor, and unconditional love.

Table of Contents

Foreword

Communism never disappeared from American awareness during the interwar period of the 1920s and 1930s. On the best of days, most people knew it as perhaps present but out of sight. The Communism of those years loomed as a monstrous specter from the new Soviet Union. Most Americans still knew the USSR as Russia and it was much more distant from them than the continents and oceans between Russia and the United States. In the late 1930s, as the world's nations slipped uneasily into global war, many Americans found Russia and its communist society easy to disparage or even to hate when it attacked tiny Finland, the only European country to repay its WWI debts to the United States. Later during World War II, increased numbers of Americans only reluctantly supported the USSR as ally, legitimated in large part as a self-serving necessity. That luxury, for both Americans and Soviets, evaporated quickly after the defeat of Hitler's legions. What the world came to know as the Cold War surely began long before Winston Churchill's eloquent Iron Curtain speech at Fulton, Missouri. Likewise, the internal red scare that was the Cold War's American civil counterpart erupted after years of dormancy.

In post-war America, certainly in Texas where I lived, the red scare assumed several guises. It alternated between virulence and silence. On the other hand, this zealous anti-communism was always present, its threats every bit as intimidating as were the actions of its supporters. Unlike a number of American teachers and school administrators, I did not lose my job due to red scare tactics. Nevertheless, I know that the atmosphere created by these groups affected adversely all of us educators and our work.

I first met the red scare in college and later during my first year of teaching. At first, I admit that many of my friends and I did not take very seriously the first red scare tactics that came along. For example, we college students opposed the loyalty oaths that the Texas legislature imposed upon all teachers in public schools and colleges and upon all students at public colleges and universities. One of my ex-GI classmates expressed his contempt of the law by signing, across several semesters, names like "Joseph Stalin" and "Vladimir Lenin" on the copy of his oath, each of which a local official in the busy registration line duly notarized. Most of my friends and I just signed "the oath" that we opposed; it was a simple nuisance. Even in that act, we joined with the vigilantes to diminish faith in and respect for both democracy and the law. These oaths never uncovered communists or "com-symps." In those heady post-war years, some good number of us loyal Americans actively debated the legitimacy of the revolutionaries' rhetoric and programs in China and French Indo-China. On occasion, we acted. For example, when J. Strom Thurmond visited Denton in the presidential campaign of 1948, two friends and I picketed his appearance. We were concerned about our future.

In 1950, I accepted a teaching post in the far west Texas ranching town of Ozona. That school year, I encountered the red scare again, this time in San Angelo, the nearest big town, 90 miles and one bend in the highway, from where I taught. The circumstance was a commonplace; the local anti-Communist vigilantes surfaced for a school board election. They stridently opposed "common learnings," a variant of the core curriculum then popular in many American junior high schools. These opponents caricatured these offerings as socialistic and intended to subvert American children with communist sentiments. Even at some distance from San Angelo, some of us teachers felt insecure and attacked. The red scare had crept closer to me as a person and to my calling as a teacher. The next year, I served as elementary school principal and high school teacher in a rural suburb of Ft. Worth. It was an interval during which I read of red scare operations in some additional American schools, but I was more interested in the expanding Korean War. That Spring, the Navy called me to active duty.

I was concerned with Soviet naval matters for the next three years, some of which time I was stationed in England. I held a Top Secret security clearance and worked in sensitive operations. Overseas, I read in the very conservative Dallas and Chicago newspapers about the growing concern about Communist subversion into American institutions. The McCarthy era was well underway at home. The really big education news that I remember focused on several dramatic events. The Supreme Court rendered its decision in *Brown v. Board of Education*. In Pasadena, California, red-baiting tactics disrupted a splendid school system and ruined the superintendency of Willard Goslin, later to be one of my professors in my doctoral studies. Some school boards, like that of

Houston, Texas, banned any teaching about the United Nations and refused to accept federal funds for school construction. Its public reasons were simplistic: a rampant local red scare convinced the board that communism underlay the UN and that feared an invasion of the locality by the "socialistic" federal government.

Only when I joined the staff of the Association for Supervision and Curriculum Development in 1958 did I realize that American teachers and public schooling had an advocate during these red scare years. That group was the National Education Association's National Commission for the Defense of Democracy Through Education. Ineptly but symbolically named, most people commonly called it the Defense Commission. Over coffee at break times and at random lunches over two years, I learned about its work from conversations with Robert Skaife, its then staff director. What stories he related. The Commission and its work profoundly fascinated me. What combined audacity and temerity it manifest in community after community across the nation. The Commission's activities, never adequately funded by the NEA, seemed then — and now, I confess — to be anemic, even puny, as it confronted the well-financed, amazingly interconnected alliances of radical-right-wing political opposition to public schooling. These groups vigorously waved the banner of anti-communism over its venomously savage attacks and insinuated, although never proved, the complicity of teachers and school administrators in alleged un-American efforts to corrupt the national spirit and American traditions. The more that I knew, the more pride I felt in the continuing work of this Commission. It provided the only significant effort during the entire period to assert a defense of American public education and its teachers. Of course, it neither blunted nor halted the red scare onslaught on American public schooling. Both teachers and programs fell victim to red scare partisans. Nevertheless, the Commission's symbolism offered hope and, in darkened days, hope can be everything to besieged educators. I also grew sad as I recognized the NEA's continued marginalization and its eventual disbandment of the Commission. For more than 40 years, I've wanted to know more about the Defense Commission.

Now, Stuart J. Foster has brought to life the activities of the largely forgotten NEA Defense Commission during the red scare. He has probed, for the first time, its long-neglected records currently unceremoniously boxed and heaped in the NEA archives. Moreover, Foster has written a graceful narrative of the Commission's work. He has told stories upon stories of its attempts, some successful and others utterly impotent, to live up to its practical charge: to defend American democracy through the defense of the nation's educators and schools. Likely, Foster's viewing of this peculiar period of American education and its politics benefits from his native English lens. His very distance from those times and institutions couples easily with his intense pursuit of American history. These qualities enabled him to add particular insights to his interpretations. Without doubt, his book opens up and displays the dramatic work and the symbolic presence of the NEA Defense Commission during the red scare for all Americans, especially American teachers, to know, to appreciate, and, especially, to value.

I invite readers to partake of this portrayal of a strikingly strange, seamy, and still unsettling period of American history. It is not a period, I candidly fear, that is fully past.

O. L. Davis, Jr.
Professor of Curriculum and Instruction
The University of Texas at Austin

April 30, 1999

Chapter I

The Red Scare: Origins and Impact

The period from 1947-1954 proved a chilling time for many Americans. Typically referred to as the "red scare" or the "McCarthy era," post-war society rapidly became engulfed by a period of fervent anti-communism that consumed all aspects of the culture. Public education was not exempt. Indeed, repeated and damaging attacks on school personnel and educational policy and practice appeared as hallmarks of the post-war era. Employing the potent tactics of the red scare, right-wing extremists damaged individual educational systems and disturbed the civic harmony of numerous local communities. Examples abound.

In New York, at least 300 teachers fell victim to the city schools' ideological purges. In Los Angeles, a state investigating committee, chaired by Senator Hugh Burns, held 30,000 educators by the throat after the Board of Education submitted its entire teaching force to invasive loyalty checks. Books were burned in Salupa, Oklahoma, for their alleged subversive portrayal of sex and socialism. The Texas legislature ordered educational institutions in the state to remove any and all literature published by the Soviet Union found in school or university libraries. Legislative act number 888, in Alabama, required all authors and publishers of "instructional materials" to state that their work, or works cited by them, were not the offerings of a "known advocate of communism or Marxist socialism." One member of the Indiana state textbook commission argued with conviction that *Robin Hood* should be banned from schools because she believed that the story was part of "a communist directive in education" which lauded "robbing the rich to give to the poor."[1] In dozens of towns and cities across the United States, boards of education and administrators withdrew from use textbooks identified and criticized as subversive, school tax elections were frustrated, and curriculum materials and teaching practices were subjected to vigorous and debilitating scrutiny.

In many schools, teachers worked within a climate of fear and suspicion. In the classroom, teachers' academic freedoms visibly were repressed. Educators avoided controversial subjects, and schools only cautiously initiated innovative teaching practices. In 1951, a committee of the National Education Association (NEA) lamented the "erosion of freedom" in schools and was equally troubled that teachers engaged in "self-censorship" that was regarded by the committee as "a far more insidious force than the overt acts of boards and legislatures."[2] In many respects, the red scare's hidden personal and professional toll often became more troubling than its more obvious manifestations. Some teachers lived in a state of constant anxiety through fear of dismissal. Others, troubled by accusations of subversion, worried for loss of their professional integrity and their status in the local community. For many, the trauma and uncertainty of the times strained personal and family relations, led to marriage break-ups, and, in some cases, prompted suicides.[3] Essentially, the period produced what historian Ellen Schrecker described as "one of the most severe episodes of political repression the United States has ever experienced."[4]

Although this post-World War II red scare had a dramatic impact on all aspects of American society, red scares were not a new feature on the American political landscape. Rabid anti-communism had been a pervasive force in American culture and politics since the founding of the communist ideology in the middle of the nineteenth century. It continued to be a powerful phenomenon in the early decades of the twentieth century. For example, the Palmer raids of 1919, the loyalty oaths of the 1920s, and the establishment of the House Committee on Un-American Activities (HUAC) in 1938 all served to fuel the reflexive fear of communism that was so deeply ingrained in pre-World War II American society.[5]

That prominent figures in the National Education Association leadership should spring to the defense of education during the anti-communist fever of the 1940s and 1950s was somewhat inevitable.[6] As the representative of hundreds of thousands of American educators and the world's largest teaching organization, the National Education Association understood and accepted its responsibility to support the teaching profession during this time of unprecedented assault. As a testament to the temper of the times and to the resolve of the NEA, in his opening speech "A Challenge to the Teaching Profession" delivered at the annual meeting of the NEA in Boston on June 29, 1941, President Donald DuShane stressed that a crisis was developing in the United States. He reasoned that "we must protect our schools from misunderstanding and unjust attack" and proposed the establishment of a specialized commission to assume this responsibility.[7] Later in the convention, the representative assembly unequivocally accepted his proposal and created the National Commission for the Defense of Democracy Through Education.

To some extent, the formation of the NEA's Defense Commission, as it was commonly known, in 1941 marked the early response of professional educators to anti-communist attacks on public schools. Typically, however, historians consider the most severe manifestations of red scare as a post-World War II phenomenon. The actions of the Defense Commission support this conclusion. Indeed, although the commission recognized the threat to education posed by anti-communist propaganda in the early 1940s, its most serious attention to red scare attack occurred between 1947 and 1954.

Historically, public schools and public school teachers have been obvious targets for red scare attacks. However, with the emergence of anti-communist sentiment and superpatriotic zeal in the years following World War II, their vulnerability dramatically increased. In 1890, high school enrollment in the United States was estimated at 200,000; by the early 1940s, the figure approached seven million.[8] Schools became one of the few public institutions that affected the lives of nearly every citizen. They existed in every community and were public institutions that were conveniently "get-at-able."[9] Moreover, because schools were perceived as a vital force in the control of the minds of America's children, the battle for their domination became intense.[10]

The struggle for control of education significantly mirrored the ideological battle being waged in the national culture and reflected the values and beliefs of American society or at least some segments of it. Schools became embroiled in bitter socio-political clashes precisely because they were wrestling with many of the issues that divided the country at mid-century. Supporters of federal aid to education, of racial integration of schools, of modern or "progressive" teaching methods, of UNESCO,[11] and of a liberal academic philosophy stood in stark contrast to those who argued for the sovereignty of states' rights, racially segregated schools, a "traditional" and disciplined educational environment, and a strongly nationalistic approach to world affairs.

Accordingly, American education became a battleground on which strikingly divisive clashes of culture and ideology were fought out. In these battles, public schools often became the targets of fierce criticism and disdain. The authors of *Public Education Under Criticism* wrote in 1954, for example, that "although ever present to some extent, criticism of public education has recently established new records for volume, breadth of coverage, and intensity."[12] A salient characteristic of this newly intensified criticism was the oft-repeated charge by extreme anti-communists that schools consciously undermined American ideals and encouraged subversive activities.

In this atmosphere of distrust, antagonists and educational professionals regularly engaged in rhetorical warfare. Educators, in particular, were under no illusion that they were embroiled in a ruthless and unforgiving battle. Prominent members of the National Education Association noted the change in climate and swiftly leapt to the defense of teachers. The NEA's Robert Skaife, for example, remarked that, although citizens were accustomed to seeing America enveloped in party politics,

> We are unaccustomed to education being enmeshed in this atmosphere of cultural conflict....Yet this is just what we have been experiencing, particularly as extreme right-wing organizations with reactionary inclinations use the national situation to attack not only such legislation as the Wagner Act, TVA, international organizations, and social security, but also instruction in the schools.[13]

In repeated speeches and publications, Skaife spoke of "enemy attacks," of "the battlefields of education," and of "waging war against the enemy."[14] Other prominent NEA leaders responded with similar passion. Before the mass gatherings of the eighty-eighth Delegate Assembly of the NEA in St. Louis in 1950, Harold Benjamin delivered an emotionally driven speech, "Report on the Enemy," that was peppered with metaphors of war. He spoke of the "campaign" to defeat "regiments" of "aggressors" and "combatants."[15] A year later, Ernest O. Melby, former chairman of the Defense Commission, in an aptly titled pamphlet called "American Education Under Fire" remarked with considerable concern that, "From Englewood, New Jersey, to Eugene, Oregon, from New York to Pasadena, in scores of cities — the entire nation is pocked with battlefields of the war against modern education."[16] In the post-war world many aspects of educational policy and practice clearly were under siege from a wide array of vociferous critics. Defense of teachers from the onslaught became an important and monumental enterprise.

The commission's original charter charged it to protect and defend the professional rights of teachers in individual cases and in selected school districts. By the beginning of the post-war period, the commission swiftly became the organized teaching profession's primary means to blunt organized and concerted red scare attacks on education in towns and cities throughout the nation. From the late 1940s to the mid-1950s, the Defense Commission concentrated the attention of its staff on efforts to defend teachers from critics who used red scare tactics and rhetoric to discredit public education and to serve the interests of reactionary forces in American society.

In the years following its establishment in 1941, the commission worked tirelessly in pursuit of its established goals. The tremendous pressures, opposition, and difficulties the commission faced in the ensuing years were revealed by Robert Skaife, the field secretary of the Defense Commission, who, in 1950, declared, "An open fight must be waged against those forces who employ subterfuge and innuendo in misinterpreting school programs and accusing teachers and the teaching profession of being communistic, socialistic, or un-American."[17] That Skaife wrote those words almost ten years after the commission's founding, and after enormous energies on the part of the Defense Commission's staff had been expended in the defense of teachers, is testament to the power and intensity of the red scare. Unbeknown to Skaife, however, worse conditions were still to come. The anti-communist steamroller was not yet in full gear, and some of the most troubling manifestations of the red scare, soon to be apparent to devastating effect, festered on the horizon.

The Emergence of "McCarthyism"

Republican Senator Joseph R. McCarthy from Wisconsin is the figure most associated with the red scare vitriol of the post-war era. As the quintessential political opportunist of the age, Senator McCarthy rode the tidal wave of fear, suspicion, and anti-communist hysteria and became the focal point of red scare politics. For all his bellicose actions, however, Joseph McCarthy was only the tip of the anti-communist iceberg. The red scare in its broadest sense existed long before he rose to infamy and continued well after his censure in 1954 and death in 1957. Indeed, although many eminent historians have disagreed over the forces that motivated the appearance of the McCarthy phenomenon, most agree that McCarthy was more a symbol of and foil for anti-communist sentiment than he was its leading force.[18] As Robert Griffith and Athan Theoharis argue, "McCarthy was the product of America's Cold War politics, not its progenitor." Regardless, McCarthy's sudden rise to prominence stands both as a striking testimony to, and as a symbol of, the power and influence of anti-communist sentiments in American society at mid-century.

Senator McCarthy catapulted to national fame following a speech on February 9, 1950, at the Ohio County Women's Club in Wheeling, West Virginia. In his speech, McCarthy shocked the audience with the declaration that, "I have here in my hand a list of 205 people — a list of names that were made known to the Secretary of State as being members of the Communist Party and who are nevertheless still working and shaping policy in the State Department." The national news media latched on to the story. McCarthy repeated the accusations the following evening in Denver, and, on February 11 in Salt Lake City, he claimed to have the names of "57 card carrying communists" who worked in the State Department. Indefatigable, McCarthy repeated his charges in a six-hour speech in the Senate on February 20. By the summer of 1950, this hitherto unknown politician had become one of the most famous people in the United States.[19] He was featured on the covers of *Time* and *Newsweek* magazines, received donations exceeding $1,000 a day, and was one of the nation's most sought after speakers. The outbreak of the Korean War on June 25, 1950, further secured McCarthy's credibility and served to enhance his prominence on the American political scene.

Over the next five years McCarthy, through a web of slander, lies, and inflamed language, was to ruin the lives and careers of thousands of innocent men and women. Historian J. Ronald Oakley ruefully noted, "he was a man without principles, scruples, beliefs, or proof of his sensational allegations. He never uncovered a single communist in the government, yet he had the support of millions."[20]

McCarthy's meteoric rise to fame could not have occurred had the socio-political climate not been ripe for his ascendancy. The early 1950s was such a period. By the time McCarthy gave his Wheeling speech, the suspicions he voiced already were deeply embedded in the American culture. British journalist and historian Godfrey Hodgson neatly characterized the context from which McCarthyism flourished:

> There was clay waiting for the potter. Long before McCarthy's speech at Wheeling, suspicion had begun to focus on the danger of communist subversion. The House Un-American Activities Committee was set up in 1938, and from the start devoted about four-fifths of its attention to investigating the Left. The Alien Registration Act of 1940, in practice and intention, a sedition act, breached constitutional precedent by embracing guilt by association. The U. S. Chamber of Commerce

began publishing in 1946 a series of reports alleging clandestine communist influence in various areas of American life....In 1947, President Truman issued an executive order requiring loyalty checks for 2.5 million civil servants, several hundred of whom were dismissed as a result. Union leaders were required by the Taft-Hartley Act of 1947 to take an oath that they were not Communists, and in 1949 the leaders of the Communist Party themselves were tried and convicted for conspiring to advocate the overthrow of the U. S. Government by force and violence. Well before the end of the 1940s, numerous states and cities had passed statutes and ordinances obliging teachers to take loyalty oaths.[21]

For Americans, passionate enmity toward "subversives," "pinkos," and "commies" also was grounded in a seemingly frustrating reality. Many people perceived that real dangers did exist. In the period immediately before McCarthy's Wheeling speech, a steady and frighteningly familiar drum beat of bad news confronted Americans. Less than a year before his notorious allegations the Soviet Union had acquired the atomic bomb. Four months before his speech, Klaus Fuchs, a British scientist working on the Los Alamos atomic bomb project was charged with spying for the Russians. Only weeks before, China, a country with a quarter of the world's population, appeared "lost" to communism. Three weeks before McCarthy's speech in Wheeling, State Department official Alger Hiss, earlier accused of treason, was sentenced to prison for five years for perjury. Just ten days before, Truman decided to build the H-Bomb, and just six days before, Fuchs confessed. With the outbreak of the Korean War only a few months away, national and international events appeared, almost chillingly, to play directly into McCarthy's hands.

These national and international events combined to create a dramatic impact on the American people. Significantly, as the gloomy news rolled into American homes, conservative politicians and special interest groups both exploited and magnified its impact. Beginning with the Congressional elections of 1950, red scare tactics and rhetoric frequently were invoked to discredit liberals and individuals allegedly "soft" on communism, to extinguish progressivism, New Dealism, and any form of social protest.[22] By the early 1950s, the use of red scare tactics by conservative forces, historically used to discredit the opposition, assumed features of a menacing orthodoxy on the American political and social landscape. All segments of society, including the public schools, fell victim to this period of new and intensified red scare attack.

To appreciate the forces that created this passionate renewal of anti-communist fervor in the country requires an understanding of American society at mid-century. The period immediately following the end of World War II was a time of transition for American society. It also was distinguished by a curious dichotomy. On the one hand, the United States emerged from the global conflict as the strongest and most prosperous nation in the world. To most Americans, the nation's and their personal futures appeared bright.[23] On the other hand, the post-war era was characterized by widespread anxiety and frustration. New domestic and foreign problems challenged a troubled generation. These anxieties and frustrations became manifest in a people who attempted to cope with an unfamiliar military "police action" in Korea, with "Cold War" tensions with the Soviet Union and Soviet bloc nations, with rapid urbanization, with intense struggles over issues of race, and with the advancement of a society consumed with increased commercialism and modernization. In addition, through its foreign policy of "containment" of communism, the United States accepted the role of the world's policeman. Thus, the nation and its people increasingly became aware of its and their continuing and awesome burden of responsibility in world affairs and of the harrowing and persistent threat of nuclear war.

The gulf between the United States' potential internal harmony and the nation's actual situation troubled many Americans. In 1949, historian Arthur Schlesinger, Jr., noted,

> Frustration is increasingly the hallmark of the century — the frustration...of the most generous hopes, of the most splendid dreams. Nineteen hundred looked forward to the irresistible expansion of freedom, democracy and abundance; 1950 will look back to totalitarianism, to concentration camps, to mass starvation, to atomic war.[24]

Robert Maynard Hutchins, Chancellor of the University of Chicago, painted an even gloomier picture,

> Examine, if you will, the problems that confront us today. We have won a great military victory and we do not know what to do with the peace. We have created the atomic bomb and we are terrified about what it may do to us. We have lost the unity which the war imposed on us, and we have abandoned even the moral slogans under which we fought. Our confusion and depression are greater than they ever have been in the memory of living man, for our problems are more numerous, more complicated, and more critical...our attitude is one of despair.[25]

Most troubling of all to the American people, however, was the belief that the American way of life was being challenged and threatened by external forces beyond their control.

Historically, a peculiar feature of American culture has been its relentless striving for social cohesion and national unity. To declare oneself "an American" symbolized a desire to uphold certain inviolate ideals and to renounce "alien" tendencies such as socialism, collectivism, and fabianism. In the late 1940s and early 1950s, therefore, "Americanism" often was irresistibly equated with anti-communism, and this explains the growth and attraction of the red scare in this period. As David Caute shrewdly observed, "one of the appeals of McCarthyism was that it offered every American, however precarious his ancestry, the chance of being taken for a good American, simply by demonstrating a gut hatred for Commies."[26] Essential to this nationalistic faith was the widespread belief that America was being betrayed at home. How else, many American citizens reasonably asked, could anyone explain the alarming gulf between the country's military power and its impotence to make the world conform to American ideals. In an attempt to explain the motivations behind the red scare and McCarthyism, Godfrey Hodgson incisively observed that,

> The tenets of McCarthyism boil down to three grand phobias. One was the idea that there was a conspiracy at work in America to undermine capitalism, free business enterprise, and the American way of life. The second was the belief that agents of this conspiracy, Communists or their dupes in education, the churches, and the media, were corrupting the nation's morale, and especially that of the young. And the third was the conviction that high places in government itself had been infiltrated by men who would sell America out.[27]

Of course, as Hodgson noted, such phobias were not new in American politics. However, strikingly different was the widespread acceptance of these essential tenets in all sectors of society, including the party that controlled the Congress and that in 1952 would win the White House.

Many educators were under no illusions that the nation's frustrations and the rising tide of red scare sentiment directly would impact their profession. Robert Skaife, for example, subtitled his widely read chapter in *Forces Affecting American Education*, "The Age of Anxiety." In his contribution he remarked pointedly that, although the United States must combat the communist threat, the country must "protect those basic freedoms guaranteed in the Bill of Rights from those who, in the name of anti-communism, would endanger the great American tradition of freedom of speech, press, conscience, and ballot."[28] Unquestionably, educators were concerned that academic freedom, the right to teach controversial subjects, and the ability to teach in a climate of trust and professional responsibility were being threatened and eroded during this time of national uncertainty.

Charles S. Johnson, President of Fisk University, similarly lamented that "a sense of insecurity" had led to some troubling national reactions,

> Some of the manifestations appear in the excited search for political heretics and for evidences of political or ideological heresy in Congressional hearings and in the demand for loyalty oaths, in the stifling of spontaneity and of courage for adventure...in a dread of innovation, in at least partial paralysis of incentives to exploration, in the urge and tendency to turn the spirit of free inquiry into indoctrination and restraint of criticism, and in sweeping attacks on modern education.[29]

Johnson's comments as a black president of a black university, demonstrated that the red scare impacted all factions in American education. He argued that these were "real" threats to the schools, ones with which the schools must reckon because "the institution of the school, like other structural institutions of our society, is facing an important crisis."

A crisis in education undeniably swelled. In 1950, state legislatures passed over 300 laws dealing with subversive practices many of which directly impacted teachers.[30] Textbook censorship was common, media criticism rife, and the dismissal of educators for alleged "un-American" activities escalated. In addition, thirty states mandated loyalty oaths for teachers and a significant proportion began investigations into alleged communist activities in the schools.[31] Across the country education fell under the intensive red scare microscope. In the post-war era, this unwanted attention and caustically negative criticism continued to deliver significant and damaging impacts on many schools throughout the nation.

Chapter II

The Power and Ubiquity of the
Red Scare in American Post-War Culture

The red scare phenomenon did not focus only on education. It permeated every aspect of American culture. The red scare induced hyperbolic Cold War rhetoric and action, intensified nationalistic sentiment, fueled what President Eisenhower named "the military-industrial complex," and contributed to the ascendancy and preeminence of corporate America. Ingeniously, capitalism, consumerism, and hedonism constituted the conceptual rebuttal of communism. At a time of increasing affluence, the argument was compelling. Writer Barbara Ehrenreich observed,

> Affluence seemed to be the ultimate rebuttal to the Soviets... *Life* frequently underscored the point with pictures of dumpy, lipstick-less Russian women sweeping streets. Forced to live without private cars, home freezers, or drip-dry clothes, the Russians appeared pathetic, practically serfs.[1]

Significantly, economists, politicians, and business leaders increasingly heralded the capitalist system as the only viable alternative to communism and to the continued achievement of widespread American prosperity. "Keynes, not Marx," wrote Arthur Schlesinger, "is the prophet of the new radicalism." "The world revolution of our time is 'Made in the USA,'" wrote Peter Drucker, the champion of industrial management. "The true revolutionary principle is the idea of mass production."[2] Enjoying the proliferation of leisure products flooding the market, buying the latest electrical equipment, consuming modern domestic gadgetry, improving the home, taking more vacations, and, above all, buying American products became the rallying cries of the age.

For example, of the 7.9 million cars sold to Americans in 1955, fewer than one quarter of one percent were manufactured abroad. In 1955, only

300 Volkswagens were sold in the United States. Americans shared the common perception that capitalism was a success. "It works," said John Kenneth Galbraith in *American Capitalism*, published in 1952, "and, in the years since World War II, quite brilliantly."[3] The affluent society, therefore, assumed the rhetoric and ideology of pro-capitalism and anti-communism. To spend and to enjoy became an easy lifestyle for Americans to adopt. More important, this lifestyle was embraced, legitimated, and at times, manipulated by all the major forces in society, including the media, corporate advertising, political figures, and big business.

Without question, the repeated emphasis about Americans living in the dangerous Cold War age served the interests of corporate America and the military-industrial complex. This repeated emphasis of the enormous threat to the United States represented by the Soviet Union, in turn, prompted massive increases in military spending and in federal contracts awarded to defense-related industries. For the corporate giants, increased government spending meant increased profits. In 1950, *U. S. News and World Report* revealingly observed:

> Government planners figure they have found the magic formula for almost endless [economic] good times....Cold War is the catalyst. Cold War is an automatic pump primer. Turn the spigot and the public clamors for more arms spending. Turn another, the clamor ceases....Cold War demands, if fully exploited, are almost limitless.[4]

The formula for continued economic growth, therefore, was simple. Create or participate in a state of alarm about the "Soviet threat," and huge contracts, guaranteed markets, and high profits surely would follow.

In the climate of the Korean War, communism, and conspiracy, U. S. defense spending sky-rocketed. At the beginning of 1950, the total U. S. budget approximated $40 billion, and the military portion of that sum amounted to $12 billion. By 1955, however, the military portion of the federal budget soared to $40 billion out of a total of $62 billion.[5] In the twenty-five years from the end of World War II to 1970, the United States federal government spent a thousand billion dollars for military purposes. It trained a standing army of three million men; it built 400 major and 3,000 minor military bases in 30 countries overseas, and it placed seven thousand tactical nuclear weapons in Europe.[6]

By the mid-1950s, the federal government nurtured 40,000 "prime defense contractors" and hundreds of thousands of lesser ones. Defense Department expenditure exploded in the post-war era. By the late 1960s, this Department possessed greater assets than the nation's 75 largest corporations, employed as many people as the top 30 firms, and spent more money than did the entire national government before the Depression.[7]

Responding to the communist threat not only entailed huge military expenditure and corporate growth, it also shackled the fortunes of politicians and geographic regions to what J. Fred Cook labeled the "Warfare State." Historian William E. Leuchtenburg remarked of this nexus between military expenditure and regional politics,

> California thrived on Lockheed, Seattle on the contracts let to Boeing; in Georgia the roll of one aircraft factory amounted to half of the value of the state's cotton crop.... Congressmen made their reputations by securing juicy military contracts...Henry Jackson from the state of Washington was known as the "Senator from Boeing," and Richard B. Russell and Carl Vinson teamed up to cram 20 military installations into Georgia. But none matched the South Carolinian who would become Chairman of the House Armed Services Committee, Lucius Mendel Rivers...who saw to it that his district housed an army depot, an air force base, a marine corps training center, a coast guard mine-warfare operation, and a navy shipyard, supply center, and weapons station, as well as defense plants with hundreds of millions of dollars in contracts.[8]

Clearly, anti-communist fervor supported the interests of many political and economic forces dominant in the United States. By the late 1950s, fifteen major corporations received two-thirds of all defense contracts. A decade later, a report by Senator William Proxmire found that just one of the hundred largest defense contractors employed more than 2,000 former upper-echelon military officers. Most contracts were not competitive, but became what was euphemistically termed "single supplier negotiable."[9] The lines between military personnel, political interests, and corporate profits blurred into extinction. As long as the communist "crisis" existed, powerful political and economic groups in American society would prevail. Unquestionably, therefore, they fanned the flames of anti-communist hysteria in order to serve their own interests.

The direct relationship between the military establishment, big business, and politics was no more evident than in President Eisenhower's choices of individuals for cabinet leadership in 1952. The President accorded prominent positions to no fewer than three men with strong ties to General Motors: Charles E. Wilson who became Secretary of Defense, Douglas McKay who headed the Department of the Interior, and Arthur Summerfield who served as Postmaster General. The only Eisenhower appointee not overtly pro-business was Martin Durkin of the plumbers' union; however, within eight months, he left his cabinet post and was replaced by a businessman. Cynically, the *New Republic* commented that the Eisenhower cabinet constituted "eight millionaires and a plumber."[10] Politicians were not slow to realize that enormous political mileage was to be made from adopting the rhetoric and tactics of anti-communism.

For example, following Truman's dramatic and unexpected electoral victory in 1948, many Republican politicians realized the power and impact of campaigns based on a platform of anti-communism. In both the 1950 mid-term elections and the 1952 Presidential elections, Republicans unashamedly accused Democrats of assisting Soviet subversion at home and of caving in to communism abroad. National scandals (e.g., the Hiss conviction) and international "failures" (e.g., the "loss" of China) legitimated Republican attacks. Taking an anti-communist stance and using red scare methods to attack the opposition also encouraged politicians to seek prominent positions on Congressional committees that investigated "subversive activities." In 1952, for example, 185 of the 221 Republicans in Congress applied for seats on the House Un-American Activities Committee, an unheard of request only a few years before.[11] Attacking communism became equated with defending Americanism. More important, the Congressional investigations brought increased media attention, popular national notoriety, and substantial political power.

To associate the red scare mentality of the age solely to the machinations of Republican politicians, however, would be inaccurate historical portrayal. Many Democrats and political liberals also succumbed to the anti-communist paranoia that pervaded culture. Historian Athan Theoharis, for example, argued persuasively that the roots of the red scare lay in the post-war rhetoric and actions of the Truman administration. In the climate of the Cold War, Theoharis suggested, red scare tactics were used to support funding for expensive and grandiose economic military programs such as the Truman Doctrine and the Marshall Plan.[12] Subsequent administrations followed the Truman example.

Without question, most liberal politicians despised — even detested — the extremist stance adopted by Senator McCarthy and his followers. However, to a significant degree, liberal politicians contented themselves with fighting McCarthy rather than McCarthyism. Fearing loss of credibility or the appearance of being "soft" on communism, most members of the Democratic Party became entranced by the zealous mood of the age. Michael Parenti strongly underlined this point,

Having accepted without debate the axiom that communism was a relentless, diabolical, conspiratorial force dedicated to our destruction, they [liberal politicians] found themselves the prisoners of their own premise and were soon supporting as necessary evils policies which did violence to their best liberal instincts.[13]

Thus, liberal figures inadvertently intensified the very aura of unchallengeable orthodoxy that strengthened McCarthyism. By the early 1950s, the political order, wittingly or unwittingly, solidified around an anti-communist consensus. In this climate, many politicians readily adopted both the inflammatory rhetoric and the dubious practices of red scare attack.

By mid-century, the intensity of the red scare manifested itself in almost every facet of American society. The red scare significantly served to suppress union activity, to hamper interracial relations and Civil Rights legislation, to undermine calls for increased equality for women, to activate a renewed fundamentalist religious fervor, to dominate the media, and to intimidate Hollywood and the American entertainment industry.[14] Accordingly, although anti-communist attacks on education proved a significant feature of the age, the assault on educators must be viewed within the broader socio-policial context of the time.

Image and Reality in the Red Scare Era

A salient feature of the red scare was the enormous gulf between peoples' perceptions of the communist threat and its reality. Few Americans, for example, appeared to understand the extent and nature of the devastation inflicted by World War II on the Soviet Union. In many respects, the post-war Soviet Union was a nation on its knees. At wars' end, by conservative estimates, over 20 million Russians were dead; fifteen of its largest cities either were completely or substantially destroyed, and six million buildings were obliterated leaving over 25 million people homeless. The war cost the country 31,850 industrial plants, 65,000 kilometers of railway, 56,000 miles of highway, 90,000 bridges, and 10,000 power stations.[15] In contrast, the United States emerged from World War II as the planet's most powerful and affluent nation. It had sole possession of the atomic weapon and a burgeoning economic and military infrastructure. In reality, therefore, the Soviets, not the Americans, had more to fear in the post-war world.

This reality, on the other hand, was strikingly different from the common perceptions conveyed by popular magazines and newspapers. By 1950, the American populace was bombarded with severely pessimistic and startlingly depressing views of the future. Typically, Americans believed that their entire way of life was under severe and imminent threat. A 1950 Gallup poll, for example, revealed that 70% of Americans believed that the Soviet Union was trying to rule the world; 41% expected the U. S. to fight a major war in the next five years; 75% believed that American cities would be bombed if the U. S. entered another war; and 19% predicted the end of the human race if another war broke out.[16] Even more alarming for the American people was their belief that the godless, immoral, and militaristic Russians threatened the comfortable tranquillity of life in the United States.

The communist was the devil incarnate, and Americans were prepared to go to incredible extremes to prevent the spread and infiltration of this atheistic ideology into the nation. For example, an opinion poll conducted by Harvard Professor Samuel Stouffer revealed that 52% of Americans favored imprisoning all communists; 42% wanted to deny the press the right to criticize the "American form of government"; 84% would deny an atheist the right to teach in public schools; and 73% felt it right to report friends and neighbors suspected of communism to the FBI. Remarkably, however, only 3% claimed to have ever known or met a communist, and only 10% said they harbored suspicions about someone they knew being a communist. Stouffer's national cross section revealed that such people identified citizens as communist because:

> He was always talking about world peace (housewife, Oregon). I saw a map of Russia on the wall in his home (locomotive engineer, Michigan). I suspected it from his conversation and manner (lawyer, Georgia). He was not like us (bank vice-president, Texas). He brought a lot of foreign looking people into his home (housewife, Kansas).[17]

During this period, Americans' perceptions of the Soviet Union and communism typically were based upon both prejudice and mis-information.[18] Anti-communist ferment pervaded the culture. In television programs, spy stories proliferated, the news media used hyperbolic headlines to "inform" and excite audiences about the Soviet threat, and political speeches displayed an obsession with issues of national security. Workers were subject to loyalty oaths and rigorous scrutiny. Even churches rallied around the American flag in an attempt to foil the advance of godless communism.

America nearly suffocated under anti-communist hysteria. Commitment to rational and critical dialogue sharply was reduced. For the American people enough "truth" existed in the fears and allegations for the red scare to possess some legitimacy. The more times the threat was repeated, the more it became "real" in the national consciousness. Indeed, by the early 1950s, the perception of danger from communist subversion had been portrayed so profoundly, so dramatically, and so often that few Americans questioned its credibility or "truth."

False impressions and distorted perceptions also caused educators grave problems during the red scare years. Exaggerated political rhetoric, loyalty investigations, ideological purges, inflammatory media coverage, and special interest group accusations offered American citizens the distinct impression that public schools across the country were riddled with communist sympathizers and indoctrinators.[19] On a daily basis, readers of America's newspapers were bombarded with sensational headlines that reported charges made against those in the teaching profession.[20] Extremists such as newspaper millionaire R. C. Hoiles exclaimed that teachers deliberately were leading students toward socialism and communism.[21] Influential politicians, such as Senator Patrick McCarran of Nevada, spoke of the "nests of communists" who had infiltrated the schools, and publications such as "How Red Are the Schools?" were distributed to Americans in communities throughout the United States.[22]

A significant feature of the red scare as it gathered momentum was the increasing tendency for ordinary Americans to accept its underlying assumptions. Persuaded by the rhetoric and the extensive coverage given to charges of educational subversion, many citizens grew steadily concerned that harmful indoctrination indeed was going on in the nation's schools. Parents' anxieties further were intensified when the sinister threat of communist infiltration from within was also matched by threats of attack from without.

From 1950 to 1952, atomic air drills became a regular feature of the school week in cities all across the United States.[23] Fearing unannounced Soviet attack, 850 public schools in New York practiced "sneak attack drill"; three million editions of the "Duck and Cover" comic strip defense brochure warned children that "the atomic bomb is a new danger," and school children in major cities were issued with dog tags, so that the lost and dead students could be identified in the event of communist atomic attack.[24] By playing on the fears, suspicions, and anxieties of the American public, red scare antagonists, therefore, effectively persuaded many citizens that the communists were proving successful in their efforts to control the schools.

If the perception existed that subversives had infiltrated the schools, what was the reality? How many teachers were avowed communists? And, what effect did their actions have on the education of America's young? Certainly, teachers who were sympathetic to the ideals of communism and who were members of the Communist Party existed in the teaching profession. Many of these educators had turned to communism in the 1930s in reaction to the troubling emergence of fascism in Europe and to the apparent failure of the capitalist system, as evidenced by the Great Depression years, in the United States.[25] In truth, however, the number of those committed to the communist cause in the 1950s was minuscule in comparison to the total number of teachers in the country as a whole. In the early 1950s, just over one million teachers worked in public schools in the United States. Even if one accepts the inflated calculations of Bella Dodd, the once communist activist turned Congressional investigation informer, the grand total amounted to no more 1,500 teachers. Dodd's testimony noted, however, that this number included those "sympathetic" to communism and those who had supported the Communist Party at one time or another. Likely, therefore, even by Dodd's generous accounting, by the early 1950s, this figure was much reduced.

Many within the NEA were infuriated by the constantly repeated claim that teachers were poisoning the minds of America's young with the ideology of the Soviet Union. In May 1953, Richard Barnes Kennan, executive secretary of the Defense Commission, told an audience of concerned citizens:

> Although Congressman Velde might have us believe that the greatest problem the schools have to face is that of subversive teachers, I am sure that anyone who is closely acquainted with the schools would disagree. Taking the worse possible view of the situation from the evidence produced to date, the number of communists in the teaching profession is extremely small, and they are concentrated in a very few urban centers. Outside our largest cities it is doubtful if there ever has been one communist in any group of 10,000 teachers.[26]

To focus solely on how many teachers actually were communists clouds much broader concerns regarding the impact that these teachers allegedly had on American students. Repeatedly, Congressional investigators and acerbic critics chastised the schools because they had "produced" traitors like Alger Hiss or Julius and Ethel Rosenberg. In many ways, charges that "red" teachers were indoctrinating children with an alien ideology exposed the ignorance of the critics. As experienced educators instinctively knew, the educative process involved far more than the mere transmission of information from the teacher and the passive reception of it on the part of students. What many of the red scare critics also failed to acknowledge was that the public schools system that had produced Hiss and the Rosenbergs had also produced Velde, Ober, McCarthy, and most other champions of the political right-wing.[27]

In reality, by the late 1940s and early 1950s, the number of communist sympathizers in the teaching profession had dramatically declined. The Stalinist purges of the mid to late 1930s, the signing of the Nazi-Soviet Pact in August 1939, and the perceived unreasonable stance adopted by the Soviet Union in the early years of the Cold War shattered the ideals of those teachers who had turned to communism in the early 1930s. Moreover, to remain an active member of the Communist Party and to be a teacher in the decade following World War II was tantamount to professional suicide. At mid-century, more than half of all teachers in the United States were untenured; their job insecurity was prevalent, and their professional status was low. To advocate communism in this climate was to invite almost certain dismissal. Even if a radical teacher had designs to propagate fervor for communism, the chances of that person continuing to hold a job for very long were remote in the extreme. The example of Frances Eisenberg, a teacher who never sought to impose her personal political views on her students, serves to exemplify the power of the anti-communist paranoia.[28]

In the red scare era, so infectious and so reflexive was the public inclination to condemn communists that to suggest that a former communist sympathizer could actually be a good teacher was considered heretical. Martha Kransdorf's intriguing biographical account of Frances Eisenberg's teaching career in Los Angeles during the red scare era suggests, however, that many such teachers did exist. Nevertheless, despite testimony to her outstanding work as an educator by colleagues, students, and parents, the fact that Eisenberg was a member of the Communist Party before World War II led, almost inevitably, to her dismissal. In the red scare period, few people — including liberal educators, the American Federation of Teachers, and the National Education Association — were prepared to stand and fight for the rights of former communists.

Another favorite tactic of red scare critics was equating the philosophy and practices of progressive education with a conspiratorial design to turn America's young toward socialism. Wherever and whenever school districts fell victim to red scare attack, the presence of "progressive" methods in the schools was heralded by the critics as a surefire indication that the "reds" were at work. In their zealous attempts to control public education, red scare critics gave the impression that the introduction of progressive methods was a new post-war phenomenon, a part of the grand design to infiltrate American public schools with communist ideals. The impression was false, however, on two counts.

First, the extent to which progressive educational philosophy truly altered the American school curriculum in the post-war era is problematic at best.[29] Second, in most school districts where progressive methods were in place, these practices often had existed for a considerable period of time. In Pasadena, California, for example, red scare criticism of the school superintendent Willard Goslin included a vicious attack on progressive education. There, the school curriculum largely had remained unaltered for more than twenty years, long before Goslin assumed his post.[30] As educational historian Arthur Zilversmit prudently observed, "The strident attacks on progressive education in the 1950s were ultimately more revealing of the mentality of Cold War America than they were reflections of what was actually happening in American schools."[31] Once again, the outward perception of communist infiltration and influence stood a remote distance from the reality of the situation.

No better examples of the gulf between the false impression created by red scare critics and the reality of the educational world exist than those centered on events in Houston, Texas, and Pasadena, California, during the late 1940s and early 1950s.

In both cities, for a period of several years, an unrelenting storm of criticism and red scare attack scared teachers and administrators. Newspapers covered the charges of communist infiltration of the schools almost on a daily basis, and radio talk shows were devoted to the issue, while pressure groups within the educational communities became locked in a desperate struggle to purge the schools of communist teachers and administrators. Anyone living in those cities in the early 1950s could not fail to be engrossed by the spectacle. Reasonably, many citizens were concerned by the prospect that "subversive" education operated under their very noses. However, despite all the rhetoric, the acrimony, the maelstrom of political invective, the teacher insecurity, and the dismissals of key administrative personnel, not one shred of conclusive evidence was uncovered to suggest that un-American or subversive acts were perpetrated in the schools.[32]

The red scare once again proved to be an effective weapon in the confusion of the public, in the exaggeration of perceived dangers, and in the creation of a false impression of the alleged threat of communist infiltration of American schools. Just as political events and media portrayals in the wider American culture were falsely presented to the American people in order to exaggerate the threat of subversive influences, so were events and occurrences in the field of public education falsely propagated.

The Red Scare as a Political Weapon

The distinguishing characteristic of the red scare was the way in which certain elite forces, special interest groups, and conservative ideologues employed the threat of communist infiltration as a weapon to discredit individuals who favored a more liberal or progressive political agenda.[33] By repeatedly emphasizing the presence of subversive forces in the public schools, the line between image and reality conveniently was blurred. Reactionary forces and powerful individuals from the political right, therefore, successfully stirred emotive and often paranoiac anti-communist sentiment in order to undermine those who opposed their ideological creed.[34]

The red scare was not a manifestation of American populist sentiment, but, rather, an expression of special interest politics often fueled by a conservative elite. In towns and cities in which educational practice and policy fell victim to red scare attack, almost without exception, conservative political forces and reactionary pressure groups played a dramatic and often decisive role in propagating intense local criticism of the schools. Use of the red scare, therefore, became a potent force in the arsenal of individuals and groups who saw the world moving away from what they believed it should be. Developments in the post-war era (such as calls for significant increases in taxes to support the expansion and development of public education, for the racial integration of schools, for federal aid to education, for the use of instructional materials produced by UNESCO, and for the continued practice of progressive teaching methods) troubled those who saw the world through a different ideological lens.

In response, many public schools throughout the United States were subjected to the tactics and methods of the red scare.[35] The target for these attacks ostensibly was the communist infiltrator. In reality, however, the critics sought out those who supported "New Dealism," progressivism, and liberalism. As the eminent historian Henry Steele Commager, who noted the same trend in higher education, perceptively remarked in 1954, "Of course, it is not communism in colleges that is the concern of the witch-hunters; it is liberalism, progressivism, controversy of any kind."[36] During the Cold War years, portrayal of the belief that schools were infested with subversive provocateurs and with alien and un-American practices became a convenient and powerful image for those from the political right. Continually stated, emphasized, and re-emphasized, the image seduced citizens in many local communities and school districts throughout the nation. A climate of academic repression resulted. Teachers and administrators grew more defensive; intellectual freedoms were curtailed; curriculum methods and materials appeared "safe" and non-controversial, and the educational philosophy of progressivism suffered a crushing blow. In many instances, the impact of the red scare on the teaching profession and on educational policy and practice was profound. That the red scare was so effective testifies to the influence of conservative forces in American society at mid-century and to the power of the ideology of anti-communism in the post-war era.

The Red Scare and the NEA's Defense Commission in Historical Perspective

Although the NEA in general, and its Defense Commission in particular, understood the damage and the impact that criticism from right wing forces had on several aspects of education, they lacked the benefit of historical perspective and hindsight fully to understand the enormous power and success that the red scare had in shaping American culture during the Cold War years. Undeniably, the NEA's Defense Commission carried out an enormous amount of commendable work in the 1940s and 1950s. It offered American educators much comfort, solace, and support in difficult times. It defended teachers who faced dismissal and investigation. It exposed and undermined many of education's most troubling and vociferous critics. It structured a means of somewhat blunting red scare attack through local, state, and national organization. It offered teachers an endless stream of information and advice about how they might deal with unwarranted attack, and it effectively garnered the support of thousands of community and parental organizations.

In addition, the Defense Commission stuck out its neck for teachers. It was the first professional organization to leap to the defense of educators

who encountered vicious attack. As a group, the staff of the Defense
Commission worked with enormous dedication and commitment for more
than a decade to challenge those who used red scare tactics to undermine
the schools. Many of those who worked for the commission received angry
and ugly criticism from segments of the media and the political arena.[37] In
carrying out commission investigations, members of the Defense
Commission, such as Field Secretary Robert Skaife, spent considerable
and uncomfortable periods away from their families as they worked to report
about local communities that had fallen victim to red scare assault. Skaife,
for example, also was subjected to intense personal attack and to repeated
threats of legal action. In many regards, therefore, in the defense of teachers,
the commission and its devoted staff conducted an enormous amount of
valuable and productive work.

Paradoxically, however, despite the commission's unceasing efforts, it
fell a casualty to the infectious tide of anti-communism that swept the
country during the post-war years. Above all, it accepted the prevailing
zeitgeist that a serious internal communist threat existed. As such, the
Defense Commission betrayed itself as a victim of the fear and paranoia of
the red scare era. Almost in a myopic desire to appear respectable and
professional to the American public, the Defense Commission often proudly
boasted of the essential social and political conservatism of the NEA. For
example, the Defense Commission followed the NEA's policy decision to
distance itself from and to renounce the wave of teacher strikes that occurred
in the late 1940s and early 1950s. The Defense Commission also repeatedly
emphasized that it explicitly opposed the employment of members of the
Communist Party as teachers in American schools. Furthermore, although
the Defense Commission consistently objected to loyalty oaths and to
Congressional investigations, not once did it encourage teachers to refuse
to sign the oaths or to shun cooperation with state and federal investigations.
The Defense Commission, like many other agencies and institutions in the
red scare era, was prepared to go only a short distance to uphold the rights
and principles of Americans living in a democratic society. In the climate
of the age, to go further and to support and defend those who espoused
more critical, radical, or progressive views was considered political and
professional suicide.

To appreciate the work of the Defense Commission, therefore, is not
only to understand the dedicated efforts of a body of professionals who
sought to defend teachers in difficult times. Nor is it only to understand the
scale, intensity, and nature of red scare criticism of schools in the post-war

period. Significantly, to understand the actions of the Defense Commission is to understand more robustly the extent to which powerful red scare forces dominated the American landscape in the years following World War II.

Chapter III

The NEA Establishes the Defense Commission

Founded in 1857 to "elevate the character and advance the interests of the teaching profession and to promote the cause of popular education,"[1] the NEA claimed nearly half a million members by the middle of the twentieth century and was the American teaching profession's most significant representative. By 1941, the NEA was a complex organization and maintained a large executive and administrative headquarters in Washington, D.C., as well as a network of local and state affiliates throughout the nation. As part of its extensive structure, the NEA sponsored thirty-one committees, commissions, and councils.[2] Its most recent creation was the National Council for the Defense of Democracy Through Education. Throughout the 1940s and 1950s, the Defense Commission became one of the NEA's most prominent and influential bodies.

The National Education Association's decision to establish the Defense Commission in 1941 revealed a shift in the NEA's philosophical and organizational approach to education in the years before World War II. Its formation also testified to the dramatic historical and political context of the times. The rationale for the formation of the Defense Commission primarily may be understood through an appreciation of three factors salient in the early 1940s.

First and foremost, the Defense Commission was created to protect and safeguard the interests of teachers in what increasingly were considered troubled times. Both in intention and in practice, the Defense Commission explicitly emphasized and championed the welfare of educators throughout the nation. Historically, however, concern for the particular interests and welfare of classroom teachers was not always considered the chief function of the NEA.[3]

From the creation of the NEA in the middle of the nineteenth century the organization chiefly was guided by two principles. It sought, first, to elevate the role and status of education in the United States and, second, to advance the interests of the teaching profession. Throughout the nineteenth and the early decades of the twentieth centuries, the first function undoubtedly received greater attention and commitment than did the second. Edgar B. Wesley, commissioned by the NEA in 1957 to write the definitive history of the organization's first hundred years, neatly captured the NEA's *raison d'être* in its formative years,

> The National Education Association, during its first half century (1857-1907), was not greatly concerned with the personal welfare of either administrators or teachers. The lofty impersonal detachment that characterized the leaders was not a pose or a revelation of indifference, but a deliberately adopted philosophy. They were mindful of the difficulties of evolving an educational system that would fit an emerging society. They believed that all educators, including classroom teachers, should seek first to establish a profession. Hence, they regarded attention to salary, tenure, and status as premature, as entirely secondary to the growth of the profession.[4]

Rather than focus on the status of teachers, the NEA focused attention on theoretical issues, such as educational philosophy, national policy, and curriculum deliberation. Consequently, although the NEA passed resolutions advocating increased pay and improved conditions for classroom teachers in 1863, 1885, 1898, 1904, and 1911, the organization devoted little energy and commitment to such issues.[5]

The reason for the relative indifference of the NEA to the welfare of the teaching profession partly stemmed from the constitution of the Association. In its founding year, the NEA had only 43 members. Twenty-five years later, in 1882, the number totaled only 290; by the outbreak of World War I, membership of the NEA hovered below 8,000.[6] In many regards, the NEA was an elite organization. Its membership primarily comprised of university professors, college presidents, and school principals and superintendents. These individuals dominated the association's conventions and guided its philosophy. Significantly, very few classroom teachers belonged to the NEA or attended its annual meetings.

During World War II, membership of the NEA soared dramatically to a figure approaching a quarter of a million members. Increasing numbers of classroom teachers joined the Association as it broadened its appeal and re-focused its original philosophical positions. Gradually, the NEA became more responsive to the needs and demands of the ordinary classroom teacher.

By the early 1940s, many school teachers believed that the NEA had the strength, power, and influence effectively to exact significant improvements in the status and welfare of the teaching profession. According to Edgar , the change in policy in the first half of the twentieth century was both incremental and dramatic,

> Teachers, administrators, professors, and all other educators came to look to the NEA and its state and local affiliates as the principal means through which they could help themselves to gain recognition and status, tenure and freedom, better conditions of work, increased remuneration, and increased security for old age. By 1910 the NEA was demonstrating some interest in teacher welfare; in the 1920's it was vigorously advocating higher salaries and tenure laws; in the 1940's it became almost militant in its defense of teachers and their rights...[7]

The formation of the Defense Commission in 1941, therefore, was emblematic of the changing focus of the National Education Association and of its increased attention to the welfare of teachers.[8]

The Defense Commission also effectively served the desire of the NEA to make the Association into a truly national organization. As early as 1917, the executive secretary of the NEA, James W. Crabtree announced the goal to achieve "100 per cent membership in local, state, and national associations."[9] Not until the 1940s, however, did the NEA adopt a vigorous policy to unite all three levels of membership into a single organization with one annual dues membership payment for all members. From the outset, the Defense Commission worked to harness the energies of educators at local, state, and national levels. As a unifying force within the NEA's structure, the Defense Commission proved immensely effective and elevated the status of the NEA in the eyes of thousands of teachers. Indeed, the formation of the Defense Commission in 1941 supported the claim of the NEA's executive secretary, Willard Givens, who boasted to the Representative Assembly in July that the NEA

> ...unifies local, state, and national forces. It brings together teachers, principals, and superintendents. It represents elementary schools, secondary schools, colleges, and universities. It is the only all-inclusive, nationwide organization of educators in the United States.[10]

When Givens addressed the 1941 NEA assembly, membership stood at 211,191. Within ten years that figure doubled. The shift in the NEA's rationale that resulted in greater attention to the welfare, rights, and status of the nation's teaching force significantly contributed to that remarkable increase in membership. In a very real and practical sense, the creation and subsequent development of the Defense Commission played no small part in affecting this important philosophical and practical shift within the National Education Association.

The second reason for the establishment of the Defense Commission in 1941 was embedded in the political, ideological, and historical context of the age. While a sub-committee of the Department of Classroom Teachers met in May 1941 to outline tentative proposals for the creation of the Defense Commission, Europe was embroiled in the fury of war. By this time, Hitler's awesome forces had occupied Denmark and Norway and had smashed their way through the Low Countries and France. Most of Europe had fallen under the domination of the Third Reich. Although the Soviet Union was soon to enter into the conflict, in the late spring of 1941 the Russians remained militarily uninvolved.[11] Furthermore, Stalin's recent actions — most notably the signing of the Nazi-Soviet Pact in August 1939 — convinced the American people that the seemingly sinister and enigmatic Russians were not to be trusted.

As the delegates for the NEA's annual meeting gathered in Boston in the summer of 1941, like most Americans, they looked across the Atlantic and saw a continent poisoned by the totalitarian evils of fascism and communism. Only Britian, supported by Commonwealth forces and pledges, remained to counter Hitler's legions. Understandably, many delegates envisaged the emergence of a new world order in which only American democracy would stand in direct antipathy to the forces of totalitarianism. The repeated belief that the vital essence of a democratic way of living was in serious jeopardy dominated the proceedings, deliberations, and speeches of this meeting. For example, in her opening speech to the NEA assembly Mary Barnes, President of the Department of Classroom Teachers told the audience, "As we see the disintegration of institutions and governments in Europe, we recognize the necessity for cooperation among all citizens if our beloved democracy is to go on." Donald DuShane, President of the NEA, continued the tenor of the meeting in the next speech. DuShane declared, "Today we are meeting when the continuance of democracy in the United States and the world is in question."[12] Other speakers laced their talks with similar rhetorical flourishes and underscored the common conviction that democracy was under direct threat. Most dramatic of all were the colorful contentions of Congressman Joe Starnes from Alabama. Starnes was a member of the Dies Committee on investigation of un-American and subversive activities (HUAC). In his lengthy speech,

Congressman Starnes told the assembled educators that he agreed with Hitler on one thing only and that was that "he spoke the truth when he said that, in this world of ours, democracy and dictatorship cannot live side by side peacefully; one or the other must be destroyed." Starnes noted the increased mobilization of the United States as it prepared for the possibility of war. He reasoned,

> All this has been made necessary because Japan ruled by a military clique, Germany ruled a madman, Italy ruled by an unspeakable man, and Russia ruled by one of the slyest, craftiest, and most cruel of men have banded themselves together in a war against democracy.[13]

Suffused with the belief that democracy was under threat, NEA members at the conference and leading protagonists within the NEA understandably sought to establish the implicit relationship between support for sound public education and the preservation of a democratic society.

Among the membership of the NEA, the belief prevailed that democracy was the antidote to totalitarianism. Educators and guest speakers at this 1941 meeting repeatedly argued a single position: if society supported public education and allowed teachers to practice the American democratic ideals of, for example, free speech, freedom of inquiry, and freedom of thought, then the United States would remain a bulwark against the unwelcome advance of totalitarianism. If democracy were to endure, many believed, then American ideals, American values, and American ways must be championed and promoted by the teaching profession. As Mary Barnes told her Boston audience, "Here we have come to rededicate ourselves to the American way of life, and to renew our faith in, and our loyalty to, American education as the only safe means through which democracy can be fostered."[14] However, despite such a loyal commitment to American values and democratic ideals among the nation's educators, many teachers and schools encountered a widespread reluctance to financially support public education in the early 1940s.

In his address to the 1941 assembly, for example, President DuShane remarked on the regrettable lack of support for education throughout the nation,

> While we take great and justifiable pride in our schools, the fact remains that much must be done before American education will be able to protect our democracy through a long period of war and privation. From a national standpoint, our schools are not sufficiently financed, developed, or protected to ensure the future of our democracy.[15]

Like other participants in the 1941 meeting, DuShane was saddened by
many of the problems besetting American schools. For example, NEA
members who attended the 1941 meeting noted that a majority of the voting
population had less than an eighth grade education, that more than 18 million
adults could not read a letter appropriately, and, despite attendance laws,
more than 800,000 children of school age were not enrolled in any school.
Troubled by these developments, questioned if the American people were
prepared to make the financial sacrifices necessary to support public
education and, by extension, American democracy,

> In this period of national crisis it is as important to support and improve our
> schools as it is to support and develop our army and navy. To maintain the schools
> of our forty-eight states on a high level of efficiency will require much legislation,
> a considerable increase in school expenditures, and a better understanding by the
> general public of the necessity of effective mass education in a democracy. That
> these requirements will be met is, under present conditions, doubtful.

In response to this unfavorable situation, the leadership of the NEA
repeatedly emphasized that by not supporting public education, American
democracy was under direct threat. Moreover, they argued that the
predicament further would be exacerbated if teachers were not afforded the
democratic rights associated with a body of professional workers and
citizens.[16]

Therefore, the NEA established the National Commission for the
Defense of Democracy Through Education in 1941 both as a direct result
of the precarious position educators experienced at this time and because
of the perceived threat to American democracy. The commission was
charged to operate on two levels. First, it was commissioned clearly to
establish the direct and explicit relationship between the preservation of a
democratic society and a national commitment to American schools. In
this regard, subsequently, the commission distributed a profusion of public
relations materials and research reports to promote the cause of public
schooling. Second, the Defense Commission was established to promote
and advance the democratic rights of teachers in the United States. The
first function was a cause to which many other individuals, departments,
committees, and commissions within the NEA were totally committed.[17]
The second function, however, almost exclusively fell within the compass
of the Defense Commission.

In formulating the policies and principles that were to undergird the
practices of the Defense Commission, NEA officials sought to delineate

the basic rights of a democratic citizen and to explore the apparent gulf between those rights established in principle and the rights of teachers as they existed in practice. The writings of Robert Skaife, Field Secretary of the Defense Commission (1949-1955), starkly revealed this apparent discrepancy. In his 1951 doctoral dissertation, in which he evaluated the program of the Defense Commission, Skaife devoted an entire chapter to the meaning of democracy and its relationship to the rights of teachers in America.[18]

Drawing extensively on the principles embodied in landmark documents, such as the Declaration of Independence, the U. S. Constitution's Bill of Rights, the Preamble to the Charter of the United Nations Organization, and the Universal Declaration of Human Rights, Skaife teased out those elements essential to the enhancement of the teaching profession. For example, part of the text of the Universal Declaration of Human Rights asserts that,

> No one shall be subjected to arbitrary interference with his privacy, family, home, or correspondence, nor to attacks upon his honor or reputation.
>
> Everyone has the right to the protection of the law against such interference or attacks.
>
> Everyone has the right to freedom of thought, conscience, and religion.
>
> Everyone has the right to freedom of opinion and expression; this right includes freedom to hold opinions without interference and to seek, receive, and impart information and ideas through any media and regardless of frontiers.[19]

Unfortunately, despite the theoretic and much-vaunted principles on which American democracy was built, Skaife and others in the NEA illustrated how teachers across the United States were deprived of many of these basic human dignities. In the early 1940s and 1950s, teachers throughout the country often were denied job security, were held hostage to the capricious whims of disgruntled superintendents or political bosses, could not exercise freedom of conscience or freedom of speech, and could be dismissed summarily without explanation or redress. Consequently, a principal mission of the Defense Commission was to establish fundamental professional rights for teachers and to promote, to champion, and to protect those democratic rights at local, state, and national levels.

Establishment of the Defense Commission, therefore, was directly related to political, ideological, and military circumstances. In the early

1940s, with the ascendancy of the forces of dictatorship in Europe, many Americans perceived that, in the near future, the world would be divided between advocates of democracy and totalitarianism. Set against this backdrop, the leadership of the NEA espoused the direct relationship between the maintenance of democracy and the advancement of public education. They contended that if schools and teachers were accorded the financial support and the rights, freedoms, and commitment of a principled nation, then democracy would prevail. The mission of the Defense Commission was to establish this link in the public consciousness and, thereby, promote the specific interests of the teaching profession and the more general interests of American education.

The third reason for the creation of the Defense Commission was related directly to the previous two justifications. In 1941, as the prospect of war approached, the NEA anticipated that an already underfunded educational system soon would reach a point of crisis. Expressing the thoughts of many, President DuShane warned the Representative Assembly that, as the country inched toward war and as increased funding was diverted for military purposes, the federal government would increase taxes and national incomes would decline. He predicted that, as personal incomes became squeezed, not only would less support for the schools be apparent, but attacks on education would increase. Drawing on the experience of the post-World War I era and the depression years, DuShane reminded the audience that all too familiar problems would re-appear. He anticipated that teachers would be dismissed, classes would become overcrowded, salaries would be reduced, criticism of teachers would become rampant, and the morale of teachers would be destroyed.

DuShane contended that, unless the NEA acted, the prognosis for education was bleak. "With the tax situation approaching and with this increased criticism and undermining of public confidence in the schools," he told the audience, "we are confronted with the most destructive situation that the schools of America have faced."[20] Participants at the 1941 meeting in Boston also were under no illusion that, as the tax situation worsened, attacks on education would mount.

Several speakers understood and predicted that many of these critics of education would utilize red scare propaganda. One member proclaimed that, in discussing these attacks, the delegates were "dealing with the most important matter before this convention." He noted that "the tax cutters, the economic councils, the research bureaus, the merchants' associations, and the chambers of commerce" were accusing teachers of "subversive activity" and invoking "the shameful misuse of our patriotic spirit...to cripple the schools of the nation."[21] Other delegates agreed. One participant noted, "We have had attacks and will have attacks more and more upon our schools, and we need to organize for defense. Let us remember that this is going to be our first and biggest job now."[22] A proposal document distributed to every member of the Representative Assembly similarly was unequivocal. It noted that "various organizations have become active in recent months attempting to create a distrust of the efficiency of the public schools and of the loyalty of the teaching profession." The proposal for the establishment of the Defense Commission implored educators that these attacks must be met by the NEA with vigor and conviction.

In his advocacy of the establishment of the Defense Commission, President DuShane remarked that, during the depression years, no individual or organization effectively spoke for American teachers. In 1941, the situation was just as serious. "When charges are made there is no method to meet them," suggested DuShane, "there is no one to speak for the profession." DuShane wanted this situation to be remedied, and he urged that the NEA take an active role in challenging the attackers and advancing the interests of the teaching profession. "The National Education Association," he emphasized,

> is the only educational organization that reaches into every state of the Union; it is the only organization that has any chance during the next few years to have the strength, courage, and public support to speak out boldly for the schools, to defend the schools from attack, and to win support for public education....[23]

Significantly, in the ensuing debate about the establishment of the Defense Commission, not a single objection was raised. Indeed, as a testimony to how serious educators at this time perceived the attacks on education to be, the deliberations that followed centered on whether the assembly had the authority to appropriate more money to the Defense Commission than its proponents originally had requested. Members of the NEA clearly understood the need for the Defense Commission and assertively supported its creation.[24]

The origins of the Defense Commission, therefore, were based upon a combination of interrelated factors that were predominant in the early 1940s. Philosophical and organizational shifts within the NEA led to an increased concern for the welfare of ordinary classroom teachers. Championing of democratic rights for teachers, fervent support for the tenets of democracy as an antidote to totalitarianism, and the desire to defend teachers from unscrupulous and destructive attack all combined to affect what soon became one of the NEA's most influential and important agencies.

The Defense Commission: Purpose, Personnel, and Policy

The idea to establish a commission with responsibility to defend teachers and to promote the interests of education was not new. In 1936, the Indiana Education Association created its own state Defense Commission. Other states also organized piecemeal agencies to deal with unwarranted attacks on local teachers.[25] By 1941, the NEA leadership believed that the time was right for the establishment of a national defense commission to protect the rights of teachers in each of the then forty-eight states. Several reasons lay behind this newly found motivation.

First, the belief existed that individual localities and state organizations might be vulnerable to concerted attack and unable effectively to respond because of the limited resources and personnel at their disposal. In contrast, NEA leaders believed that a national organization would be able to defend teachers with all the machinery, personnel, and commitment possessed by a coherent and unified organization. NEA officers reasoned that a professional organization supported by hundreds of thousands of members had the power, influence, and political force to blunt the charges of those who criticized education.

In addition to this primary reason for the decision to establish the Defense Commission, the NEA also was concerned that attacks on education in certain communities often had their roots in the machinations of national level organizations. A nationwide organization, therefore, was needed to investigate the origins, motivations, and tactics of these groups in order that educators at local and state levels could be warned of their potentially destructive influence. "We need also to ascertain," Donald DuShane explained,

> what is going on on the part of some of these organizations organized specifically for the purpose of injuring schools. We should all know what they are doing in their various communities. Very often the people of Louisiana or Indiana or Colorado may be injured through attacks upon their schools starting in New York and those people can do nothing about it, because they are a way off from the center of propaganda, and so those problems must be faced nationally.[26]

Another important argument that supported the creation of a national organization centered on the belief that those working to defend teachers must be "protected people." In other words, members of the commission must be secure in their jobs, free from outside pressure, and willing to confront inevitable criticism. At state and local levels, the NEA was concerned that every time members took a stand they might well be vulnerable to the pressure of possible dismissal. Only at the national level, with the support of a unified and devoted association, the NEA leadership argued, could members of the Defense Commission stand protected from the political chicanery of the critics.[27]

The Defense Commission was established formally at the NEA's Annual Meeting in June 1941. Earlier, in the spring of 1940, the Executive Committee considered the creation of a national defense commission. It asked two of the chief advocates of the commission, President Donald DuShane and Executive Secretary Willard Givens, to draw up plans for serious consideration at the Atlantic City Convention later that year. Subsequently, a subcommittee was established to look further into the details and logistics for the creation of the Defense Commission. The subcommittee invited various educational groups to consider the outline proposals and to return written criticisms by May 10, 1940. After a very lengthy consultative process, the formal proposal was laid before the Representative Assembly in Boston in the summer of 1941.

At the 1941 Annual Meeting, each member of the Representative Assembly received a copy of the proposal for the creation of the National Commission for the Defense of Democracy Through Education. The document clearly stated the essential purposes of the Defense Commission,

> To create public understanding and support of education through informing leaders of lay organizations concerning educational purposes and needs, and to strengthen education through analyzing and evaluating educational activities and recommending the discontinuance of those found to be unsound.
>
> To investigate criticisms and movements against education, school systems, teachers colleges, textbooks, teachers organizations, and members of the teaching profession; and to publish the results of such investigations as are found to be significant and constructive.
>
> To catalog the various groups opposing education; to investigate the sources of their funds; and to make resumes of their activities available to local and state teachers' organizations.
>
> To cooperate with state teachers' associations in analyzing sources of taxation and financial conditions; and to help coordinate the work of local and state associations with lay organizations.

To investigate alleged subversive teaching; and to expose any teacher whose attitude is found to be inimical to the best interests of our country.

To acquaint individual teachers with their responsibilities for participating in the public relations program of the schools; and to help them with their work in this field.

To bring to the teaching profession a greater unity of purpose in education for democracy and a better knowledge of methods of securing public understanding and support.[28]

To execute these stated purposes, the NEA recognized the need for robust and committed personnel.

From the creation of the Defense Commission and throughout its existence, its actions were guided by a group of ten people. The executive committee of the NEA appointed seven members for three-year terms. Also serving were the current president of the NEA, the chairman of the NEA's Board of Trustees, and the NEA's executive secretary. In addition, each state and regional teachers' association named one representative bringing the total to approximately sixty members. In intention and in practice, therefore, the Defense Commission was a national organization that boasted the inclusion of some of the NEA's most influential and powerful members.

The NEA Executive Committee also charged the steering committee to select a leader for the Defense Commission. This person would be employed by the NEA. Without hesitation, the committee appointed Donald DuShane to the new post. Undoubtedly, as the current president of the NEA, DuShane's impending leadership provided the newly created Defense Commission immediate substance, stature, and credibility.

Selection of the seven members of the commission, appointed for three-year terms, also was based upon the desire to assemble a group of educators at once representative of the teaching profession and actively committed to the ideals of the NEA. Specifically, the NEA's executive committee discussed eleven criteria on which selection of Defense Commission members was based:

1. an understanding of the problems faced by the commission,
2. an enthusiastic and sympathetic interest in these problems,
3. willingness to make the work of the commission the first professional obligation,
4. security of position,
5. reasonable geographic distribution,
6. classroom teacher representation,
7. equitable division between men and women,
8. tolerance and charity in working with others,

9. individuals with strong convictions, but who will give 100 per cent support to the decisions of the group,

10. individuals who are nationally known, and

11. individuals with various types of backgrounds and opinions.[29]

After deliberation, three distinguished figures from higher education were asked to serve on the commission: Frank Graham, President, University of North Carolina; Ernest O. Melby, Dean, School of Education, Northwestern University; and Alonzo F. Myers, School of Education, New York University. In addition, Orville C. Pratt, Superintendent of Schools, Spokane, Washington, and three classroom teachers, Mary D. Barnes (Elizabeth, New Jersey), Kate Frank (Muskogee, Oklahoma), and Frederick Houk Law (New York City, New York) were named to join the Defense Commission.[30] Significantly, two years later, Kate Frank became embroiled in her own personal school battle in Muskogee, Oklahoma. During the controversy, which initially led to her dismissal and eventually resulted in her reinstatement, Frank drew upon the influential support of the Defense Commission.

From the outset, therefore, the NEA recognized the need to have a strong and resolute Defense Commission comprised of influential leaders in education and able and committed classroom practitioners. Led by Donald DuShane and supported by individuals significant in the NEA hierarchy, such as Executive Secretary Willard Givens, the association seriously understood the potential impact of an effective commission in the defense of the teaching profession and in the vigorous support of public education.[31] Indeed, Donald DuShane articulated the considerable promise of the Defense Commission. He advised that if the right type of commission were created, with "the right kind of staff back of it," and if it were given "all the financial support" required, then, he believed, "The National Education Association can come into its own, can speak for the teaching profession of the country as it has never done before, and can occupy the field that needs to be occupied."[32] DuShane's confident assertion reflected both the troubled world of education in the early 1940s and the critical importance that he, and many others within the NEA, attached to the creation of the Defense Commission.

Chapter IV

The Defense Commission
During Its Formative Years, 1941-1948

Fundamentally, the activities of the Defense Commission were driven by two guiding aims and principles. First, the commission sought to protect and defend the rights of teachers; second, it desired to increase public awareness of, and support for, the needs of public schools throughout the United States.

The desire to accomplish the first of these goals primarily resulted from the vulnerable position in which educators found themselves at the beginning of the 1940s. In addition to the low salaries teachers received, the overcrowded classrooms in which they worked, and the low social status accorded to them by society, teachers across the country faced acute job insecurity. Fewer than half of the nation's million teachers enjoyed the protection of a state's tenure law that assured a teacher's continued service providing he or she worked satisfactorily. A quarter were employed under "continuing contracts," which, despite some concessions, still enabled the employing school district to terminate without cause a teacher's contract at the end of the school year. The remainder of the nation's teachers — approximately a quarter of a million of them — held no legal protection whatsoever with regard to their employment.[1] As the defender of the rights of educators, the Defense Commission feverishly worked to remedy this appalling lack of security in employment.

The commission was very concerned that as teachers could be dismissed without notice or explanation, many would fall victim to the whimsical actions of disgruntled or politically embattled superintendents or to the arbitrary meddling of powerful business leaders or local politicians in school administration. At the NEA's 1947 annual meeting in Cincinnati, one speaker echoed the sentiments of many others by noting that "teachers in many parts of the country lived in fear."[2] Not surprisingly, in this perceived climate of repression, both teachers and administrators often avoided controversial issues and refrained from classroom practices or discussions to which influential individuals in the community might object.

In its campaign for tenure protection for teachers, the Defense Commission understood the need to garner the support of the general public. Its work dovetailed with that of the NEA, in general. For example, every year throughout the 1940s and early 1950s, Willard Givens, the Executive Secretary of the NEA, produced his widely distributed "Annual Report of the Profession to the Public."[3] In repeated issues, Givens argued that increased tenure protection for teachers would result in better education for the nation's children. For example, in his 1946 report, "Our Schools," Givens asserted,

> Teacher tenure makes possible better schools for our children. Teachers who are secure in their employment grow in the practice of their profession and enter actively into the affairs of the community in which they live.... We must protect our teachers from the domination of those who seek to control them for political or selfish purpose. Every child has a right to the best possible instruction from a teacher unharried by constant pressure and fear.[4]

The Defense Commission also argued that increased tenure protection significantly would reduce the mounting exodus of teachers from the profession that had occurred in the years since Pearl Harbor. The number of teachers who left the profession during and after the Second World War amounted to a staggering 350,000 and resulted in "one of the greatest vocational migrations in the nation's history."[5] In the immediate post-war years, the nation's teachers' colleges attracted half the intake of the pre-war period, and acute teaching shortages were commonplace across the nation. The problem was further compounded by the overwhelming number of inexperienced and uncertified teachers who practiced in American schools during the 1940s and early 1950s. The Defense Commission eagerly sought to draw attention to these troubling developments and, thereby, elicit the support of the American public for secure tenure for American teachers.

The actions of the Defense Commission were underpinned by the NEA's concern that teachers enjoyed employment conditions concomitant with a professional organization in a democratic society. The NEA leadership believed that these circumstances included "the right to economic security," the "right to job security," and the "right to discuss and teach issues that may prove controversial."[6] Importantly, officers of the NEA asserted, "Every teacher should have the right to express his sincere opinion without fear or retaliation." They added, "Every teacher is entitled to be fully informed about any teaching weakness, to be given time to correct them, and to be given supervisory help in so doing."[7] Above all, the NEA campaigned for the rights of teachers to be secure in their jobs unless tangible evidence discredited their status as an employee in an honorable profession.

The Defense Commission, therefore, devoted considerable efforts to the issue of tenure protection. It lobbied state legislatures, stirred local school districts to action, and conducted a concerted public relations campaign. However, perhaps the most effective method of defending teachers and of bringing the tenure question to widespread attention was through the increasingly well-publicized and well-known Defense Commission investigations.

Of all the activities in which the Defense Commission engaged during its existence, none were more celebrated than its investigations. From its inception, one of the commission's primary purposes was, "to investigate criticisms and movements against education...and members of the teaching profession, and to publish the results of such investigations as are found to be significant and constructive."[8] Requests for NEA Defense Commission investigations originated at the local and state level. The commission then undertook a preliminary review of the particular situation and determined whether or not an investigation was warranted. As the reputation of the commission grew, requests for investigations at the local level escalated. As personnel and resources were limited and investigations consumed time, talent, and resources the commission carefully had to select which cases to pursue. Consequently, rather than become embroiled in essentially local issues, the Defense Commission focused attention on those cases that it believed held national significance and that would strengthen the teaching profession in the eyes of the public.

Typically, the Defense Commission conducted two forms of inquiry. Based on the nature of the local situation and on the time and resources it considered necessary to investigate the complaint or conflict, the Defense Commission conducted either a preliminary inquiry or a full-scale investigation. Between 1942 and 1949, the commission undertook nineteen preliminary defense cases. Although they were important to educators and often achieved favorable results, these preliminary inquiries remained unpublished and received limited national prominence. Nevertheless, the unpublished defense cases illuminated many of the problems common in the teaching profession in the 1940s. That these matters also were geographically scattered suggests that teachers across the United States encountered similar problems.

From Gardiner, Maine, to Valencia County, New Mexico, and from Natchez, Mississippi, to Omaha, Nebraska, the Defense Commission investigated numerous cases that impacted the lives of local teachers.[9] Almost without exception, the issues addressed by the investigations also represented matters germane to educators across the nation. Often, as in the cases of Kenosha, Wisconsin, and of Cambridge, Ohio, educators were dismissed for their active participation in local teacher associations. In 1947, in Pampa, Texas, two teachers were dismissed because of their campaign for a local increase in teacher salaries. In Hot Springs, Arkansas, Syracuse, New York, Shorewood, Wisconsin, and Las Vegas, New Mexico, teachers, principals, and/or superintendents also were discharged because their personal political affiliations conflicted either with those of the local school board and/or with influential groups in the communities. In Valencia County, New Mexico, for example, a local teacher was dismissed because he refused to contribute $75 and 2% of his monthly income to the activities of local politicians.

Although adequate documentation remains incomplete and elusive, use of red scare propaganda and rhetoric in many of these politically charged cases seems likely. Certainly, in 1942, taxers organizations in Omaha, Nebraska, readily adopted the tactics and methods of the red scare in a concerted effort to thwart a teacher-led campaign for an increased tax levy. Tangible evidence of the red scare also existed in Buffalo, New York, in 1948. At the time, a Buffalo teacher was dismissed for alleged "un-American" activity and for "bringing politics into the school system." In addition, in Lebanon, New Hampshire, the Defense Commission investigated a case in which a Canadian-born female teacher was discharged because she was an "alien" and in which the troubled superintendent questioned what would "happen to democracy when aliens led a crusade against constituted authority."[10]

In the six full-scale investigations conducted by the Defense Commission between 1942 and 1949, however, explicit evidence of red scare activity was scarce.[11] Most of these investigations focused on areas of "educational controversy" and unwarranted "political interference" with the democratic rights of teachers. For example, the Defense Commission's first full-scale investigation targeted New York City, in February 1944. It exposed the political interference and corruption of Mayor LaGuardia in the New York City school system.[12] The second investigation, in Chicago during May 1945, revealed "evidence of dishonest political interference and other unfair practices" on the part of the Chicago Superintendent Dr. William H. Johnson.[13] McCook, Nebraska, in May 1947 was the site of the third investigation that questioned the motives of the local school board's "dismissal of teachers without cause."[14] Other investigations followed in North College Hill, Ohio, Chandler, Arizona, and Grand Prairie, Texas. In each of these cases, the NEA's Defense Commission supported local teachers, exposed wrongdoing, elevated public awareness of illicit educational practice, and promoted a more democratic, professional, and just system of public education.

The Defense Commission, through these investigations, met with varying degrees of success in its appointed role as the defender of teachers. The commission always was hampered by the fact that its investigating committee lacked legal authority. Its influence, consequently, only could be exerted through appeals to the local community, to the media, and to the fair-mindedness of local school officials. In each case, the commission published detailed recommendations that, if carried out, the committee believed would improve the particular grievances as well as the educational environment in the particular school district. Significantly, in many cases in which full and preliminary investigations were conducted, the Defense Commission's recommendations often were followed, and notable improvements resulted.[15]

Unquestionably, as the commission continued its work, its credibility and stature grew in the eyes of the teaching profession and the public at large. In many cases, educators found to be unfairly discharged were re-instated following a Defense Commission investigation. Even in those cases in which teachers fell victim to allegedly unscrupulous practices in one school district, the Defense Commission effectively supported them as they sought employment elsewhere. The commission's ability to give discredited teachers a "clean bill of professional health" inured educators against unwarranted attack and served to strengthen the professional influence of the NEA throughout the nation.

The investigations also exposed those school districts that blatantly infringed the democratic rights of teachers. The Defense Commission used media attention and conducted public relations campaigns to great effect in the illumination of the unfair practices of several school districts.[16] "School boards, responsible to the community," wrote the field secretary of the Defense Commission,

do not welcome unfavorable publicity. If they are inclined to overstep their
responsibilities, the fact that the teaching profession has a commission that will
enter into the local situation if the conditions warrant such action, is a deterrent,
a potential threat in their minds.[17]

The effectiveness of the Defense Commission in the promotion of change
favorable to the teaching profession at the local level also strengthened the
NEA at the national level. The leadership of the NEA and the Defense
Commission passionately believed that the defense of teachers in particular
communities vigorously strengthened the teaching profession throughout
the nation. Protection for teachers in one community provided protection
for teachers everywhere. By the late 1940s, therefore, although the
commission lacked legal authority, its investigations proved successful in
the support of the democratic rights of teachers in school districts across
the length and breadth of the country.

Despite the Defense Commission's successes, the continued need for
investigations underlined the precarious positions in which teachers found
themselves during the 1940s and early 1950s. Essentially, in communities
throughout the United States, teachers often were dismissed without
explanation, and they enjoyed little opportunity for redress. Therefore,
although the Defense Commission was relatively successful in those areas
in which it focused its attention, unscrupulous and undemocratic practices
by school boards and superintendents in other areas often occurred in this
period. In response to this situation, rather than concentrating solely on
individual cases, the Defense Commission decided to attend to national
legislation that impacted the lives of every teacher in the nation.

The Hatch Act was one piece of national legislation opposed by the
Defense Commission. The Hatch Act, passed in 1939, sought to prevent
"pernicious political activities."[18] Fundamentally, it prohibited any employee
paid from federal funds from participation in political activities, such as
local, state, or national elections.[19] In many school districts, the act was
used by local officials to prevent educators from becoming involved in
local elections. At a time when the teaching profession needed political
allies and when education desperately needed increased funding, the Hatch
Act had damaging implications for educators. The NEA, therefore,
vigorously asserted the democratic right of educators to participate in
legitimate political affairs. A resolution passed at the annual meeting of the
NEA in 1941 urged an amendment to the act. In support of the resolution,
one delegate noted, "we have a solemn obligation to restore to the teachers
of the nation the right to full and active participation in the affairs of the

American government."[20] As testimony to the organizational skills of the Defense Commission and to its growing political influence, the Brown Amendment to the Act was finally signed into law by President Roosevelt on October 24, 1941.

The passage of the Brown Amendment, which stated that educators could lawfully participate in political matters, signaled an important and highly visible early victory for the Defense Commission. "It means that the Congress of the United States," noted Donald DuShane, the executive secretary of the commission, "now gives full recognition to the political freedom of the teaching profession...it means that teachers may wholeheartedly enter into campaigns to elect public officials favorable to the support of public schools."[21] The NEA repeatedly asserted the right of educators to involve themselves in civic affairs.[22] The campaign to elevate public regard for teachers, however, was difficult and — despite the passage of the Brown Amendment and regular assertions by the NEA leadership that educators must enjoy the same democratic privileges as any ordinary citizen — teachers and administrators continued to face dismissal for political activities throughout the 1940s and 1950s.

Significantly, the allegedly political acts of dismissed high school teacher Kate Frank in 1943 occasioned the formation by the NEA of a national teachers' defense fund. The establishment of the fund provided further illustration of the Commission's desire to achieve national recognition through involvement in local cases.

In 1942, the local Board of Education in Muskogee, Oklahoma, cut the school year from nine months to eight and one-half months. Due in part to the efforts of Kate Frank, an original member of the Defense Commission, the Muskogee Board of Education paid the teachers for the two weeks income due them under their contracts. Disturbed by the political campaigning of Frank, the school board dismissed her and two of her colleagues. Despite twenty-three years of devoted service to the Muskogee schools, Frank learned of her dismissal from a story in the local newspaper. She received no written or verbal notice of her dismissal, nor did she receive an explanation. In a lengthy case, vigorously supported by the Defense Commission, Frank eventually was reinstated.[23]

Of greater significance, even than its efforts to defend Frank and her colleagues and to finance the legal costs of her defense, the NEA established a fund to be administered jointly by the Committee on Tenure and Academic Freedom and the Defense Commission. Monies were collected directly from voluntary contributions proffered by NEA members. In its first year, the fund amounted only to $3,795.60, but enough to pay Frank's salary for the year and a half for which she was unemployed. Steadily the fund increased. By 1957, for example, annual expenditure amounted to $82,620.[24] With the death, in 1949, of Donald DuShane, the commission's influential leader, the fund was named in his honor. Between 1949 and 1955, the DuShane Memorial Defense Fund allocated monies to persons who requested assistance from the $37,000 contributed by members of the NEA from 1949 to 1954. The money chiefly was distributed to educators judged unfairly treated by local school districts. Typically, the funds paid for teachers' legal expenses or for their living costs during the period under investigation. Despite the limited financial support available and the relatively few recipients of the money, the defense fund symbolized the Defense Commission's commitment to support teachers in difficult times. Importantly, the defense fund received national attention and elevated the status of the NEA in the eyes of many within the teaching profession.[25]

In achieving the first of the Defense Commission's two primary purposes (i.e., to protect and defend the rights of educators), the commission enjoyed some notable success. For example, its formative years saw the development of the increasingly influential Defense Commission investigation. Other activities included the establishment of a teacher's defense fund, legislative amendments to the Hatch Act, and vigorous campaigns for improved tenure laws. Yet, within the profession, impressively large and knotty problems remained unattended. In the 1940s and early 1950s, many teachers remained insecure in their teaching positions and appeared vulnerable to reflexive criticism and dismissal. Ironically, just as the Defense Commission was making progress in securing and defending the rights of teachers, the situation worsened. Indeed, by the late 1940s and early 1950s, attacks on education appeared rampant. In this renewed climate of hostility, the need for an effective Defense Commission became both more apparent and more acute.

The second major function of the Defense Commission, particularly in its formative years, sought to capture the support of the general public. The rationale behind this policy was simple. If citizens fully appreciated and understood the problems facing education, the NEA believed, then, that the public would support local schools. Furthermore, a logical corollary to this development would be the improvement of the status, income, and welfare of the teaching profession.

The NEA leadership reasoned, perhaps simplistically, that Americans' lack of enthusiastic support for education stemmed not so much from widespread public apathy, but more from ignorance of the serious problems faced by public schools in the 1940s. Accordingly, the NEA leadership supported the Defense Commission because they believed it was a useful and dynamic agency both to promote the cause of educators and to explain the problems that challenged public education during this period.

America's one million teachers and administrators faced a severe social and economic plight during the 1940s and 1950s. In 1941, the year the Defense Commission was formed, the average salary of an American public school teacher was $1,470. In contrast, the average salary for a lawyer or a doctor in independent practice amounted to $4,794 and $5,047 respectively. The NEA often focused on the income of individuals in other professions as a way of emphasizing the gross disparities that existed. More troubling to educators, however, was that the average federal government employee received an annual wage of $4,150, almost triple teachers' average salaries.[26] Indeed, in his annual report, the executive secretary of the NEA expressed his disgust that, "Fully one-third of the teachers in this country are now working for a salary which is substantially less than the wages of the women who scrub the floors and polish the furniture of its offices in the nation's capital."[27] In 1944, the average annual pay for teachers was $464 less than the average worker in private employment.

The relatively low salaries of teachers became a constant source of complaint at NEA conventions throughout the 1940s and early 1950s. At the 1945 conference in Chicago, for example, Ralph McDonald, Executive Secretary of the NEA Department of Higher Education, regretted that the federal government spent a large sum to teach pig farmers, but "not one cent" to aid in the professional education of teachers of children. "Do the people of the United States want good schools and teachers?" the speaker asked the assembly,

> With a thousand voices they say they do. Businessmen, statesmen, leaders of all kinds say "We must have better teachers." Their words are in contrast with the hard, cold facts: Teachers are leaving the profession; college students are shunning teacher preparation; teaching salaries are pitifully low; we spend $7,000 million annually on liquor as compared with $3,000 million on education; we pay $12,000 million for a peace time Army and Navy, four times as much as we pay to educate 25 million students. These and other facts speak louder than words.[28]

NEA members also became alarmed by the grave disparities within the profession. Although the national average salary of teachers in 1944 was a paltry $1,728, in four states salaries averaged less than $1,000. Additionally, more than 40,000 teachers earned less than $600 for their year's work.[29] In some rural areas, teachers were paid a mere $300 a year for their labors, and, in the early 1940s, in several states, "colored" teachers earned less than $300 per annum.[30]

The problem of low income was compounded and exacerbated by the low social status accorded to teachers in the post-war years. Many citizens tended to place teachers in a somewhat special category. Often, educators were denied personal freedoms enjoyed by others in the community. For example, in some school districts school boards censored teachers for engaging in "amusements and recreation commonly enjoyed by other responsible citizens."[31] Teachers who purchased clothing and other personal items outside the town in which they worked frequently were criticized. Leaving the area of the school district for weekends also was frowned upon.[32]

Restrictions on economic and personal liberties were most pronounced among female teachers. In 1948, for example, the NEA's annual "Report of the Secretary," asserted that in the early 1940s married women were ineligible for appointment as regular teachers in 58% of the city-schools systems and a further 29% of American school districts appointed married women only under special conditions. In many communities, women teachers who married after appointment were subject to immediate dismissal.[33] Teachers complained that, unlike other professions, they were singled out for unfair practices. One female educator expressed anger that teachers were denied the "right to be a person" and noted the restrictions local communities placed on their social activities. "It is not true," Vera M. Butler told the NEA delegation in Cleveland,

> that a teacher wishes to drink, smoke, or dash out to dances, but she does resent the fact that teachers are the only group singled out by society for control...Socially the teacher is invited out to dinner with the gray beards as a dull duty, but is seldom included in the gay party or the family outing.[34]

Limits on the professional and democratic rights of teachers often were most acute in rural school districts.

At the end of the Second World War, one half of the nation's children attended, and 54% of its teachers taught, in rural schools. Although some excellent rural schools existed, millions of children in agricultural communities were handicapped by serious educational problems. Often, the money expended on education in rural areas was significantly lower than that spent in urban school systems. For example, in 1945, rural schools spent $86 per year per pupil compared to an average expenditure of $124 in town and city schools. Indeed, according to the NEA Executive Secretary Willard Givens, the average annual income for a rural teacher in 1945 was less than half that of the average teacher in the larger cities and towns.[35]

Furthermore, grave teacher shortages, classroom overcrowding, lack of tenure protection, restrictions on social freedoms, and inadequate wages exemplified some of the very real problems facing the post-war teaching profession. Formation of the Defense Commission in this period explicitly related to these conditions. The NEA's leadership believed that a robust and active Defense Commission would not only blunt the criticisms of those attacking education at this time, but that it also would elevate and promote the interests of the teaching profession in an aggressively proactive way.

Throughout the existence of the Defense Commission, its leaders believed in the value and importance of a cogent public relations program. Consequently, as an extremely effective way of communicating the various issues crucial to education in the 1940s, the commission convened a series of educator-lay conferences. The first of these meetings was held in conjunction with representatives of the National Association of Manufacturers (NAM) in 1942.[36] A traditionally conservative group, the NAM had been critical of public education and, in particular, troubled by its increasing cost. However, in 1943, following a series of 15 conferences held in cities throughout the country, the attitude of the NAM leadership appeared to shift. The conferences enabled educators and industrialists to discuss crucial educational issues and to reconcile mutual misconceptions and suspicions. In addition, the NAM passed a resolution that supported adequate funding for schools, and, throughout the conferences it evidenced a genuine concern for the plight of public schools.[37] That the Defense Commission considered these conferences successful is expressed by Chairman Alonzo Myers' 1943 commission report,

Resulting from these conferences there has been a notable change in attitude toward education and its adequate financial support on the part of the nation's business and industrial leaders.... [W]e plan greatly to extend our program of cooperation and conferences with all important lay groups in the United States. It is our conviction that this kind of activity will pay huge dividends in the form

of better understanding of education, its problems, and its needs and will lay a
sound basis for support for the adequate financing of public education.[38]

The undoubted early success of these conferences spurred the Defense
Commission to extend the magnitude and scope of the commission's
conference program.

Impressed by the work of the Defense Commission, the NEA Executive
Committee granted the commission $25,000 in October 1943 from its War
and Peace Fund to organize conferences in order that a fuller understanding
of the war and post-war role of the public schools might be developed by
all groups in American life. In 1944, the commission used the funds to
establish a program of conferences in 27 cities throughout the United States.
Conference attendees represented a wide spectrum of American society.
They included leaders of business, industry, labor, agriculture, civic
organizations, chambers of commerce, parents' groups, patriotic groups,
the American Legion, the League of Women Voters, and a host of other
professional organizations. By the end of 1945, these educator-lay
conferences had brought together an estimated 12,000 citizens in 40 states
in order to discuss the problems encountered by public education in the
modern era.[39] The NEA considered these conferences to be of enormous
value in its solicitation of lay support for public schools and to counter
unwelcome attacks. As a consequence, educator-lay conferences continued
to be a feature of the work of the Defense Commission throughout the
1940s and 1950s.

The National Commission for the Defense of Democracy Through
Education supplemented its valuable educator-lay conferences with other
vigorous public relations campaigns. The commission became heavily
involved in the promotion of the work of the NEA's Citizenship Committee
and in achieving mass public participation in "American Education Week."
The commission also regularly distributed pamphlets and information sheets
to NEA members and to influential public figures in order to extol the
benefits of widespread support of the public schools.

With the active cooperation and leadership of the Defense Commission,
the NEA had made some important gains by the mid-1950s. Indeed, NEA
historian Edgar B. Wesley noted that the "phenomenal growth" of the NEA
from 219,334 members in 1943 to 659,190 in 1956 was, in part, explained
by the sterling work of the Defense Commission in its role as defender of
the teaching profession. He noted that "fifty years ago a teacher or a principal
or a superintendent could be discharged at the whim of the school board."

"Today," Wesley wrote in 1957, "the more than a million professional personnel of the nation's schools know that in the event of unjust dismissal they can call for help from the NEA's Defense Commission."[40]

As a result of the ambitious efforts of the Defense Commission and of the Committee on Tenure and Academic Freedom, public school educators by mid-century displayed a more professional appearance. In 1920, only five states recognized in law the principle of permanent teacher tenure. In contrast, by 1955, 32 states had established tenure laws. In 1946, 123,000 emergency sub-standard certificates were held by teachers; in 1955, only 71,589 such qualifications existed. In 1946, only 41,000 degree-holding teachers were professionally educated; in 1955, the number doubled to 86,696. In 1946, 882,980 teachers belonged to their state associations; in 1955, 1,026,932 were so affiliated. In 1946, 78% of teachers had some form of legal tenure; in 1955, 82% enjoyed tenure protection.[41]

Despite many setbacks to the education profession during the post-war era, public education accomplished some notable achievements. Without question, the NEA's Defense Commission played a major role in affecting these changes and in bringing about a significant improvement in the lives of many classroom teachers.

Red Scare Attack, 1941-1948

The 1940s proved a difficult time for American education. Despite the notable achievements of the Defense Commission during the decade, serious problems continued to plague public schooling. In the late 1940s and early 1950s, these problems intensified. Criticism of the public schools assumed a more disturbing and ominous tone. The use of red scare methods and tactics to attack educators increasingly became a dominant feature of the age.

Although these attacks burgeoned in the late 1940s, the Defense Commission appeared conscious of their existence in the early years of the decade. Attacks on education extensively were reported in the commission's regular publication, the *Defense Bulletin*. As the commission's mouthpiece, the *Bulletin* reported on a range of issues in which the NEA actively was involved. Although the contents of *Defense Bulletins* issued between 1941 and 1948 indicate that the commission was not absorbed with red scare attacks, they nevertheless reveal an increasing concern for the emerging phenomenon.

Critics who used red scare rhetoric and tactics encompassed a curious assortment of individual and groups. Curriculum scholar William Van Til disparagingly described those "hard core adherents" as a "mixed bag of economic royalists, tax cutters, superpatriots, and religious zealots, plus assorted racists, bigots, and other monomaniacal kooks."[42] The attackers of America's schools during the period between 1941 and 1948 reasonably may be separated into three major categories: first, patriotic organizations and groups that specifically appeared as vigilantes of public education; second, business and tax-payer associations that fervently adopted red scare tactics and propaganda to attack pubic schools' need for increased financial support, and, third, politicians and political groups who used their influential positions publicly to accuse the teaching profession of "subversion" and "un-American" activities.

Recognizing the special threat of the patriotic groups and educational vigilantes, the Defense Commission accorded them special attention. In particular, the commission was troubled by the growing body of widely distributed literature that emanated from the innocently named *Bulletin of the Friends of the Public Schools*. As an organization, the Friends of the Public Schools, led by retired army General Amos A. Fries, proved to be one of education's fiercest and most prolific critics. In 1942, the organization's propaganda bulletin boasted regular distribution to 33,000 individuals. Copies of his *Bulletin* were sent "free to as many city school boards as possible, to county superintendents, and to members of Congress and other government officials."[43] The charges made by Fries were familiar: teachers were advancing communism, instilling un-American values in children and youth, and generally advocating acts of subversion.

Unashamedly, Fries also targeted the NEA for particular criticism. In the summer of 1946, Fries spoke to Chicago members of the Friends of the Public Schools and described the NEA as an organization "completely dominated by communists and fellow travelers."[44] He attacked the NEA for promoting the cause of socialism and for sponsoring textbooks that affronted patriotism. Fries' comments were reported sympathetically in the press, and they stirred Frank C. Waldrop of the Washington (D.C.) *Times-Herald* to suggest that HUAC should "have a look at" the "peculiarities of the NEA." He excoriated, "Lift the veil, gentlemen, and see what you find. There are red rats in the schools. Shoo them out."[45]

Another aggressive and influential red scare organization was the Committee for Constitutional Government (CCG). By the mid-1940s, this group had produced a plethora of pamphlets that attacked public school methods and practices. Furthermore, it eagerly distributed copies of John T. Flynn's *The Road Ahead*, which argued that the New Deal and Democratic Party legislation lead straight to communism.[46] The CCG sold more than 10 million copies of Flynn's opus in its first four years of publication. The committee promoted sales of the book through direct mail campaigns to more than three and a half million addresses.[47] Significantly, by 1950, the Committee for Constitutional Government had spent almost $2 million for lobbying purposes and had distributed 82 million booklets and pamphlets during the previous seven years.[48]

Several self-described patriotic organizations launched attacks on teaching materials and textbooks commonly used in the public schools. For example, the Guardians of American Education, Incorporated, was formed chiefly to question the loyalty of textbooks written by Harold S. Rugg. In 1946, the Defense Commission also noted venomous criticism from both the Sons and the Daughters of the American Revolution. The DAR condemned an eighth grade history textbook as only being favorable to "New Deal Democrats, pinks, or socialists." In addition, Aaron Sargent, an attorney who represented the California branch of the SAR, similarly poured invective on the widely used "Building America" series and further suggested these textbooks were clear evidence of communist infiltration of the schools.[49]

Mindful of the early warnings of NEA President Donald DuShane, the Defense Commission proved extremely vigilant of the second category of critics: the business groups and the tax-payers' associations. In an effort to reduce taxes, these groups often used red scare propaganda to extinguish calls for federal aid and increased local financial support for public education. In 1941, for example, the Citizens Emergency Committee consorted with 19 state tax-payers' associations to declare that schools and other public services represented "luxuries which the ordinary community can no longer afford."[50] The Defense Commission monitored similar attacks from such organizations as the National Hardware Manufacturers' Association, the Conference of State Taxers' Organizations, the Employers Association of Chicago, and the American Bottlers of Carbonated Beverages.[51] Typically, these and other groups contended that educators routinely advanced the cause of communism through their subversive classroom practices. An early example of such criticism appeared in the comments of Les Allman, Vice-President of the Fruehauf Trailer Company, in an address to the Michigan Trucking Association,

> Is it so strange that many of our young folks come out of the schools and the
> universities with cockeyed impressions about America and about our marvelous
> way of life, of doing business? A prominent industrialist picked up a textbook —
> used by his nephew, attending a modern high school in the midwest — and
> found it definitely and poisonously colored with communistic thinking.[52]

Other organizations expressed similar concerns. Late in 1945, Schipper
Associates issued a news release that expressed the increasing concern of
businessmen that school textbooks openly were critical of the American
system of free enterprise. Among influential elements of the American
business community, therefore, existed the commonly held belief that public
education both explicitly disavowed essential American ideals and
championed the cause of socialism and communism.

The third group that received the serious scrutiny of the Defense
Commission included individual politicians and political associations who
actively sought to suppress what they perceived to be "subversive activity"
in the schools. Significantly, many references to red scare attacks by
politicians were voiced long before Senator Joseph McCarthy made his
renowned and widely publicized accusations in Wheeling, West Virginia,
in February 1950.[53] For example, in September 1946, the commission's
Defense Bulletin revealed a sweeping indictment of education articulated
by Republican Congressman George A. Dondero of Michigan,

> This country is being systematically communized, perhaps unconsciously, through
> its educational institutions. These institutions are instruments through which left-
> wing theories and philosophies may be and are taught to large groups of young
> Americans....We now have an entire generation of voters who do not appreciate
> our Constitution, or our national history, who believe the profit system to be
> wrong and private ownership as undesirable, who are easy victims of demagogy,
> and who listen with credulity to false and leading propaganda, of or from
> Russia...[54]

On many other occasions, the *Defense Bulletin* portrayed the accusatorial
rhetoric of state representatives, such as Ealum E. Bruffet and Erastic Davis
of Missouri and Hamer McKenzie of Mississippi. National politicians such
as Sam Hobbs of Alabama, Joseph McCarthy of Wisconsin, and Harold H.
Velde of Illinois also featured prominently.[55] The vast majority of these
attackers were identified as members of the Republican Party. Indeed, a
1946 *Defense Bulletin* specifically noted that the annual convention for the
National Federation of Republican Clubs charged that "subversive literature
is being distributed in the nation's public schools and that certain faculty

members are deliberately misrepresenting American ideals."[56] However, passionate anti-communist sentiment was not solely the preserve of the Republican Party. As early as March 1947, the acerbic rhetoric of Representative John E. Rankin, a Mississippi Democrat, was brought to the attention of the Defense Commission because of his demands that Congress investigate "pink teachers" and the "subversive influences of some of the leading educational institutions."[57] Repeated issues of the *Defense Bulletin* and the archival records of the Defense Commission testify to the consistently hostile and damaging rhetoric of other local, state, and national politicians who alleged subversive and un-American activities in schools before 1948.

The increasing use of red scare tactics and methods to undermine public education in the late 1940s occurred chiefly as a result of the political and ideological polarization manifest in American society at this time. As a flagship of the NEA, and as the education profession's primary defender, the activities of the Defense Commission were perceived to typify the liberal and progressive wing of the American political spectrum. In both policy and practice, the work of the Defense Commission represented the antithesis of conservative and reactionary thought.

Whereas, for example, the Defense Commission supported intercultural education and policies to promote the unity of human brotherhood, the American political right wing defended segregated education and school zoning policies designed to keep the races apart. Whereas, the Defense Commission promoted the United Nations and UNESCO and established links with the World Organization of the Teaching Profession, conservative figures lauded isolationism and resorted to an intense distrust of non-American and "alien" influences. Whereas the Defense Commission opposed universal military training for young people in the post-war years, the political right fervently advocated its introduction. Whereas the Defense Commission and the NEA often heralded the achievements of progressive education, right wing agitators championed traditional and old-fashioned teaching practices. Finally, whereas the Defense Commission campaigned for increased tax levies and federal aid to support public schools, political and economic conservatives argued for tax cuts and increased limits on government control.

To some extent, these oppositional forces likely always existed in American society. However, set against the backdrop of the Cold War, the ubiquitous fear of atomic attack, and the perceived threat of the Soviet Union, these political divisions gravely intensified. Significantly, by the late 1940s, national and international events appeared to play into the hands of conservative forces. If progressivism and New Dealism could be tainted with the smear of socialism or communism, many from the political right reasoned, then those espousing a more liberal creed would lose both the credibility and the support of the American people. Whether the malicious charges made against liberals or liberal ideas and practices were true or false mattered not at all. From the perspective of the political right, what counted was that people should believe them and that conservatism should prevail.

The increasing virulent attacks on public education in the late 1940s and early 1950s should be viewed within this context. Victory for the conservatives augured a reduction in tax support for public education, the maintenance of racially segregated schools, the removal of federal interference, the rejection of allegedly un-American instructional materials, and the passionate celebration of nationalist ideals. Understandably, therefore, in the closing years of the 1940s and the early 1950s, American education increasingly represented a battlefield in which competing American ideologies fought for cultural dominance and control. Into this fray the Defense Commission stepped. As the red scare intensified, the commission worked with unrelenting energy and considerable commitment to protect and to defend the rights of teachers and to extinguish the protests of those who sought vehemently to undermine public education.

Chapter V

Red Scare Attackers and Their Methods

The steady trickle of red scare criticism of education which had featured sporadically in the early 1940s soon exploded into a raging torrent of vicious assault. Between 1948 and 1954, many educators throughout the United States fell victim to the devastating intensity and crushing power of the red scare.

In this troubled climate, education came under the suspicious microscope of the national media. Television, radio, newspapers, and magazines accorded increasing attention to the public schools.[1] In particular, publications such as *Time*, *Life*, *McCall's*, *The Saturday Review of Literature*, *Collier's*, and *The Atlantic Monthly* regularly focused on educational issues. In October 1950, for example, *Life* magazine devoted a special edition to education that reached an audience in excess of 24 million people.[2]

Some in the media were angered by the perceived failures of public education and appeared concerned that schools had become seedbeds of socialistic activity. Others were more generous in their assessment and encouraged citizens actively to support the schools. Few doubted, however, that education was engaged in a desperate struggle. John Bainbridge writing in *McCall's* in October 1952, poignantly remarked that,

> A bewildering disease that threatens to reach epidemic proportions has infected the public schools of America. It has struck in scores of communities from coast to coast. It is spreading at a gallop. It contaminates the rich and poor community alike, and its effects are malignant.[3]

Bainbridge, like other commentators of the age, recognized that education increasingly was being subjected to bitter assault and "hysterical attack."

As the most significant representative of the teaching profession, the National Education Association appeared particularly perturbed by the accumulating attacks. Repeatedly, speakers at NEA national meetings expressed their grave concerns that public education was in serious jeopardy. "There have been increasing attacks in the various communities of our nation." Earl J. McGrath, U. S. Commissioner of Education, told the NEA in 1952, "These attacks, though not entirely new in our history, are today matters of more serious significance because they are at present more intense and widespread than usual."[4] In response, criticism of education was afforded increased attention in NEA conference deliberation and debate, and strategies and methods to meet the emergent attacks appeared as a consistent feature in annual meetings from 1948 to 1954.[5]

An indication of the mounting concern among educators was the reaction of delegates to the 1951 convention of the American Association of School Administrators to a conference session devoted to "Pressure Groups and the Schools." Significantly, whereas in 1950 hardly any interest in the topic was evident, the next year, according to former Defense Commission Chairman, Ernest O. Melby "there was interest, great interest." He noted, "Some 600 men and women crowded into a small auditorium to discuss the nature of the attacks on public education, to determine some means of combating them."[6] Acutely aware of the damage caused by the mounting assault against teachers and their schools, the NEA turned to its Defense Commission for action. From 1948 to 1955, the Defense Commission assumed a more intense and vigorous role in blunting red scare attack.

At a time when educators had no other established agency or mechanism to challenge the stinging attacks on education, the Defense Commission came into its own. Prior to 1948, the Defense Commission flirted with activities designed to discredit those who assailed education. Subsequently, at least through 1955, those efforts dramatically intensified. Indeed, by mid-century the Defense Commission became almost totally consumed by the desire to extinguish attacks from red scare critics. Not wishing to appear overly sensitive to the arguments of all critics of education, members of the NEA and the Defense Commission repeatedly asserted that they welcomed and valued reasoned and sensible criticism of public education. "By attacks on education," a 1951 commission *Defense Bulletin* declared to its readers in typical fashion, "we do not mean the normal, sincere, often justified protests against unsatisfactory conditions that may...exist in a particular school building or school system."[7] This sentiment was echoed and substantiated by resolutions consistently adopted at national meetings throughout the 1950s that asserted,

> The National Education Association believes in and welcomes constructive criticism of the public schools. It recognizes that the growth and development of American schools throughout their history have come in response to honest criticism and community thinking.[8]

In the late 1940s and early 1950s, criticism of public education featured prominently. The NEA leadership appeared concerned that, by branding all critics of education "rabble rousers" or "enemies," the Association might appear too self-righteous in the public eye. In meeting considered charges against the schools, therefore, the NEA recognized the need to adopt a rational, dispassionate, and professional approach.

Differentiating between critics proved to be a slippery process. Some simply were hostile to progressive education. In 1949, for example, Bernard Iddings Bell's *Crisis in Education* and Mortimer Smith's *And Madly Teach* offered sweeping indictments of American education.[9] The trend was continued by a host of other detractors most noted of which arguably was Albert Lynd whose *Quackery in the Public Schools* launched a savage attack on the "superpedagogues" who, Lynd alleged, blindly controlled education.[10]

Of all the criticisms levied at public education the sharpest and most intellectually penetrating undoubtedly were authored by Arthur Bestor. In a series of publications that culminated in the widely read *Educational Wastelands*, Bestor criticized education for increasingly ignoring the essential lessons of the academic disciplines.[11] Bestor, however, was regarded as a critic and not an enemy of public education. As a former academic at Teachers College, Columbia University, and a self-confessed product of a progressive school, he was not unsympathetic to some aspects of and frequently treated the views of John Dewey with dignity and respect.[12] To the NEA, therefore, Arthur Bestor, and others like him, symbolized the more acceptable face of educational criticism. Consequently, although these critics' incisive comments often troubled the NEA and angered educators, they were accorded a certain professional respect. Thus, the commission accorded little attention to intellectual and honest criticism of the schools. Almost exclusively, the commission concerned itself with front organizations who used red scare methods and tactics to destroy public support for education.

In an effort to distinguish between those who used acceptable methods to reprimand public education and those who adopted what the Defense Commission regarded as a more aggressive, "unprincipled," and "dishonest" approach, it drew upon the frequently cited template established by Virgil Rogers at the NEA convention in San Francisco in 1951:

HONEST GROUP TYPE

1. Meets under auspices of regular organization, e.g., PTA or school advisory council.
2. Has sanction of school authorities and cooperates with local teachers and officials.
3. Makes criticisms that are constructive and specific.
4. Welcomes teachers and administrators in meetings, usually jointly held with them.
5. Gives evidence of sincerity by seeking the truth based upon facts.
6. Avoids use of propaganda literature, shuns sensationalism.
7. Rejects the inflammatory orator, radio commentator, or newspaper letter-writing addict.
8. Uses American way of getting at the truth — let all be heard, listen to both sides and make up your own mind.
9. Keeps on issues and avoids bringing up personalities.
10. Makes decisions based upon all available evidence and only after exhaustive study.
11. Makes open and objective reports without attempting to embarrass officials, such reports having been previously submitted to the whole group for study and consideration.

DISHONEST GROUP TYPE

1. Meets initially under authorized group, perhaps; may then begin holding secret or off-record sessions.
2. Tends to work under cover and to use devious means of evading school officials and faculty.
3. Attracts emotionally unstable people to it and often these are given command of the group.
4. May break away from an honest, firmly established group and set up its own splinter organization with high-sounding title, indicating patriotic motives or unselfish concern for public education.
5. Uses smear literature, poison pamphlets, usually imported from the outside, or lifts phrases, slogans, and titles from them.
6. Introduces extraneous issues, rather than concentrating on the agreed-upon area of discussion.
7. Accepts rabble-rousing techniques, "dust throwing," "name calling."
8. Permits only one side of the issue to be presented fully.

9. Frequently passes resolutions without thoughtful deliberation and regardless of all the evidence. Persons making such resolutions are frequently fanatically critical of the schools.
10. Attacks personalities — the superintendent or principal frequently becomes the "whipping boy."
11. Makes a pretense at getting the facts, then issues ultimatums to be answered in a limited amount of time. Sometimes these attacks take the form of a list of questions to the school officials or to the board, often given to the press simultaneously.
12. Frequently uses the press in the campaign.
13. Secures funds through collections and through gifts solicited, not through regular constituted membership.[13]

Officers of the Defense Commission regularly identified the involvement of dishonest critics in front organizations that, the commission argued, principally operated in such a way as to conceal their purpose, clientele, financial backers, and methods of operation.

An editorial in the April 1951 edition of the *Nation's Schools* similarly argued that the earmark of a front organization was its explicit refusal to answer questions such as,

Who are the individuals back of the movement? From whom do they obtain money, and how do they spend it? By whom are the policies made? To whom are the leaders responsible? Is it controlled by self-appointed, self-anointed cliques answerable to no one other than itself? By whom is it endorsed? Who are its co-workers? Have impartial, reliable groups studied and approved the organization and its program?[14]

Concerned that these front organizations were using deceptive methods and harmful propaganda to attack the schools, the Defense Commission gravely understood the need to expose these organizations and blunt their assault.

Robert Skaife, Field Secretary for the Defense Commission, was particularly disturbed by these "front organizations." Unashamedly, he labeled them "enemies" and castigated them for their "blanket use of the expression 'communists' or 'reds' to categorize liberals as a group." Skaife and his colleagues also were angered by the perpetual use of "cleverly contrived arguments clothed in half-truths, innuendoes, and outright falsehoods," and he appeared concerned that these red scare critics ultimately "would like to see public schools disappear."[15]

In the years that followed the end of the Second World War these front organizations suddenly proliferated. Numerous societies, leagues, committees, councils, and crusades emerged to challenge, to discredit, and often, to seriously damage public education.[16] In response, the NEA's Defense Commission devoted feverish activity to checking their assaults. As testimony to how serious and how damaging the Defense Commission considered these attacks on education, the archival files of the commission almost choke with reference to these venomous critics. From 1948 to 1954, therefore, the Defense Commission's committed staff devoted their considerable energies in efforts to extinguish the ferocious challenge from individual critics like Allen A. Zoll, one of public education's most poisonous opponents.

A Proliferation of Red Scare Critics

Allen A. Zoll, regarded by historian Robert Iversen as "the most spectacular of the post-war vigilantes,"[17] and his organization, the National Council for American Education (NCAE), emerged as the leading group in the battle to destroy progress in the schools.[18] Zoll's virulent and fanatical use of anti-communist propaganda typified attacks at this time and appeared as the embodiment of developing red scare assault.

Founded in New Jersey in the summer of 1946, Zoll's organization quickly received the serious attention of the Defense Commission. The January 1949 issue of the *Defense Bulletin*, for example, provided extensive coverage on Zoll's activities. In the following eight years, the Defense Commission monitored the machinations of the NCAE. The most blatant public exposé of Zoll's organization was Robert Skaife's article in the January 1951 issue of the *Nation's Schools*.[19] However, in numerous other publications, pamphlets, bulletins, and information sheets, the Defense Commission continued its vigilant scrutiny of the NCAE throughout the early 1950s.

Although Zoll burst on to the scene in 1946 in a fury of activity, he was not new to the world of political extremism. Before World War II, he initiated and supported the activities of extremist organizations such as the American Patriots, Inc., and the American Federation Against Communism.[20] As evidence of his racist and anti-Semitic convictions, in 1939, Zoll appeared before the Senate Judiciary Committee to oppose the appointment of Felix Frankfurter to the Supreme Court on the grounds that Frankfurter was Jewish. Zoll also was a committed supporter of the extremism of Father Coughlin.

In 1948, Zoll's National Council for American Education was dealt a crushing blow due to revelations by the Friends of Democracy and journalist Frederick Woltman about Zoll's former political affiliations. Woltman's article in the *New York World-Telegram* on August 25, 1948, entitled "Zoll, Hate Monger, Promotes New Racket," was particularly effective and caused many hitherto supporters of the NCAE immediately to resign from Zoll's organization and publicly to renounce its policies.[21] Despite the setback, however, Zoll remained an extremely powerful figure in the years that followed. By appeals to the patriotic loyalties of many influential citizens and wealthy businessmen, Zoll continued to operate a well-financed and effective organization throughout the red scare era. Indeed, the mass distribution of anti-communist propaganda throughout the United States over many years suggests that Zoll's organization continually was flooded with significant financial support.[22] Zoll employed a series of widely distributed publications as the NCAE's primary vehicle to attack public schools. They appeared with rapid regularity and employed revealing titles including "How Red Are The Schools?" "Progressive Education Increases Delinquency," "The Yale Whitewash," "They Want Your Child," "Socialism is Stupid," "Red-ucators at Harvard," "A Fifty-Year Project to Combat Socialism on the Campus," "Awake, America, Awake, and Pray!" "Should Americans Be Against World Government?" and "Harvard Red Hunting Ground."[23]

Central to the arguments expounded in these publications appeared the conviction that American schools were infiltrated by subversive teachers and communist sympathizers. For example, in "They Want Your Child," Zoll contended,

Early in the conflict, the strategists of the Kremlin saw that the key to the future of America lies in the education given to America's children. AND SO THE INFILTRATION AND CONTROL OF AMERICAN EDUCATION BECAME COMMUNISM'S NUMBER ONE OBJECTIVE IN AMERICA. THEY WANT THE CHILDREN OF AMERICA. THEY WANT YOUR CHILD.[24]

Zoll's pamphlets enjoyed mass circulation and proved particularly influential as a result of their appeals to the loyalty of American citizens.

Typically, NCAE's publications were laced with emotional rhetoric, vivid imagery, and a particularly direct style. Above all, they championed American values and warned readers of the emergent dangers of un-American and alien ideologies. In one blistering attack on "subversive" teachers Zoll preached that,

For a generation, *your* tax money has helped the salaries of many propagandist-teachers who have been endeavoring to make socialists, or worse, of America's youth; attempting to rob them of their self-reliance and substituting dependence on the government, on doles, on subsidies; seeking to ensnare them with the false doctrine that it is better to have statism than liberty; undermining the Christian principles and ethics upon which this nation was founded; scoffing at everything American and exalting everything collectivist.[25]

Repeatedly, Zoll and his followers spoke of the "threat from within," the proliferation of "Marxist propaganda in the schools," and of "the plot" to "destroy American society."

From Zoll's perspective, the agents of collectivism and socialism in the United States were the luminaries within the progressive education movement many of whom emanated from Teachers College, Columbia University. "Does it not inescapably follow," Zoll wrote in his widely received "Progressive Education Increases Delinquency," "that the purpose of education as conceived by John Dewey, George Counts, and their like, is to prepare children for adult life in a society in which competition has been eliminated?"[26] Convinced that progressive education was conspiring to subvert the true values and ideals of American society, Zoll passionately assailed its practice. "So called progressive education," Zoll complained,

denies the necessity of every factor necessary for our survival as a free people. It has robbed growing youth of the ability to think independently, it spawns its millions mentally conditioned only for the collectivist state, it robs those it blights of the moral standards by which alone a people may maintain a secure, free, coherent society.[27]

Although many educators treated Zoll's hyperbolic rhetoric and frenzied writing with contempt,[28] the Defense Commission appeared acutely aware of the damage to public education that the NCAE triggered in the early in 1950s. From the viewpoint of the officers of the commission, Zoll could not be dismissed casually as an eccentric critic. Rather, they recognized the extreme and disturbing influence of his red scare tactics and methods.[29]

The NCAE's anti-communist vigilance also was directed toward school textbook adoptions. Verne P. Kaub, Zoll's principal associate, directed much of this activity. Kaub was NCAE vice president, and Zoll delegated to him responsibility for the regular dissemination of the *Educational Guardian,* the NCAE's semi-monthly publication. Formerly, Kaub had worked with Zoll in a Chicago organization called Citizens U.S.A. Committee, and both had appeared as contributors to the anti-Jewish publication, the

Individualist.[30] Zoll and Kaub also had collaborated in campaigns to oust alleged socialists and communists from the Protestant clergy.[31] In the field of education, however, Kaub achieved his greatest notoriety as the editor of the *Educational Guardian*.

Convinced that schools were being infiltrated by dangerously subversive teaching resources, Kaub used the *Educational Guardian* to lash out at textbook authors and their publications for their supposedly un-American stance. He criticized textbooks that, he believed, not only undermined the American way of life, but also that championed the achievements of the Soviet Union. For example, he was particularly angered by the popular *Building America Series* for portraying "such ugly pictures of American life and such glowing pictures of life in the USSR."[32] Consistently, he argued that children were being indoctrinated with collectivist ideas,

> ...in examining several scores of [graded and high school] texts I found not one which I could recommend either as having been written from the viewpoint of a firm believer in the American system or which fairly presented the system in comparison with the European collectivisms.[33]

The *Educational Guardian* was widely distributed and had significant impact in communities throughout the United States. Allen A. Zoll used Kaub's textbook reviews as evidence to discredit instructional materials in Pasadena, California, and Englewood, New Jersey. Furthermore, in Tennessee, the *Guardian*'s allegations gave rise to a public outcry and led to the creation of a full-scale legislative investigation of that state's adopted series of textbooks.[34]

Zoll was not a lone vigilante of education. Much evidence suggests that Zoll and his organization interacted and colluded with an array of other disgruntled parties, groups, and individuals who were critical of education in the post-war era. Zoll, for example, extensively collaborated with the founder and national chair of the Minute Women USA, Suzanne Silvercruys Stevenson. Repeatedly, he addressed local meetings of the Minute Women in towns and cities throughout the country.[35] Zoll also enjoyed close ties with Merwin K. Hart's influential anti-communist organization, the National Economic Council, which, according to the Defense Commission, was noted for its "reactionary economics and bigotry."[36] Significantly, therefore, Zoll's association with a variety of right-wing pressure groups and student organizations served as further testimony to the ubiquity of his red scare propaganda machine.

Unquestionably, Zoll's greatest influence resulted from activities fostered in local school districts and communities throughout the United States. The large number of communities in which his impact was felt constituted a remarkable feature of the Zoll campaign. Often, local criticism of the schools initially appeared without Zoll's interference. Once criticism surfaced, however, Zoll's involvement proved immensely effective. "Even in those cases where Zoll's group has not been directly involved," one contemporary observer noted, "its ideas and materials have often set the pattern of attack." Similarly, "Zoll, may not have personally set off the series of local attacks," remarked Robert K. Bingham in *The Reporter* in October 1951, "but he has certainly done all that lay within his power to keep the attacks going."[37]

Masterfully, Zoll exploited local discontentment and fueled an explosion of red scare activity in communities across the nation. Citizens in school districts small and large were inundated with propaganda literature, information sheets, and accusatorial anti-communist pamphleteering. Frequently, these materials were used by local tax groups, patriotic organizations, or ultra-conservative citizens to attack public schools. For example, between 1950 and 1952 alone, evidence of Zoll's powerful influence turned up in communities in Michigan, California, Texas, Florida, Colorado, New Jersey, New York, Tennessee, Illinois, and countless other troubled towns, cities, and states.[38]

Zoll's influence also appeared prominent in political affairs at the local, state, and national level. In November 1948, for example, Zoll wrote to mayors throughout the nation:

> Dear Mayor_____,
>
> May we make a suggestion which will be of genuine benefit to your city, to the United States, and which probably also will benefit you personally.
> The suggestion is this: that you appoint a commission to ascertain whether there are any un-American or communistic teachings and activities in the schools of your city.
> ...As you know, there is great concern on the part of the public these days in regard to Communist and Socialist activities. There is also beginning to be an interest on the part of parents and taxpayers generally as to what is being taught in the schools and colleges. Accordingly, we sincerely believe that the right-thinking people of your city will greatly appreciate your appointing a commission to determine the situation in your schools regarding both textbooks and personnel.[39]

The letter suggested additionally that once mayors had established a committee, the NCAE would send to the appointed councils, "lists of subversive textbooks and other data that will be helpful to them."

No doubt many mayors and local politicians ignored this NCAE offer and those of other similar organizations. However, the proliferation of investigating committees, textbook investigations, and loyalty checks for school personnel that occurred at the local and state level suggests that many political officials believed that subversive infiltration of the schools existed. Zoll's materials and activities, difficult to assess in particular settings, nevertheless, fueled the anti-communist fever. Historian Robert Iversen remained convinced of Zoll's destructive influence,

> He, his followers, and his literature can be found near the center of many post-war campaigns against the schools. His dossier on the University of Chicago was almost the sole basis for the Broyles Commission's attack in 1949.... He was successful in getting the American Medical Association to demand an investigation of the schools for teaching socialized medicine. He addressed audiences from Harvard to Pasadena.[40]

Other educational historians also have recognized Zoll's devastating impact on education in the post-war era. Marjorie Murphy, for example, argued that Zoll and other red scare propagandists severely damaged the NEA's quest to secure federal support for education. "It was no coincidence," remarked Murphy, "that the House Un-American Activities Committee (HUAC) began investigating education in 1948 just one month before Congress began considering the NEA's funding bill."[41] Essentially, Zoll and others like him effectively portrayed the relationship between the desire for federal funding and the ideology of the collectivist and communistic state. Classic red scare tactics were at play and, in the Cold War era, they worked with an alarming degree of success.

More than any other organization in the United States in the post-war era, the NEA's Defense Commission recognized the explicit threat that Zoll and his supporters posed for public school education. Whether through direct appeals to influential politicians, through exhaustive propaganda campaigns in local communities, or through extensive media coverage, Allen A. Zoll provoked intense red scare furor. The Defense Commission understood the danger he represented. Throughout the late 1940s and early 1950s, it tracked, monitored, challenged, and exposed his activities. Yet, despite the concerted efforts of the commission, Zoll proved remarkably resilient to rebuff and effective in his attack on the educational community. Some contemporaries scoffed at his extremism and his crude methods. Others considered him a passing aberration. In truth, however, Zoll arguably was one of the greatest enemies of American public schooling. As Robert Iversen neatly concluded, "the fact is Zoll took his toll."[42]

Although the National Education Association considered Zoll and his organization to be a prime threat to education, the Defense Commission also was troubled by the profusion of other red scare groups that operated contemporaneously. In particular, the commission focused on two organizations, the Committee for Constitutional Government and the Friends of the Public Schools of America.

The Friends of the Public Schools of America was founded by Mrs. Greta Deffenbaugh as a vehicle to counteract Catholic influence in the public schools of Chicago. Gradually, the organization expanded its constituency into several other states and broadened the scope of its activity. In the late 1930s, Amos A. Fries, a retired Major General in the U. S. Army, became the organization's leading protagonist.[43] Fries focused most of his attention on alleged communist infiltration of the schools, and, as editor of the *Bulletin of the Friends of the Public Schools,* he wielded considerable influence on educational policy.

To the chagrin of the Defense Commission and of the NEA, Fries appeared as a major figure in his support of The National Tax Conference and the U. S. Chamber of Commerce in their successful endeavor to prevent federal funding of public education.[44] Frequently, Fries attacked the teaching profession for harboring "subversive elements" and for welcoming the collectivist state. "The general," remarked *McCall's* journalist Arthur D. Morse in 1951, "stands four-square against nurseries and kindergartens, health, welfare, and recreational activities, service for handicapped pupils, and vocational guidance."[45]

Throughout the late 1940s and early 1950s, the Friends of the Public Schools of America continued its damaging attacks on contemporary education. The organization's *Bulletin* assailed the Kellogg Foundation for its sponsorship of a project to improve public school administration, repeatedly accused the NEA of promoting communist-inspired activities and, according to the Defense Commission, never hesitated to "besmirch the character and try to destroy the influence of some of our best schools and most substantial educators."[46] As with many other red scare organizations, the Friends of the Public Schools of America often captured public support because it campaigned to reduce taxes and appealed to patriotic sentiment. A questionnaire survey conducted by the Defense Commission noted that individuals widely received the *Bulletin of the Friends of the Public Schools* and that it wielded considerable influence in communities throughout the United States.[47] Accordingly, as an organization aimed at discrediting educators and reducing financial support for schools, the Friends of the Public Schools of America appeared to be immensely influential.

Founded by the wealthy publisher Frank Gannett in New York City in 1937, the Committee for Constitutional Government (CCG) quickly developed into another extremely powerful right-wing lobbying organization in the 1940s and 1950s. Led by a highly paid executive director, Edward Rumely, the CCG actively campaigned for "lower taxes," "for economic freedom as against encroaching big government," and for the elimination of "socialized education, socialized housing, and socialized medicine."[48] Throughout the existence of the CCG it sought fervently to remove alleged "Marxist influences" in the public schools.

In the red scare era, the CCG developed into a prominent and well-financed political pressure group. As a measure of its financial clout, the Counsel for the federal House Select Committee on Lobbying Activities reported that the CCG spent almost $2 million for lobbying purposes, and in one seven-year period alone, "distributed 82 million booklets, pamphlets...at the rate of about 12 million pieces a year."[49] In addition, according to the Defense Commission's *Bulletin*, much of the propaganda of the CCG was distributed under the postal frank of Representative Ralph Gwinn, a fierce opponent of federal aid to education, actions—saving Rumely's organization an estimated $240,000 to $300,000 in postage.

A feature of the activities of the CCG was its strenuous efforts to disguise the organization's financial backers and its involvement in the creation of several sister organizations. The 1950 House Select Committee on Lobbying Activities, however, claimed that the CCG had

> spawned no less than four subsidiary organizations: Fighters for Freedom, America's Future, Constitution and Free Enterprise Foundation, and Features for America. One group specializes in political action within Congressional districts, a third in syndicated columns and releases, a fourth in contacts with educational institutions. But what appears to be a number of distinct groups is in reality the Committee for Constitutional Government.[50]

Undoubtedly, in efforts to conceal the origins and development of these subgroups, the CCG wished to shield prominent supporters from adverse criticism, to partition significant financial contributions into smaller amounts for tax reporting purposes, and to convey the appearance that many additional Americans simultaneously shared its concerns with regard to the loyalty of public schools and their educators.[51]

Of the Committee for Constitutional Government's four creations, America's Future best encapsulated the vigorous propaganda activities of the umbrella organization. In an assortment of media outlets, America's Future regularly chastised public schools for the induction of high taxation, for the promotion of "encroaching socialism," and for the encouragement of wasteful government spending. Through radio, books, pamphlets, and newspapers, America's Future proved immensely influential in communicating its passionate political ideology.

The radio activities of America's Future chiefly centered on support for weekly radio broadcasts by John T. Flynn. Flynn's bombastic radio commentaries reportedly were carried on more than 500 network stations throughout the United States and enjoyed a significantly large radio audience. The book program of America's Future included a quarterly review of "All-American Books" and an *All American Book Digest.* The tone of the material included in the *Digest* was established in its first issue with contributions from John T. Flynn's *While You Slept* and Mary L. Allen's *Education or Indoctrination.*[52]

Additionally, America's Future orchestrated a prolific program of political pamphleteering. The contribution of a pamphlet written by the organization's secretary, Rosalie Gordon, entitled "What's Happened to Our Schools?" typified the ideological orientation of other contributions. In her offering, Gordon launched a vicious attack on progressive education. She claimed that education's alleged failings amounted to a "planned, slyly executed, and almost successful attempt to deliberately under-educate our children in order to make them into an unquestioning mass who would follow meekly those who wish to turn the American Republic into a socialist society."[53] The sentiments of Gordon and other critics of education similarly were echoed by John T. Flynn in newspaper commentaries sponsored by America's Future. As a measure of its potential impact on American society, Flynn's 700-word editorial regularly was distributed to 4,016 weekly newspapers and carried the message of America's Future to an estimated 20 million readers.[54]

As the parent organization, the CCG appeared particularly fond of John T. Flynn's political stance and regularly distributed his book, *The Road Ahead*. In its first four years of publication alone, the Committee for Constitutional Government sold more than 10 million copies of Flynn's book and promoted sales by mailing 3,500,000 postcards. Littered with anti-communist rhetoric, *The Road Ahead* attacked the *bêtes noires* of the red scare movement: progressive education, textbook authors, and subversive teachers. "The favorite roosting place" for exponents of "revolutionary" philosophies, argued Flynn, "is in the editorial sanctums of textbook publishing places."[55] Flynn also received notoriety for an article in the October 1951 issue of the *Reader's Digest*, "Who Owns Your Child's Mind?" in which he wrote of "guilty teachers," the communist "invasion," and the "drive to infect our schools with collectivist propaganda."[56]

Heralded and financially assisted by the CCG, Flynn epitomized red scare rhetoric and conviction in the post-war period. Flynn, however, formed only part of the red scare arsenal employed by the CCG. As a creator, promoter, and distributor of red scare propaganda in the late 1940s and early 1950s, the CCG severely damaged public confidence in American education. Supported by wealthy business interests, media magnates, and patriotic organizations, the Committee for Constitutional Government proved particularly influential in attacking many aspects of American schooling including progressive education, federal aid to schools, "un-American" textbooks, and "subversive" teachers.

In 1953, in *Forces Affecting American Education*, the Defense Commission's Robert Skaife identified six groups that he believed warranted particular attention as a result of their destructive red scare activities.[57] Included in his selection was the National Economic Council (NEC). Originally founded in 1930 as the New York State Economics Council, the organization was reformed as the NEC in 1943. For the next twenty years the NEC was led by Merwin K. Hart, a noted right-wing activist, neo-fascist sympathizer, and head of New York's oldest chapter of the John Birch Society.[58]

Hart operated out of an expensive suite of offices in the Empire State Building in New York. As a champion of the extreme political right, Hart secured the support of many vested business interests and powerful political figures. His ideological platform rested on familiar foundations. As an arch-conservative, he bitterly opposed federal aid to education, public housing, further immigration, civil rights measures, the TVA, and the United Nations.[59]

The mouthpiece of the NEC was the *Economic Council Letter*. Published twice a month on conspicuously yellow paper, it viciously attacked liberal and progressive causes. Many issues of the *Letter* also revealed the NEC's ardently anti-Semitic stance:

> ...the founding of Palestine was the price paid the Zionists for their bringing America into World War I.... Had it not been for the Zionists, America would undoubtedly never have got into that War. Probably there would have been no I. Soviet Russia might never have existed. There probably would be no world communism...
>
> If there were six million Jews within reach of , which number is widely questioned, and if they have all disappeared, where are they?
>
> Is it not likely that many of these six million, claimed to be killed by Hitler and Eichmann, are right here in the United States and are now joining in the agitation for more and more support for the State of Israel — even if the American Republic goes down?[60]

As an archetypal nationalist, Merwin K. Hart unleashed a similar invective on the United Nations. He argued that the UN was explicitly "un-American" and conspired to support the "socialization of American industry," and "the illegal immigration of perhaps a million European and Asiatic undesirables" in an attempt to "bring all American life under absolute domination."[61]

The NEC's relentless attacks on education brought its activities to the attention of the Defense Commission. In line with other red scare critics, Hart's organization condemned progressive teaching methods, accused educators of subversion, attacked un-American textbooks, and vehemently opposed federal aid to education. Hart also appeared suspicious of free inquiry in the classroom. In a letter written in 1949, he complained that the policy of telling students everything and encouraging them to make their own minds up spelt doom for America. "I always thought it was the purpose of a teacher," Hart asserted, "to guide young men in their thinking along the right lines. From the number of educators among the 'fringe' group, it looks as though too many brains call for too much free thinking."[62]

The extremist views of Merwin K. Hart and his colleagues, however, did not represent the position of an isolated reactionary fringe. Significantly, among Hart's supporters and financial backers appeared some of America's prominent economic leaders. In the late 1940s and early 1950s, for example, Hart received substantial contributions from leading officials in the General Motors Corporation, the Bethlehem Steel Corporation, Eastman Kodak,

Beech Aircraft, the Shaeffer Pen Company, and the Los Angeles Chamber of Commerce. In addition, Hart revealed to a House Select Committee on Lobbying Activities that the NEC received more than $60,000 from Lammot du Pont and his brother Irenee from 1947 to 1950.[63]

Hart was a skillful and adept campaigner. He solicited funds from a range of corporate giants and had the ear of influential political figures. In a lavish NEC-sponsored gala banquet held at the Waldorf-Astoria Hotel in October 1949, for example, Hart enjoyed distinguished company. Apart from corporate figures such as Lammot du Pont, J. Howard Pew, President of the Sun Oil Company, and Benjamin Freedman, also in attendance were Congressman Ralph W. Gwinn of New York, Senator James P. Kem of Missouri, and ex-Senator Albert W. Hawkes of .[64]

Casually to dismiss red scare organizations, such as Merwin K. Hart's NEC, as a fanatical aberration in American politics, therefore, ignores political reality. Many of these groups were supported extensively by powerful business interests and influential politicians.[65] These organizations undoubtedly influenced political decisions, legislative investigations, and local, state, and federal governmental policy. Importantly, as a natural target for red scare propaganda American public schools often fell victim to their seemingly harmful influences.

As a result of the multifarious activities of prominent right-wing organizations and pressure groups, educators often resorted to safe and non-controversial instructional practices and teaching materials. For many in the teaching profession, self-censorship was engaged in widely, academic freedoms were extinguished, and disturbing job insecurity prevailed. In many regards, therefore, the machinations of red scare organizations impacted educational policy and practice in important and often dramatic ways.

Established Patriotic Organizations and Influential Individuals Fuel the Red Scare

Whereas many influential red scare organizations were formed in the 1930s and 1940s in direct response to the perceived spread of communism within and outside the United States, some American organizations manifested a history of patriotic affiliation. Salient among these older organizations were the Sons of the American Revolution (SAR) and the

American Legion. Significantly, during the post-war red scare era, these established patriotic groups played no small part in fueling fervent anti-communist sentiment in the country and explicitly questioning the loyalty of American educators.

The Sons of the American Revolution demonstrated particular success in its anti-communist purges in the schools in California. In the late 1940s, renowned communist witch hunters, State Senators Tenney and Dilworth, extensively used reports commissioned by the SAR successfully to attack and censor textbooks commonly used in schools.[66] Buoyed by these early triumphs, the SAR soon undertook the more ambitious project of urging legislative investigations of school textbooks on a national scale.

In April 1949, the SAR filed with Congress its much vaunted and widely publicized *Bill of Grievances,* warning legislators of "interstate traffic in propaganda textbooks and teaching materials." The lengthy bill urged Congressional investigation of subversive textbooks that, the SAR argued, unconditionally were slanted to favor "socialism and communism." In the foreword to their *Bill of Grievances*, for example, the SAR warned,

> Our schools are being converted into agencies for the dissemination of radical propaganda, much of which originates in communist front organizations and other pressure groups. Gullible or indoctrinated 'liberals' supporting these organizations appear to be responsible for this condition.
>
> We believe the people and, particularly, the parents of children in our public schools, have a right to know what is going on, and what is proposed for American youth.[67]

Contained within the *Grievances*, a document approximately 50 pages in length, the SAR attacked many of the traditional targets of red scare activists including the NEA, Rugg textbooks, and the *Building America Series* that, the SAR contested, proffered "material originating from one hundred and thirteen fronts." In the compilation of its document, the SAR relied heavily upon the files of the Tenney Committee, the mysterious Appendix IX acquired from the Dies commission, the writings of Allen A. Zoll, and the reports of their own passionately anti-communist attorney, Aaron Sargent.[68]

The *Bill of Grievances* attacked "liberal" educational policy, labeling it "Gulliberalism" and explicitly pointed an accusatorial finger at "communist inspired" progressive education. For example, the *Bill* included "briefs" on such topics as "'Gulliberalism' and 'Progressive' education in California"; "Vilification and class consciousness put in the curriculum under the 'progressive' method"; "Propaganda of 'progressive' educators aimed at nullification of the Constitution"; and "Recent propaganda activities of 'progressive' educators."[69] The SAR angrily denounced the designs of progressive educators that, the SAR argued, amounted to the desire to "convert this country into a social welfare type of state." The *Bill* asserted, "Inexperienced children at an impressionable age are being indoctrinated with...propaganda against the will of their parents."[70]

The activities of the SAR and its *Bill of Grievances* impacted American education. In response to the SAR's report, for example, John S. Wood, then chairman of HUAC, promptly requested from 71 colleges lists of textbooks used in their classes in order that their contents might be scrutinized for pro-communist sentiment. Many legislative bodies at the state and local level followed suit. Educators acutely became aware of the dangers of using identified texts and, in an increasing climate of repression, often avoided tackling subject areas that might provoke controversy.

The Defense Commission appeared enormously concerned by the debilitating effect that the SAR had on education. Robert Skaife, for example, identified the Sons of the American Revolution as one of six leading red scare critics.[71] The commission's field secretary also was troubled that the SAR repeatedly campaigned for a reduction in tax support for schools. In May 1950, for example, the SAR produced a report entitled "A Socialistic Public School System" that deliberately linked mounting taxes with the cost of progressive education. With harmful simplicity, the report invited readers to "dig up your tax return for last year. Re-figure the tax according to the 1939 rates and subtract. The difference in your bill is for the projects and schemes of 'progressive education.'"[72] At a time when the NEA vigorously campaigned to preserve academic freedoms for educators and for increased tax revenues to support public schools, the SAR's well-orchestrated attacks proved immensely destructive.

As one of America's oldest and most established patriotic organizations, the American Legion was a pioneer of anti-communist sentiment. The long established relationship between the NEA and the American Legion, therefore, was curious. On the one hand, the American Legion, as a fiercely patriotic organization, often was a loyal and devoted ally of the NEA. The two organizations began their collaborations in 1921 and, in 1938-39, established a joint committee to promote mutual interests that included the sponsorship of "American Education Week" and support for federal aid to education. In addition, each year representatives from the American Legion and the NEA were invited to address each other's at their respective annual conventions.[73]

On the other hand, tensions between the two organizations regularly surfaced. The NEA often expressed concern that the American Legion readily embraced red scare tactics to attack public school educators. The NEA's ambivalence toward the Legion neatly was reflected in a 1955 report issued by the Defense Commission reporting that many local teachers listed the American Legion as both an "active supporter" of public schools and a powerful "source of criticism."[74]

Typically, the American Legion, at both national and local levels, firmly supported public education if the schools adhered to ardently patriotic and American principles. However, with the proliferation of attacks on progressive education and on subversive teachers, many Legionnaries openly questioned the loyalty of school teachers and the materials that they used in the classroom. In the *American Legion Magazine* of May 1949, for example, John Dixon penned a savage attack on un-American U. S. history textbooks. Peppered with inflammatory rhetoric, the article fiercely criticized social studies and progressive education. Dixon wrote of the "debunkers of history," the "traitors in the classroom," and "the enemies of America who infect the minds of the young." The author asserted,

> Above all else we need a renaissance of patriotism in America's history classrooms, an informed and aggressive patriotism. We need more militant Americanism. We need a veritable revolution in the attitudes and methods of a great number of American classrooms. No teacher should be employed in any American history classroom who does not believe whole-heartedly and without any reservation in American free enterprise, in representative government, and in the preservation of the dignity and independence of the individual citizen.[75]

Received by each of the Legion's four million members, the *American Legion Magazine* repeatedly expressed its concern that communists had infiltrated the schools. Furthermore, the Legion's renowned Americanism commission, which "blossomed with former FBI agents and military-intelligence veterans," regularly furnished Legion posts with anti-communist materials. Significantly, the Commission's *Counter-Subversive Manual* contained a lengthy chapter on how to discover communists in the schools.[76]

Of all the attacks perpetrated by supporters of the American Legion, however, none received more attention from the NEA than an article which appeared in the *American Legion Magazine* in June 1952. Written by Irene Corbally Kuhn, the article summoned forth all the conventional red scare criticisms of education. Progressive educators who controlled the schools, argued Kuhn, constituted a gang of "pinkoes, commies, collectivists, and

Marxists." She named names. Singled out for particular criticism were John Dewey, William Heard Kilpatrick, George Counts, Harold Rugg, and John Childs, who together, Kuhn asserted, perpetrated a "conspiracy to commit the American public schools to communism."[77] Significantly, the article also charged the NEA with "propagandizing for a socialistic America." Kuhn continued,

> They [the NEA] have had things pretty much their own way for a long time...Some of its performances have been more typical of the tactics of a captured labor union complete with goon squads than of a respectable national organization of more than half a million teachers.[78]

Outraged by the bitter attack, the NEA mobilized its defense. Passionate speeches were heard at the Association's national convention in Detroit. The NEA passed a resolution that condemned Kuhn's outpourings. The August 1952 *Nation's Schools* launched a stinging counterattack of Kuhn in an article entitled "Who Speaks for the Legion?"

Appalled by the apparent betrayal of the American Legion, an ostensible ally, the Defense Commission produced its own response to the Legion's activities. The September 1952 edition of the *Defense Bulletin* conveyed its reaction on the *Bulletin*'s headline pages and assertively defended the principles of "free public education."[79] Nevertheless, Kuhn's attack deeply troubled the commission. Ruefully, the commission noted that, a decade before, Kuhn's comments would have been dismissed summarily as the rantings of an eccentric extremist. However, in the summer of 1952, with the McCarthyite tide nearing its peak, Kuhn's contentions alarmingly typified mainstream political discourse.

Anti-communist tactics and methods were not, however, solely the preserve of organized red scare groups. Significantly, throughout the red scare era, many notable individuals and colorful personalities also exerted considerable and damaging pressure on American schools. As propagandists and leaders of key anti-communist organizations, individuals such has Allen A. Zoll, John T. Flynn, Amos A. Fries, Merwin K. Hart, and Edward Rumley dramatically stand out. Other individuals who used red scare tactics and methods to attack education also played supporting roles. The Defense Commission tracked the smaller as well as the more prominent players. Right-wing author and editor Frank Chodorov, for example, represented the type of critic whom the commission also followed.

Throughout the 1940s and 1950s, Chodorov frequently surfaced as an exponent of arch-conservative views. As editor of right-wing journals, magazines, and broadsheets that included *Analysis*, *Human Events*, and the *Freeman*, Chodorov glorified libertarian and individualistic philosophies and savagely renounced what he perceived to be America's steady march toward collectivism.[80] In 1952, supported by the wealthy business interests of the Foundation for Economic Education, Chodorov formed the Intercollegiate Society of Individualists (ISI). Using the ISI's considerable financial resources, within two years of its formation, the society reportedly distributed to American university students 160,000 pieces of right-wing propaganda and literature. The organization emerged as a fierce critic of public schools, progressive education, and socialistic professors and teachers.[81] Cognizant of the damage caused by Chodorov and the ISI, the Defense Commission endeavored to expose its methods and tactics. In "The Conflict Continues," published in the *Nation's Schools*, for example, Robert Skaife explicitly linked Chodorov's organization with Allen A. Zoll and published a revealing critique of their joint ventures.[82]

In addition, the Defense Commission became alarmed by Chodorov's widely reported views on public school education. Following the dismissal of Superintendent Willard Goslin from his position in Pasadena, California, for example, Chodorov wrote a stinging editorial in the July 14, 1951 issue of the *Saturday Evening Post*. In it he ruthlessly attacked progressive education. Fundamentally, his editorial argued that progressive education with its emphasis on "collectivism" was alien to American individualism and that Goslin was "a traitor to American tradition."[83]

As an antidote to "creeping socialism in the schools," Chodorov, with Zoll's support, produced a widely distributed pamphlet "Private Schools: The Solution to America's Educational Problem." Chodorov argued that, because public education had failed America, parents should be encouraged to turn to the private educational sector. With chilling simplicity, Chodorov asserted that parents who were dissatisfied with the un-American nature of progressive schools would leave these public schools in dramatic numbers and that public education would collapse under the competition. Although many dismissed Chodorov's views as too extreme to receive serious support, the Defense Commission was troubled by Chodorov's activities. At a time when the NEA vigorously campaigned for increased funding for schools, Chodorov's attacks appeared as another vexing thorn in the flesh of public education. Thus, the Defense Commission reasoned that Chodorov's criticism could not be ignored, should be treated seriously, and should be met with the various defensive and offensive strategies available to the commission.[84]

Of all the red scare critics, however, for the use of his own personal wealth and for his extreme political convictions, no individual in the post-war era matched the exertions of publishing millionaire Robert C. Hoiles. During the 1940s and the 1950s, Hoiles presided over a chain of newspapers under the umbrella of Freedom Newspapers Inc., with publications in Colorado, California, Florida, New Mexico, Texas, Nebraska, and Ohio.[85] Typically, he used the editorial columns of his newspapers to deliver some particularly bruising and radical attacks on public education.

As an ardent individualist, Hoiles represented a man of unique ideological conviction. His fierce anti-government stance, for example, led him to object to government-supported highways, post offices, the police, and the armed forces. Not surprisingly, he vigorously and passionately opposed public education. He argued that tax-supported schools violated both the Biblical commandment, "Thou Shall Not Steal," and the U. S. Declaration of Independence, which asserted government by the consent of the people. "This means INDIVIDUAL consent [sic]," Hoiles contended and, "since I have not given my consent, it is a violation of the Declaration to tax me for something I don't want to pay for."[86] In numerous editorial and public debates Hoiles launched a barrage of vitriol against the schools. Commonly, he argued,

> Government schools are leading us to socialism and communism.... It is impossible for tax-supported educators to teach American principles. They can only teach foreign principles, collectivism, fascism, might-makes-rightism, and that the end justifies the means.[87]

A common editorial feature of publications owned by Hoiles was the frequent tendency to employ red scare rhetoric and argument.

Lewis C. Fay, Sunday editor of another paper, the *San Antonio Light*, for example, noted that "a favorite device" of Hoiles was "associating schools with Communism." Hoiles preached a violent distrust of public schools because he believed they supported the government's desire to infuse the young with un-American and Socialist ideals. "We believe that it would be next to impossible," Hoiles claimed,

> to find anything taught that preaches old-fashioned American individualism as against our modern New Deal fraternalism in government. Hitler and Hirohito used government schools to promote their regimes. Stalin is using Russian government schools to promote his regime. Karl Marx made free public schools one of the points in his famous 'Communist Manifesto.' Any government delights in having schools to propagandize its doctrine.[88]

In repeated newspaper editorials, Hoiles took his campaign for the abolition of public schools directly to his readers. He vocally attacked anti-American school textbooks and subversive teachers, and he openly declared that "the most harmful person in every community is the superintendent of compulsory education."[89]

Significantly, in the places where Hoiles' newspapers were published, he faced little or no direct media competition. Almost without exception, Hoiles acquired newspapers in towns and cities in which he could enjoy a monopolistic advantage in his attempt to mold public opinion. In the Texas Rio Grande Valley, however, Hoiles' newspaper chain encountered some unusual opposition. Repeated attacks on the public schools in Hoiles' newspapers led to much indignation among the local citizens of Brownsville, McAllen, and Harlingen. The controversy culminated in a series of bitter public debates during February 1952 between R. C. Hoiles and influential Houstonian, Judge Roy Hofheinz. Broadcast by the local radio and staged before packed audiences at the McAllen High School auditorium and football stadium, Hoiles and Hofheinz debated the desirability of public education.[90]

The debates served to expose Hoiles' extreme political disposition. Many commentators and observers considered him a crackpot and believed that he did not warrant serious attention. Even Robert Skaife wrote that "Mr. Hoiles' views are so unusual that very few people agree with him."[91] Others, however, argued that, despite Hoiles' extremism, he represented both a menace and a threat to public education.

The extent to which Hoiles and his newspaper chain seriously affected public support for schools remains open to conjecture. Likely, however, Hoiles had some deleterious impact. Lewis Fay, for example, believed that because Hoiles' editorials remained unchallenged in dozens of communities, local schools were harmed. "Bond issues for schools, teacher salaries, and other avenues of improvement of public education," reasoned Fay, "appear bound to suffer to a greater or lesser degree."[92] Gould Beech, manager of the local Harlingen radio station, recognized that Hoiles' threat appeared not so much from overt actions against public schools, but rather from the creation of an unhealthy educational climate:

> The question is not whether the newspapers can eliminate the schools. Of course, they can't do this today or tomorrow. But the atmosphere of opposition they inevitably create imposes a handicap on the teachers and administrators who must work in this atmosphere.[93]

In this simple statement, Beech illuminated the red scare's most potent weapon. By creating a public suspicion of educators and their practices, by perpetually hanging a skeptical question mark over schools and their activities, critics sowed seeds of doubt in the public consciousness. Wary of being singled out as subversive or as an agent of communism, teachers became cautious in their actions and conservative in their methods. As teachers regularly operated under the debilitating shadow of repression and mistrust often they considered it prudent to play safe, to boast one's loyalty, and to steer clear of issues and personalities that might be construed controversial. If nothing else, therefore, R. C. Hoiles and others like him fueled this unsavory climate of red scare fear.

Hoiles' impact on public education appeared in other forms too. For although Hoiles often has been portrayed as a lone figure fighting a zealous crusade against the schools, he was inexorably linked to other red scare organizations. For example, he was associated with numerous other attackers including Leonard Read, President of the Foundation for Economic Education, John Chamberlain, editorial writer for *Life* and the *Freeman*, and the notorious Frank Chodorov.[94] In addition, the Defense Commission, at one of its joint conferences on "Public Education in a Dangerous Era," noted Hoiles' links with the Committee for Constitutional Government and his support from the renowned red-baiter, John T. Flynn.[95]

Possessing a fortune in excess of $20 million and as a newspaper owner, Hoiles represented enormous potential for seriously injuring American public schools. Unequivocally, he used his newspapers to promote his views and those of other radical figures who agreed with his ideological convictions. In addition, he used his personal funds also to support prominent anti-communist organizations. As with other red scare zealots, therefore, individuals like Hoiles must not be dismissed easily. For no matter how radical or extreme their political position appeared to some, they fueled both the anti-communist crusade and the use of the red scare as a fierce weapon of attack against teachers, administrators, and the school curriculum.

Chapter VI

Politics, Propaganda, and Public School Textbooks

The opening years of the 1950s represented a tense period in American history. Communist forces in China secured their ascendancy in the most populous nation in the world. The Soviet Union appeared increasingly aggressive. The media sensationalized stories of communist espionage and subversion at home, and the McCarthyite juggernaut powered onward with irresistible and devastating force. Furthermore, by the end of the Korean War in 1953, 33,651 young Americans had lost their lives to the communist foe.

American activities in Korea frustrated many back home in the United States. In particular, critics objected to the symbolism that military action was governed by the United Nations, and not by the United States. Any military failings, therefore, easily could be attributed to this cause. Right wing critics of education were not slow to equate inadequacies in UN policy with the implicit denial of the rights of Americans. Gerald L. K. Smith, a notorious advocate of "vigorously American" education complained in September 1951,

> The UN is such a babble of voices and mixed opinions that on numerous occasions our boys in Korea have been forced to stand back, giving the enemy time to kill and slaughter our sons, while waiting for some technical decision to come from the UN.
> Down with the UN! Out with the UN! Abolish the UN! Away with the UN! The Constitution is good enough for me, and Old Glory is my flag.[1]

Merwin K. Hart, influential leader of the National Economic Council, similarly denounced the UN for propagating socialism and rejecting Americanism. "It is a mechanism," he claimed, "for fastening upon the world an international collectivism which, if it prevails, will destroy human freedom. More than anything else, it will destroy our priceless American liberty." Other right-wing critics charged that the UN was "a communist inspired organization" led by "Marxist plotters" and full of "leeches, traitors, molly coddlers, and perverters of Christian teachings."[2]

Not surprisingly, hatred of the UN spilled over into the arena of public education. Extremely active in this regard was the American Flag Committee of Philadelphia. Organized by W. Henry McFarland Jr., in the summer of 1950, the American Flag Committee enjoyed the support of many influential individuals noted for their attacks on the public schools. Allies included Allen A. Zoll, Merwin K. Hart, Gerald L. K. Smith, and other leaders and organizations known to be associated with anti-Semitic and fascist causes. The American Flag Committee soon became a focal point for attacks on the United Nations and its organizations.

UNESCO appeared as an obvious target for red scare attack. In October 1951, the *Philadelphia Newsletter*, the official organ of the committee, claimed in a report that UNESCO was,

> ...a subversive association. It is consciously furthering a campaign calculated to pervert the teaching profession in this country, and so destroy the worth and integrity of America's first bulwark of freedom — our tax-supported public schools.[3]

Fewer than a thousand subscribers received the report of the American Flag Committee. Standing in isolation, it probably would have caused little or no public outcry. However, on October 18, 1951, Republican Congressman John T. Wood from Idaho dignified the report by including it in the appendix of the *Congressional Record*. Within a matter of months, reprints of the report, now dramatically retitled "The Greatest Subversive Plot in History," exceeded half a million copies. Wood's opening remarks to Congress demonstrated his unqualified endorsement of the committee's work,

> Mr. Speaker, I am herewith appending an article published by the American Flag Committee, 876 Granite Street, Philadelphia, Pa., bearing the title, 'A Report to the American People on UNESCO.'
> How anyone who venerates and loves Old Glory as the symbol of the deathless march of the United States through the years to fulfill its destiny as a free and independent Republic can read this documented evidence of the greatest and most malignant plot in history against the future of this country, and its children, is more than I am able to comprehend.

It is my sincere hope that every parent of every child in America may be able
to read the inroads that this infamous plot has already made in the educational
system of America, and, reading, may feel impelled to do something about it,
both locally and nationally; and particularly at the voting booth [sic].[4]

Paraded on this much broader political stage the report caused a stir in
school districts throughout the land. Public fears and anxieties were fueled
by the combined activities of red scare pressure groups, the local media,
wealthy business interests, and influential politicians.

In several communities, UNESCO materials were banned and
discussion of the UN was eliminated from the school curriculum. For
example, in Houston , in 1952, not only were students barred from entering
into an annual UN essay writing contest, but all references to the UN were
deleted from school workbooks and a debate exercise using UN materials
"was expunged from the ninth grade curriculum."[5] Schools in Los Angeles
became embroiled in a similar controversy that finally resulted in the board
of education's decision to abolish the district's entire UNESCO program.[6]

The attacks on UN materials in both cities demonstrated the incredible
power of the red scare at mid-century. As an example of how anti-communist
hysteria could be exploited to discredit aspects of a school curriculum or
school instructional materials, the UN episodes in Los Angeles and in
Houston provide a dramatic cameo. In both communities, what started as
the rabid claims of the American Flag Committee, a seemingly insignificant
extremist organization, soon snowballed into an avalanche of invective and
red scare criticism that, ultimately, deeply affected teachers, the curriculum,
and the education of thousands of students.

In Texas and in California, attacks on the UN quickly were supported
by powerful interest groups, right wing politicians, and influential forces
in the media. In Los Angeles, for example, the campaign against the UN
vigorously was championed by the Hearst press. Under the banner headline,
"Outlaw in Schools! A Victory for Americanism," the *Herald and Express*
extended its "congratulations to the patriotic organizations and the fathers
and mothers of Los Angeles whose battle against foreign propaganda
resulted in the outlawing of the whole program."[7] Red scare activists in
Houston enjoyed similar support from the *Houston Chronicle*. In addition,
concerted attacks on UN materials from powerful business interests, political
conservatives, and right wing pressure groups all combined to make effective
use of the red scare in order to undermine liberal opposition.[8]

In many respects, these UN incidents exemplified how local or national politicians could dramatically impact educational policy and practice. Significantly, in the late 1940s and early 1950s, legislators and politicians throughout the United States almost became consumed by red scare activity and fervor.

The primary catalyst for these widespread political attacks on education undoubtedly was the House Committee on Un-American Activities (HUAC). Formed in 1938 under the leadership of Congressman Martin Dies of Texas, HUAC became, in 1945, the first permanent committee established to investigate subversive and un-American activities and propaganda. The Committee operated across the entire country and established a forum for those who wished to charge individuals of subversion.[9] Between 1945 and 1957, HUAC appeared particularly active. It held in excess of 230 hearings and gathered the official testimony of more than 3,000 people, of whom more than 100 individuals were cited for contempt.[10] During this period, teachers became an obvious and vulnerable target for concerted red scare criticism.

Although HUAC's most destructive attacks on the integrity of educators did not occur until the early 1950s, ominous signs of the gathering storm appeared frequently in the late 1940s. In December 1946, for example, the Defense Commission noted the public comments of John E. Rankin, a Mississippi Democrat and a member of HUAC, who, in an article in the *New York Times*, questioned the loyalty of teachers and called for the assistance of patriotic organizations to drive out communist teachers and "pink professors."[11] Two years later, the editors of the *Defense Bulletin* also noted with alarm that a 40-page HUAC publication, "100 Things You Should Know About Communism," charged that, "taken as a whole the Communist Party depends for its strength on the support it gets from teachers," and those within other occupations.[12]

As a result of the Republican sweep in the 1952 national elections, investigations into, and attacks upon, educators dramatically intensified. Until 1951, HUAC appeared as the only Congressional investigating committee in existence. However, as anti-communist fever assumed a tighter grip on the nation, this situation soon changed. In 1952, HUAC acquired a new chairman, former FBI agent Harold Velde, and a new chief counsel, Robert L. Kunzig. Velde made his intentions clear from the outset, "I feel that we should look into the field of education. That has been left largely untouched up till now but I believe that it is a very fertile field for investigation."[13] Significantly, in his relentless pursuit of subversives in education, Velde was not alone.

In 1952, Senator McCarthy, as a result of assuming an investigating committee of his own, gleefully announced that he would be "going into the education system" and "exposing communists and communist thinkers."[14] In addition, between September 8 and October 13, 1952, the Senate Internal Security Subcommittee (SISS), chaired by fiercely anti-communist Senator Pat McCarran, conducted a series of vigorous hearings into "subversive influences into the nation's educational system."[15] These resourceful politicians implicitly understood the enormous political capital to be gained from attacks on communism and alleged communist sympathizers. On a regular basis, McCarran, McCarthy, and Velde were quoted in the national press — radio stations clamored for their bombastic statements, and television networks eagerly covered their dramatic Congressional investigations.[16]

The investigating committees of Velde, McCarthy, and McCarran combined to induce an extremely repressive climate in many of the nation's schools. Each forceful prong of this immensely effective red scare trident claimed dozens of victims. In Philadelphia, for example, 26 educators, who either invoked the Fifth Amendment or refused to answer questions before the Velde Committee, later found themselves dismissed by the Board of Education.[17] In March 1953, educators in Los Angeles experienced similar repression after Velde cast his red scare cloak over Southern California.[18] In addition, in New York City, out of 31 educators who refused to cooperate with McCarran's SISS investigations, only five later kept their jobs. Not surprisingly, by July 1953, the *Harvard Crimson* estimated that over one hundred school teachers had been dismissed for non-cooperation with Congressional committees.[19]

Many teachers subpoenaed to appear before state and Congressional investigating committees spoke of personal anxiety and tension. Variously, they claimed to "live in terror," to be consumed by "fear," and to be "terribly frightened."[20] Others, who actually avoided being called before investigating committees, appeared similarly disturbed. For example, one California teacher who was active in the local teachers' union remarked that "in my last year of teaching I was always afraid that I would be called in and investigated. Every time I would get a call to go to the office on my way there my heart would be pounding."[21] In many respects, therefore, the relatively small number of those dismissed as a result of Congressional investigations often disguised the intense concerns that afflicted thousands of educators in this period. Indeed, in many cases, the fear of being called before a committee, the worry that one might be labeled a "communist," the concern that classroom activities might be misconstrued as subversive, likely produced an atmosphere that intimidated many teachers and often led to inherently conservative classroom practices.[22]

A salient characteristic of state and Congressional investigations into education was their frequent and blatant disregard for the legal principle of due process. Although hundreds of teachers were accused of subversion for their actions and were later dismissed, in no case was *prima facie* evidence produced to demonstrate that individual teachers were indoctrinating students or advocating the overthrow of the government.[23] Regularly, Congressional witnesses appeared with damaging charges against educators for purported un-American activities. Almost without exception, however, the accusations were unsubstantiated, based upon rumor and innuendo, and influenced by the political affiliation of the accuser. In addition, teachers often were denied proper legal representation. Frances Eisenberg, for example, who appeared before the Tenney Committee, the State of California's investigating committee for un-American activities, was denied the services of the teachers' union lawyer. "This was a kangaroo court, and lawyers couldn't take part," Eisenberg recalled with alarm many years later.[24]

Confronted by the threat of being called before an investigating committee often to answer spurious and implausible, but nonetheless fiercely damaging charges, many teachers, particularly in major urban areas such as Los Angeles, New York, and Philadelphia, increasingly became intimidated. Unquestionably, teachers who were former members of the Communist Party had most to fear from the renewed zeal of the post-war red scare. In the Cold War climate, few Americans supported the rights of communist teachers or sympathized with those who refused to confess their personal links to the Communist Party. A public opinion poll conducted in 1954, for example, found that 90% of a national sample of citizens believed that communist teachers should be fired.[25] Accordingly, teachers who were smeared as communist agitators in Congressional investigations, irrespective of their innocence or guilt, received virtually no public support and appeared extremely vulnerable to dismissal.

Guilt by accusation and innuendo also was bolstered by the principle of guilt by association. When witnesses identified individual teachers as former members of the Communist Party, the committees could justify their ideological purges. Accordingly, witnesses, who were prepared to name names and to expose communist teachers were gold dust to the investigating committees. Not surprisingly, investigating inquisitions clamored for the testimony of witnesses such as Bella Dodd who exposed links between members of the New York City teachers' union and the Communist Party in the SISS hearings in 1952.[26] Following Dodd's revelations to SISS, she was enthusiastically borrowed by HUAC to repeat her story and to identify other potential victims for further red scare attack.

Other teachers were coerced into testifying against fellow educators. High school teacher Wilbur Lee Mahaney Jr. was a case in point. In February 1954, he informed a HUAC investigation that he was prepared to talk about his own record, but declined to discuss the activities of other. He was cited for contempt and suspended from his job. In July 1954, under enormous pressure, he agreed to rectify his "false sense of loyalty" by identifying 16 teachers as being Communist Party members. Purged of his own personal guilt, Mahaney's confession condemned his colleagues to the full force of red scare attack.[27]

Although state and Congressional investigating committees profoundly impacted many educators, a peculiar feature of these committees was the limited legal authority they explicitly had available to them. Congress did not enjoy any direct control over educational policy, and, certainly, it had no jurisdiction over the employment practices in public schools. Rather, the power of the Congressional committees lay within their ability to expose and to identify individuals including teachers who were communists or former communists. The committee's purpose, therefore, was to invite "public exposure" in order to "instruct, to deter, to punish, and to destroy."[28] Members of the investigating committees believed that, once exposed, communist teachers readily would be dismissed from their teaching positions by local school boards and boards of education. Accordingly, Ellen Schrecker argued that McCarthyism resembled a two-stage process,

> First, the objectionable groups and individuals were identified — during a committee hearing, for example, or an FBI investigation; then, they were punished, usually by being fired. The bifurcated nature of this process diffused responsibility and made it easier for each participant to dissociate his or her action from the larger whole. Rarely did any single institution handle both stages of McCarthyism.[29]

McCarthyism as a process was strikingly effective. Once HUAC, SISS, McCarthy, or a state investigating committee questioned a teacher's loyalty, school authorities rushed to investigate the individual. As a result, scores of educators were dismissed.[30] Furthermore, blacklists and dossiers of those educators who appeared before HUAC and SISS often found their way to the homes of school board members, or to the desks of school administrators. A blacklist of the names of 90 teachers who had invoked the Fifth Amendment during the SISS investigation of subversion in education, for example, received wide circulation.[31]

Significantly caught up in the hysteria of the red scare, few school board members or school administrators appeared prepared to defend teachers accused of harboring communist sympathies. For many teachers, once tainted with the blemish of the communist label they could not eliminate the stain. Historian Arthur Zilversmit similarly remarked how professional education organizations often succumbed to the prevailing anti-communist mood of the period. He noted how publications, such as the *American School Board Journal*, which argued that innocent teachers had nothing to hide from the inquisitors, frequently defended Congressional investigations. Zilversmit also contended,

> Virtually everyone who attended the 1953 [Association of School Board Administrators] annual meeting agreed 'that any person who was a communist or subversive in any other way should not be permitted to teach.' Despite the obvious threat to academic freedom, educators refused to take a clear stand against the Congressional investigations, which increasingly turned into witch hunts.[32]

The position of the Defense Commission on state and Congressional investigating committees is particularly revealing. Throughout the late 1940s and early 1950s, numerous issues of the *Defense Bulletin* reported the activities of Congressional committees that investigated alleged subversion in the schools. Undoubtedly, members of the Defense Commission were troubled by many of the investigations' proceedings and appeared dismayed by the conclusions reached by them. Richard Barnes Kennan, the commission's executive secretary, was particularly contemptuous of the inquisitors. He accused them of acting like "modern day Quislings" and suggested that "some of our American governmental probes are as inharmonious and disagreeable as a phonograph record run in reverse."[33] The Defense Commission also eagerly publicized the remarks of Mrs. Agnes Meyer who denounced the Congressional inquisitions and called for a powerful "counter-offensive against" them. Meyer claimed that, "the independence of our whole education system will be jeopardized if Velde, Jenner, and McCarthy are not stopped in their tracks."[34] In addition, other members of the Defense Commission spoke out against state and

Congressional investigations in several issues of the *Defense Bulletin*, in education conferences, and in the nation's media.[35]

Yet, despite their dislike of Congressional investigations and despite their rhetorical objection to them, members of the Defense Commission appeared reluctant to back their words with actions. For example, they failed to defend or stand up for any teacher explicitly accused of being a communist in a Congressional investigation. Furthermore, although they objected to the practices of Congressional investigations, not once did members of the commission advise members to avoid cooperation with them.

Very often many of the activities of the commission lacked substance and conviction. For example, the only positive suggestion that the authors of the *Defense Bulletin* urged to counter harmful investigations appeared in January 1953. This edition of the *Bulletin* published the names of all the politicians who served on Congressional committees investigating education. Under the dramatic, but essentially misleading, heading "ACTION," members were encouraged to, "Keep in touch with members of these committees in your state or locality. Help to keep them informed of the contribution the schools are making to our American strength and unity."[36] This advice reflected both the timid nature of the Defense Commission's response to Congressional investigations and the extent to which the commission often misunderstood the power and motivation of red scare attack. The very notion that politicians like McCarthy, Velde, or McCarran might be influenced by letters that celebrated the achievements of schools revealed a complete lack of appreciation of the political motivations behind the red scare.

Of greater significance, by supporting the NEA's decision to deny the right of any educator to be a member of the Communist Party, the Defense Commission assumed the same stance as virtually every other liberal or conservative organization in this period. The commission readily embraced the prevailing belief that no citizen could be both a communist and a respectable educator. Consequently, once a Congressional investigating committee branded someone a communist, the Defense Commission distanced itself from that person's claim to defense. Chillingly, the Defense Commission became trapped by the logic of its own political position.

The paradoxical dilemma of the Defense Commission testified to the strength and power of the red scare in post-World War II America. The rhetoric and practices of the red scare fueled anti-communist fervor throughout the nation. It popularized and legitimized both the claims and invasive actions of the political right. It served the interests of conservatives in business and in the media, and it offered a perverse legitimacy to extremist and nationalist organizations. More revealingly, however, the red scare sucked in those with more progressive and liberal ideals. In the climate of acute repression scarcely any democratic organization, including the NEA and its Defense Commission, actively and vigorously opposed Congressional investigations and the red scare motivations that underpinned them.

School Textbooks Fall Victim to the Red Scare

Criticism of school textbooks for religious, political, philosophical, or ideological reasons have been a pervasive characteristic of education throughout the history of American public schools. In the post-World War II period, however, this criticism became unusually prolific and caustic. Scores of ultra-conservative and reactionary individuals regularly attacked school textbooks for their alleged pro-communist and anti-American viewpoints. Trapped in this frenzied atmosphere of red scare assault, publishers, school boards, teachers, and administrators operated with extreme caution in fear of antagonizing these powerful critical forces.

As a soft target, school textbooks fell victim, almost automatically, to the acerbic charges of the critics. Virtually every organization associated with the red scare participated in reflexive assaults on textbooks. Officers of the Defense Commission expressed extreme concern about the damaging impact that red scare criticism of textbooks might have on American schools. For example, a storm of red scare criticism had plagued the textbook series of Columbia's Harold Rugg and reduced circulation of his texts from 289,000 copies in 1938 to 21,000 copies in 1944, to virtual elimination by the early 1950s. Members of the commission painfully remembered this episode in American educational history.[37] In the late 1940s, many editions of the commission's *Defense Bulletin* referred to increasing attacks on school textbooks and to the widespread intensification of censorship and academic repression.

In January 1948, for example, the *Defense Bulletin* observed censorship of textbooks in California and the District of Columbia.[38] In February 1948, the *Bulletin* alarmingly noted that a House subcommittee was considering a recommendation to ban all textbooks written by Harold Rugg, Louis Adamic, and Louise Kreuger. In addition, the *Bulletin* noted the subcommittee's intense scrutiny of *Building Citizenship* by Ray O. Hughes on the basis of its allegedly favorable portrayal of the Soviet Union. Critics, the subcommittee learned, objected to the book because it contained a picture of Stalin, even though the text labeled him a dictator.[39] The attacks continued with striking regularity. In November 1948, the *Defense Bulletin* reported other cases of academic repression and textbook censorship. In California, for example, the NEA supported *Building American Series* suffocated under an avalanche of criticism and controversy, and, in Iowa, an eighth grade textbook, *The Building of Our Nation*, by historians Eugene Barker, Walter Prescott Webb, and Henry Steele was attacked "as a glib piece of propaganda intended to deceive."[40] By the end of the 1940s, attacks on textbooks became both a regular feature on the American educational landscape and a familiar weapon in the arsenal of many red scare critics and organizations.

Within this vicious whirlpool of red scare activity, however, one group, the Conference of American Small Business Organizations (CASBO), remained unparalleled for its invasive and single-minded scrutiny of school textbooks. CASBO originally was formed by pro-business leader Fred A. Virkus, with its headquarters in Chicago. CASBO's foremost activities soon were centered in New York around the effective and calculating leadership of Lucille Cardin Crain. As editor of CASBO's notorious *Educational Reviewer*, Crain and her associates launched a passionate crusade to rid American schools of "dangerously subversive" and "un-American" texts. CASBO's obsessive concern with school instructional materials stemmed from a resolution passed at the organization's ninth annual meeting held in Washington, D.C. in February 1948. CASBO proclaimed,

> Whereas...educators have secured the adoption of textbooks which are essentially documents of propaganda with the aim of changing the 'climate of opinion' in the United States; now, therefore
> Be it resolved that the Conference of American Small Business Organizations assembled emphatically condemns the perversion of our educational system through so-called social science courses and the neglect of instruction in history, geography, and civics; and
> Be it further resolved, that the Conference does hereby urge its members and affiliated groups, and all other patriotic groups throughout the nation to inquire of the local school authorities whether American history is being taught well and whether un-American textbooks are being used...[41]

The resolution prompted CASBO's creation of the *Educational Reviewer,* which, during a five year period from July 1949 to October 1953, actively campaigned to rid the schools of subversive materials and literature.

Under the editorial stewardship of Lucille Cardin Crain, the *Educational Reviewer* undoubtedly had an impact on school textbook adoption practices and policies in communities throughout the United States. Indeed, one of the *Reviewer*'s avowed purposes was to involve as many citizens in the process of textbook vigilantism as possible. This was a policy that Crain neatly explicated to a gathering of businesspeople in New York City in June 1950,

> The purpose of the *Reviewer* is two-fold. It is designed to not only be a source of information concerning educational materials currently used in the schools and colleges, but also a tool in the hands of its subscribers who wish to work with the school authorities in their communities. In fact, every reader of the *Reviewer* is urged 'to get in on the act' by sending in a list of textbooks and other materials used in his school in connection with the subjects where the American idea is most likely to be under subtle attack.[42]

Crain's address was typical of her regular activities. Although Crain used the *Reviewer* as the primary vehicle for assailing American school textbooks, she also wrote for other noted publications and often spoke before local and national audiences on the subject of communist infiltration of the schools.

Once described by Allen A. Zoll as a "charming woman, very lovely," Crain operated out of an office in New York City. Arthur D. Morse, *McCall's* reporter, remarked that Crain appeared "the most attractive figure in the anti-school movement" and further noted, "She is 50, she has cool blue eyes, a cameo face, and a fondness for using rather fancy words."[43] In political, business, and social terms, Crain was well connected and enjoyed the support of many influential figures on the political right. Senator Karl Mundt, columnist Arthur Krock of the *New York Times*, and President G. D. Humphrey of the University of Wyoming, to name but a few, approved and supported *The Educational Reviewer*. In addition, in order to add an air of credibility to the publication, *The Reviewer* boasted a consulting staff composed of Lewis H. Haney, professor of economics at New York University, William Star Myers, professor emeritus of politics at Princeton University, and O. Glenn Saxon, professor of business administration at Yale University.[44]

The practice of *The Educational Reviewer* was simple. Based upon the scrutiny of *The Reviewer*'s staff or upon the advice of "loyal informers," selected school textbooks were subjected to meticulous review. Singled out for inevitable attention were those books that either contained passages allegedly advocating socialism, collectivism, and government interference, or that were perceived to be anti-business, anti-capitalist, and inherently un-American.

From the outset, the Defense Commission's Robert Skaife understood the destructive intentions of *The Educational Reviewer*. "A reading of several issues of *The Educational Reviewer* indicates," he wrote in May 1951, "the approach that appears to be used is to search through textbooks concerned with controversial issues for sentences or ideas reflecting what *The Reviewer* would call 'collectivism.'"[45] Once a range of textbooks underwent review, copies of *The Educational Reviewer* were distributed to people in communities throughout the nation. In particular, the staff of *The Reviewer* understood its audience included business leaders, influential politicians, patriotic groups, and school board members.

One issue, published in April 1951, typified the tone and content of *The Reviewer*. In this issue, fourteen textbooks were identified for their purportedly subversive influence. Appraisals appeared venomously critical and damaging accusations were hurled at selected materials. Representative comments included the charges that the textbooks "were undermining the principles of private enterprise," using "slanted arguments and data by governments," and "indoctrinating" the young "toward a socialistic state by the surreptitious presentation of half-truths under the guise of education."[46]

The Reviewer's critical examination of school textbooks triggered action in communities throughout the United States. For example, as a result of *The Reviewer*'s comments *The American Way of Life* by Harry E. Barnes and *Modern Economics* by James F. Corbitt and Minna Colvin fell under the scrutiny of school boards in several local school districts.[47] *The Educational Reviewer* also stirred emotive attacks on textbooks used in Council Bluffs (Iowa), Detroit (Michigan), Birmingham (Alabama), and Jackson (Michigan). Textbooks singled out for particular scrutiny in these towns included *The Story of American Democracy* by Casner and Gabriel, *The Challenge to Democracy* by Blake and Baumgarten, and the *Building of Our Nation* by Barker, Webb, and Commager.[48]

Stinging attacks by *The Educational Reviewer,* however, did not remain unchallenged. Many within the fields of education and political science, as well as the media questioned the methods and the conclusions drawn by Crain and her colleagues. U. S. Attorney General McGrath, for example, was troubled by the persistent tendency of textbook critics to smear opponents with the label of communist. "The loose application of the words 'subversive' or 'collectivist' to the textbooks with the idea of getting the textbooks labeled un-American," remarked the attorney general in 1951, "is to abridge beyond reason our tradition of democratic freedom."[49]

The strongest official condemnation of CASBO and its activities appeared in the final report issued by the House Select Committee on Lobbying Activities in 1950. Chaired by Congressman Frank Buchanan, the committee was disturbed that groups like CASBO had "long since recognized that lobbying of the traditional variety is not enough to ensure lasting legislative success. As a consequence, they have entered upon a far reaching and infinitely ambitious struggle to control public opinion." Buchanan's committee appeared extremely concerned that CASBO, as a "long range pressure group," had no objective other than to establish its "philosophy as the standard educational orthodoxy in the schools of the nation." Alarmed by this possibility, they poignantly concluded,

> We all agree, of course, that our textbooks should be American, that they should not be the vehicle for the propagation of obnoxious doctrines. Yet the review of textbooks by self-appointed experts, especially when undertaken under the aegis of an organization having a distinct legislative axe to grind, smacks too much of the book burning orgies of Nuremberg to be accepted by thoughtful Americans without foreboding and alarm.[50]

Not only did Buchanan's report provide the NEA and the Defense Commission a tremendous boost in morale, it also offered the Defense Commission powerful ammunition in its efforts to blunt red scare attack. The *Defense Bulletin* enthusiastically publicized the select committee's conclusions, which had appeared in the *Congressional Record*. Mass reprinting of the *Record* was ordered by the commission, and it was widely distributed to local educational organizations across the United States. In addition, Robert Skaife and Arthur H. Rice, editor of the *Nation's Schools*, solicited the political support of Frank Buchanan as a result of a series of meetings with the Congressman.[51]

Skaife and Rice explicated similar opinions with regard to CASBO's activities. Both shared the conviction that the authors of *The Educational Reviewer* had the right to vent their criticisms of American schools. Rice's editorial column contested, however,

> the function of any self-appointed interest group to decide what shall or shall not be taught in the schools.... Such decisions are the responsibility of the school board or the state legislature, legally representing the interests of the people.[52]

Skaife concurred, "No responsible education leader wants or expects public education to be immune from criticism." "But," argued the commission's field secretary in May 1951, "he does expect the criticism to come from responsible sources and to be justifiable in terms of the welfare of the entire community."[53] In repeated issues, the *Defense Bulletin* hammered home this point.

In back-to-back issues of the *Defense Bulletin* published in January and February 1951, the Defense Commission additionally condemned CASBO and *The Educational Reviewer* for printing unsubstantiated and "unprovable generalizations" for the explicit intention of "undermining the schools."[54] To illustrate the transparency of CASBO's methods, the *Defense Bulletin* printed the following paragraph from *The Educational Reviewer*,

> That collectivist theories are tending to suppress, if not destroy entirely, our American governmental theory, is evident from a statement of a student...who believes, 'that very few young people finish school today without having a tinge of collectivism ingrained into them...'[55]

The authors of the *Bulletin* challenged the flimsiness of the evidence, the gross oversimplification of the case, and the sweeping generalizations made by *The Reviewer*. In addition, the *Bulletin* argued that educators had "a right to know the background of the reviewing agency...and the duty to protest the generalized editorial allegation."[56] Still, despite the tenuous and radical claims of *The Reviewer* and the vigorous efforts of the Defense Commission to expose its brittle arguments, the commission painfully was aware of the destructive influence that CASBO and *The Educational Reviewer* had on many educational communities.

The effectiveness of *The Educational Reviewer* was considerably boosted by the explicit support given to the publication from influential politicians and figures in the media. Fulton Lewis Jr., for example, a nationally known commentator, specifically promoted *The Educational Reviewer* in his popular radio broadcasts during the winter of 1950. Newspapers such as the *Chicago Daily Tribune* also championed CASBO and *The Educational Reviewer*. Indeed, an editorial of the Chicago paper, released on January 29, 1950, urged readers to support the publication. *The Tribune* maintained, "Every school trustee in this country and every school administrator ought to subscribe to *The Educational Reviewer*."[57]

The Educational Reviewer also was strengthened by the support it received from other red scare groups and organizations. For example,

CASBO sponsored the Committee on Education, a right-wing group centered in New York, and frequently consorted with Allen A. Zoll and his burgeoning anti-communist organization. John Bainbridge of *McCall's* magazine remarked on the close association between groups such as Friends of the Public Schools, Pro-America, the American Education Association, and the National Council for American Education. "These extreme right-wing organizations, though having no official connection," noted Bainbridge, "keep in touch with one another's activities, exchange literature, and, with other groups, constitute an informal coalition to spread destructive propaganda about the schools."[58] Consequently, as a result of the combined assistance of other red scare organizations, powerful business interests, favorable media coverage, and sympathetic political support, *The Educational Reviewer* proved remarkably successful in its pillory of instructional materials used in public schools.

No better example of CASBO's profound influence on school textbooks existed than the organization's concerted attack on the Magruder texts which first occurred in the summer of 1949. Magruder's *American Government* had been a classic school textbook read in schools for more than a quarter of a century. Used by the U. S. armed forces and by thousands of schools in each of the then 48 states, Magruder's book overwhelmingly was the most widely used text in its field. Its author, Frank Abbott Magruder, was a professor of political science at Oregon State College. Ironically, Magruder, a devout churchman who used the royalties from his book to support a camp for victims of polio, died just as the most vicious attacks on his work commenced. Undoubtedly, had he lived he surely would have been stunned by the fierce and, at times, hysterical criticism that his book received.[59]

The catalyst for the assault on the *American Government* text was a review published in *The Educational Reviewer* in July 1949. Authored by Edna Lonigan, *The Reviewer* claimed that Magruder's text followed "the Communist Party line." Meticulously she pointed out passages in the text which, she alleged, exemplified the subversive nature of the book. As testimony to the effectiveness of the network of red scare organizations and their influential supporters, her "review" triggered a sensational storm of protest in many communities throughout the country.

Almost immediately, boards of education banned the book in Houston, Texas, New Haven, Connecticut, and Washington, D.C. Schools in Little Rock, Arkansas, removed the text from classroom use and relegated it to the reference shelves of school libraries. Censorship campaigns against the book, many of them extremely successful, mushroomed in communities in Georgia, Iowa, New Jersey, Michigan, Oregon, Ohio, California, Montana, Alabama, and Washington.[60]

In Florida, the Committee for American Action spearheaded an explosive attack on the Magruder text. In Georgia, despite the *Atlanta Constitution*'s protest that Governor Talmadge had used the Magruder text when he was in school, Mrs. Julius Y. Talmadge, a member of the Georgia School Board and a former national regent of the Daughters of the American Revolution, asserted that the book's "controversial material" had no place in Georgia's classrooms. Oddly, however, Mrs. Talmadge had no qualms about selling the then redundant 30,000 copies of the text to other school systems outside Georgia. As Robert Iversen noted, "Having saved Georgia she had no compunction in subverting neighboring states."[61]

The school children of Houston, Texas, also suffered from the Magruder controversy. In October 1949, the *Defense Bulletin* informed readers that the Houston School Board voted to ban the book.[62] As a consequence, educators in the Houston Independent School District went without a standard civics text until 1954 when the book was re-edited in accordance with the wishes of the censors. Significantly, in the intervening five-year period, some of Houston's teachers opted to use John T. Flynn's right-wing books, which Texas millionaire Hugh Roy Cullen conveniently made available to schools free of charge.[63]

The avalanche of red scare activity triggered by *The Educational Reviewer* profoundly impacted many educational communities throughout the United States. Significantly, the chaos caused by its critical revelations illuminated two of the classic hallmarks of the red scare.

In the first place, as with other aspects of educational criticism, many of the accusations leveled at Magruder's text patently were spurious and often depended upon misquote, rumor, and blatant falsehood. The Magruder text controversy provided stark evidence of typical red scare tactics in operation. According to Lonigan, for example, the Magruder text alleged that, "Italy and Germany were dictatorships, but not the Soviet Union." In reality, however, the Magruder text actually stated, "Russia is the leader of the dictatorial nations, most of which are communistic." Lonigan asserted that Magruder openly advocated collectivism. As proof she cited the following extract, "By democracy we mean that form of government in which the sovereign power is in the hands of the people collectively." However, by omitting an ellipsis after "collectively," Lonigan deliberately failed to add, "and is expressed by them either directly or indirectly through elected representatives."[64] In addition, whereas Lonigan claimed the Magruder text stated, "The United States and the Soviet Union are equals fighting for world leadership." The text actually stated, "The United States and the Soviet Union, the most powerful of all allies in the Second World War, now find themselves as the only two powerful contenders for world leadership." *The Reviewer*'s biting condemnation of the Magruder text was replete with other misrepresentations and selected editorial statements that typified red scare criticism of school texts.

The second feature indicative of the red scare was the stark realization that when textbook criticisms were subjected to rational investigation, virtually no evidence of subversion was uncovered. Benjamin Fine, educational editor for the *New York Times*, for example, noted that the Magruder text had been under fire in many states. "Yet, upon a thorough reading of the book," Fine remarked, "the school board and educators give it a clean bill of health. They maintain there is nothing subversive about it, nothing contrary to the American ideals and traditions."[65] Accordingly, in Council Bluffs (Iowa), Jackson (Michigan), New Haven (Connecticut), Trumbull County (Ohio), and scores of other places where the book originally was withdrawn, subsequent meticulous investigation deemed the text highly appropriate for school use.[66]

Despite the text's absolution and reinstatement in some school districts, the red scare proved devastatingly effective in altering the educational climate in other communities. School boards were thrown into disarray as a result of the charges against the Magruder texts. Endless hours of acrimonious debate and discussion were expended on the issue. Many school boards and textbook selection committees were forced to commit precious time to the scrutiny of textbooks, paragraph by paragraph. As in New York, often special textbook commissions were established to investigate charges of subversion. Significantly, at a time when schools confronted the very real problems of overcrowded classrooms, dilapidated buildings, and acute teacher shortages, the desperately needed attention of school boards was diverted to chasing numerous illusory allegations against school textbooks.

The red scare climate induced what Kalman Seigel of the *New York Times* described as a "subtle creeping paralysis of freedom of thought and speech" in communities across the nation.[67] Teachers often were afraid to speak out; they became defensive, invoked self-censorship, and grew increasingly wary of engaging in controversial or unpopular topics. Even in communities where attacks against the schools were declared unfounded, irreparable damage had been done. As one contemporary commentator revealingly observed,

> In the case of Englewood, New Jersey, after exhaustive hearings to investigate alleged subversion in the schools, the Board of Education concluded that the charges were based on hearsay and rumor, and absolved the teachers of any implications of 'subversive activity.' But Englewood was not unscathed. Teachers reported afterwards that they were afraid to discuss controversial issues in their classes. *The Englewood Press-Journal* reported that, 'There is a community menace that is growing here like a cancer.'[68]

School materials and the school curriculum also fell victim to the attacks. On October 27, 1951, *The Nation* commented that the "seeming calm" in thousands of communities was "actually retreat: experimental courses and controversial library books have been renounced; reduced appropriations for buildings, equipment and salaries have been accepted."[69] The Defense Commission's *Bulletin* of September 1952 lamented the impact that unwarranted attacks had on textbook publishers. Increasingly materials appeared that were cautious, bland, sterile, and non-committal.[70] In school districts throughout the United States freedom to inquire and to explore in the classroom frequently was crushed.

Complexities of Red Scare Attack

As the rhetoric and activity of the Cold War dramatically intensified in the late 1940s and early 1950s, the ideology of anti-communism dominated America's view of the world. On the domestic scene, anti-communist legislation, loyalty investigations, and the ever present suspicion of soviet infiltration proved dangerously fertile ground for increased red scare attack. In the battle for ideological control of the culture, schools became a natural target for concerted attack.

Discerning a clear and coherent pattern of red scare attack on the schools proved a complex and multifaceted proposition. Nevertheless, members of the Defense Commission believed that an identifiable process was evident. For example, numerous publications and information bulletins produced by the Defense Commission essentially reasoned that attacks on the schools progressed through four discernible phases.[71] First, a few citizens "who are especially eager to keep taxes low" or who were pushing a clear political agenda "are corralled into a self-styled and self-appointed 'citizen's council.'" Second, according to the leadership of the Defense Commission, these groups, which were often highly organized and financially well supported, showered the local community with "demagogic pamphlets and leaflets." At this phase, the officers of the Defense Commission noted, the attackers invited others dissatisfied with the schools to join with them to demand changes in school personnel, policy, practice, and curriculum. The third phase was characterized by "the heavy pressure campaign" in which critics vocally and vigorously outlined their complaints. One NEA-sponsored pamphlet, for example, asserted that these attacks incorporated

> —Demands that the schools "return to the 3R's."
> —Attacks on textbooks that encourage inquisitive thinking and reasoning.
> —Attempts to malign leading educators and any teachers, principals, or members of the local school board who dare to defend sound, modern educational methods.
> —A hue and cry about the need for stronger discipline in the schools.
> —Calls for a legislative investigation of teachers, textbooks and school administrators.[72]

A significant feature of the third phase appeared to be the widespread and extensive use of materials from national organizations eager to discredit the schools. A Defense Commission "fact sheet," "The Current Attacks on Public Education," produced for the benefit of NEA members in January 1953, noted, for example, the increasing menace of national organizations and their orchestrated campaigns to undermine public education.

The fourth and final stage of the attacking process often produced harmful and damaging results. At this stage, Defense Commission publications asserted, "the entire school issue becomes confused and charged with emotion. Epithets such as 'communist,' 'socialist,' 'collectivist,' 'secularist,' and 'un-American,' are thrown around freely to exploit the sentiments of genuinely patriotic, anti-communist citizens." In this climate, "teachers are intimidated and school boards coerced."[73]

The Defense Commission's four-phase model offered an incisive, coherent, and neatly packaged analysis of a complex and indeterminate process. Without question, the commission's observations somewhat accurately reflected occurrences in scores of communities across the country. For example, in many respects, the attacks on school superintendent Willard Goslin in Pasadena, California, closely mirrored the four-stage process outlined by the commission.

In other respects, however, red scare attacks were subject to irregularities, inconsistencies, and factors peculiar to local situations. Sometimes attacks originated as result of propaganda materials distributed by national organizations at the local level. On other occasions, attacks on schools began as a result of local frustrations and, subsequently, were substantiated by the actions of powerful pressure groups, wealthy business interests, and national red scare organizations. Some attacks enjoyed devastating success, while others met with enormous community resistance.

For instance, the concerted process of red scare attack, which proved so effective in undermining the activities of school personnel in Houston and in Pasadena, had limited success in other communities. In Scarsdale, New York, for example, the community was subjected to many of the ingredients of red scare attack that featured so powerfully in Houston and Pasadena. The effects of the attacks, however, appeared strikingly different. In Scarsdale, in 1949, an orchestrated campaign by a local reactionary group known as the Committee of Ten used familiar tactics and methods to discredit the local schools. These critics received the support of influential businessmen, patriotic organizations, and red scare pressure groups. The attackers were successful in that they effectively embroiled the schools in a furious debate on the issue of whether or not the local schools were infiltrated with un-American materials and teaching practices. However, largely as a result of the conservative minded Town Club and other community groups, the attacks eventually were blunted. Significantly, in the school board elections of May 1950, candidates supported by those who attacked the schools fared miserably.[74]

Understanding the process of attack also proves complicated when the motivations of the critics are analyzed. In some instances red scare attacks were deliberately and consciously used by powerful forces in the community to exact political gain and to assert the ideological agenda of particular interest groups. On other occasions, attacks succeeded because many people firmly believed that schools systems did support socialist ideals and un-American ways.[75] Some citizens also used the apparent failings of the schools as a convenient scapegoat to explain social ills such as increased juvenile delinquency or as a vehicle to explain the academic failings of their own children.

Whatever the motivations of the critics and whatever the exact process of attack, two conclusions appear reasonable. First, in the late 1940s and early 1950s, national and international events made the use of red scare tactics and methods enormously effective weapons to discredit the schools. That the persuasive use of anti-communist rhetoric and accusation often hid the true agenda of the critics mattered not at all. The reflexive use of anti-communist tactics to attack the perceived plurality of social, cultural, and political evils proved an effective and alluring proposition for many on the political right and explains the extensive proliferation of red scare attacks on public schools in many communities across the nation.

Second, the many red scare critics and organizations were enormously influential in changing and shifting the atmosphere and culture of public schools in communities throughout the United States. Significantly, although their rhetoric and charges often appeared extremist, sensational, and in almost every case, unsubstantiated, often they enjoyed the support of business leaders, media representatives, and influential politicians. Typically, these extremist organizations colluded through an informal and effective national network.[76] Among the groups that regularly attacked the schools, information was exchanged, literature disseminated, and individuals and institutions singled out for special attention and assault. Furthermore, these red scare organizations often operated on a national scale. For example, The Minute Women USA, Inc., founded in 1949 by a group of 127 Connecticut women, boasted organizations in more than 40 states in 1952.[77] Many other organizations followed a similar pattern and enjoyed considerable success in their attacks on public schools.

The archives of the Defense Commission attest the plethora of organizations that emerged to discredit American schools at this time. Unquestionably, these organizations and their political and business allies wielded considerable influence throughout the United States. Red scare attacks emerged both in large urban areas such as Los Angeles, Philadelphia, and New York, as well as in small communities such as San Angelo (Texas), Muskogee (Oklahoma), and Tenafly (New Jersey). Attacks appeared on the west coast in cities like Portland (Oregon) and on the east coast in such places as New Haven (Connecticut). America's red scare knew no geographical boundaries. Birmingham (Alabama), Columbus (Ohio), Denver (Colorado), and Battle Creek (Michigan), for example, also fell victim to attack. As a consequence, although some towns and cities may have emerged from the post-war era with little direct experience of the red scare, and, although attacks sometimes met with resistance in a few local communities, the records of the Defense Commission clearly demonstrate that the red scare threw scores of communities across the United States into turmoil, and, in many towns and cities, it exacted an enormous educational price.

Red scare organizations and their political allies clearly were effective in determining significant dimensions of the climate in which educators worked. By mid-century, many teachers appeared acutely fearful of engaging in any subject matter which might be construed as subversive or controversial. They used textbooks and other instructional materials cautiously; self-censorship among teachers appeared common, and teachers used curriculum materials judiciously for fear of alienating political forces in the community. Caught up in the vortex of red scare propaganda and other post-war conservative attacks, teachers and public schools suffered. In these difficult times, teachers and administrators looked to the NEA for support and protection. Accordingly, by the late 1940s, the Defense Commission assumed a more prominent, active, and influential role. The next three chapters present a detailed examination of the work of the Defense Commission. They offer both an insight into its effectiveness in blunting red scare attack and an insight into the power and ubiquity of the red scare phenomenon in the decade immediately following World War II.

Chapter VII

The Activities of the Defense Commission, 1947-1954: Exposing Critics and Supporting Educators

Throughout the existence of the Defense Commission, its staff diligently sought to defend teachers from virulent criticism. As the nature and frequency of red scare attack dramatically intensified in the late 1940s and early 1950s, commission members and staff increasingly recognized the need to become more vigorous, more defiant, and more active in their defense of America's educators.

Harold Benjamin encapsulated the Defense Commission's renewed zeal in his passionate address to the NEA assembly in July 1950.[1] In his speech, "Report on the Enemy," he graphically illustrated the crisis that contemporary educators faced. Benjamin noted the growing proliferation of attacks, their motivations, and the organized and financially well-supported groups that orchestrated them. Dean Harold Benjamin asserted that the NEA must take a firm and resolute stand against education's critics and prepare vigorously to blunt their charges against the schools:

> To the Zolls and their National Councils for American Education, to the tax-haters and the school development councils and school protective leagues which they have set up in many places throughout the country, we need to pay close attention. We need to get more information about them and their tactics, and we need to pass that information back to our great combat team.[2]

Benjamin reasoned that the "combat team" comprised not only the NEA and the Defense Commission, but also the "armored columns" and "heavy weapons" of parents organizations, community and civic groups, and trade assemblies. In the face of an "enemy" that was "stronger than he looks," he argued that the time for positive and vigorous action had arrived. Optimistically, he asserted, "If we get our combat team together...get the information it needs for its decisions swiftly and accurately before it, even a stronger enemy than this one would make hardly more than a ripple in the smoothness of our advance." In the climate of the times, Benjamin's emotional address to NEA delegation undoubtedly received warm and empathetic approval.

Benjamin's desire to be more resourceful and proactive in response to red scare attacks was shared by many others in the NEA. Significantly, at the 1949 NEA conference in Boston, several delegates campaigned to increase the Defense Commission's budget and staffing allowance. Sarah Caldwell, for example, horrified that many teachers appeared "victims of petty jealousies, unjust attacks, and cold-blooded reprisals," demanded that the NEA approve increased funds to defend teachers.[3] Similarly, Miss Vail, a delegate from Arizona, asserted that "there was a crying need" to appoint a field secretary to work for the Defense Commission on the behalf of teachers throughout the nation.[4]

The NEA's sympathetic response to such requests indicates the seriousness with which members of the Association regarded the attacks on schools at this time. Throughout the late 1940s and early 1950s, the commission's budget allocation climbed significantly. Indeed, in 1954, the commission received almost five times the amount it secured ten years previously, and, apart from the Department of Classroom Teachers, it received more funds than any other NEA commission or Department.[5] Concomitant with its rapid growth in financial resources was the significant increase in the Defense Commission's staff. In its formative years, the commission operated with a full-time staff of only two individuals, and a stenographer.[6] By 1950, however, it enjoyed a full-time staff of ten. Personnel included an executive secretary, a legal counsel, an assistant secretary, a field secretary, and five secretarial assistants. As the 1950s progressed, the number of full-time staff members continued to grow.

This escalation in financial support for the commission and the rapid expansion of its personnel dramatically illustrated the NEA's growing concern with red scare attacks. The importance of defending teachers further was underscored by the decision of the leadership of the Defense Commission to concentrate much of its attention on those attacking the schools. Indeed, by 1951, the commission "devoted practically all of [its] time to combating criticisms."[7]

Unquestionably, one of the NEA's most important and telling moves was its decision in 1949 to appoint Robert Skaife as field secretary to the

Defense Commission. Essentially, Skaife's role was to provide direct support to educators in troubled school districts throughout the United States.

At the height of the red scare, Skaife served as an energetic and unapologetic defender of American teachers. He wrote numerous articles in educational publications to expose critics and inure teachers against attack. He spoke to educator-lay audiences in communities across the country. Furthermore, he led important Defense Commission investigations into hotbeds of controversy, such as Houston and Pasadena. Like many other influential figures in the NEA, Skaife realized that to be more effective required the Defense Commission to meet attacks against education head on. In 1951, he wrote that,

> deliberate, forthright steps should be taken to challenge untrue statements and false propaganda which are increasingly becoming a part of the stock in trade of the enemies of public education. The point has been reached where the profession can no longer sit back and ignore the charges being made.[8]

Skaife repeated this message to educators and lay people throughout the country. For example, at one of a series of educator-lay conferences on "Public Education in a Dangerous Era," Skaife asserted,

> As members of a profession vital to the preservation of the American democratic way of life, we must courageously stand up for the things in which we believe. We must not allow ourselves to be intimidated by bigots and cranks.[9]

Skaife's defiant rhetoric typified the stance and position of the Defense Commission at mid-century. Of course, the commission always had appeared vigilant of, and responsive to, red scare attack. By the closing years of the 1940s and the opening years of the 1950s, however, that vigilance and responsiveness rapidly intensified.

The increasing realization that red scare organizations were both growing in number and effectiveness considerably alarmed members of the Defense Commission at mid-century. The leadership of the commission appeared particularly concerned that many of these national organizations could damage the reputations of local educators in such a way as to leave the organizations' poisonous influence largely undetected. Skaife, for example, firmly believed that many of these "right wing 'front' organizations" were a danger to American democracy. "Yet," he lamented, "with the searchlight of public attention focused on communism these pseudo-patriotic groups escape attention."[10] Increasingly, therefore, many leading educators understood the need to provide teachers, administrators, media interests, political figures, business representatives, and the general citizenry with abundant information on the attackers in order to publicly expose their methods, practices, beliefs, and sources of support.

Several educators reasoned that ignorance of the source and nature of attack potentially could prove fateful to teachers and administrators throughout the nation. Significantly, Willard Goslin, who, through his dismissal as Pasadena's school superintendent in 1950, painfully understood the power of concerted red scare attack, remarked upon the need for educators to be alert to the "elusive sources" of attack. "In a battle," Goslin pointed out, "it is about as important to know who is shooting at you and from what direction, as it is to know what kind of ammunition is being used."[11]

By the end of the 1940s, therefore, the Defense Commission shared the belief that concerted efforts were required to track down the sources of local attack and, as appropriate, to reveal to the community any national red scare organizations fueling the discontent. Robert Skaife clearly articulated the Defense Commission's renewed focus:

> The Commission's part will be to expose the activities of the sowers of distrust in the *Defense Bulletin*; to continue the "Off Record Conferences" concerning attacks on education, educators, and educational publications; to work with other national organizations in exposing these extremists; to get material into the hands of classroom teachers which will help them meet attacks against textbooks and against the school program. In other words, the 'defense' aspect of the Commission's program may become the major part of its work.[12]

Skaife's desire to expose the sources of criticism reflected the fervent belief held by members of the Defense Commission that once the public received reliable information about red scare critics and their extreme opinions, then they would be rapidly discredited, and their views, widely rejected.

Essentially, the Defense Commission's efforts to expose red scare critics were directed at two audiences. First and foremost, the commission offered information to teachers and administrators. It provided valuable intelligence on the methods, practices, and powerful forces behind red scare extremists in the hope that educators at the local level could use the information to weaken the influence of emergent attacks. Second, the commission sought to inform and educate parents, business groups, and community organizations about these radical groups and their deleterious impact on public education.

The officers of the Defense Commission used a variety of methods to inform educators and to expose the damaging influence of red scare attack. Typically, members of the commission used educational journals as vehicles to convey their message. In the early 1950s, for example, Robert Skaife, authored a series of articles in the *Nation's Schools* that dealt exclusively with red scare attacks. Published under the revealing titles, "They Sow Distrust," "They Want Tailored Schools," "They Oppose Progress," and "The Conflict Continues," these articles portrayed the extremist position of the attackers and launched a punishing and forthright criticism on their methods and practices.[13] Similar articles written by Skaife and other colleagues within the Defense Commission also appeared at this time and unquestionably proved an effective medium to communicate valuable information to America's teaching profession.[14]

In December 1951, the *Connecticut Teacher* published Skaife's article, "Know the Enemy." The article typified the approach that Skaife and his colleagues at the Defense Commission took in their efforts to expose red scare criticism of the schools. Initially, Skaife outlined the types of people likely to criticize the schools. Essentially, he believed they amounted to four forces: "(1) politico-economic extremists, (2) patrioteers, (3) anti-pragmatists, (4) sectarians."[15] Skaife determined the underlying characteristic of each of these groups and noted that often they operated as "huge propaganda organizations" and consorted with powerful interest groups and "wealthy individuals and business organizations." He informed readers that these groups often used the term progressive, socialist, or collectivist to smear educators "in their desire to preserve *their* version of the American way of life." Significantly, Skaife warned educators that these critics were dangerous and influential forces and that, "although they may have been 'laughed off' in the past, today [1951] they must be taken seriously." Accordingly, he remarked,

> ...as the hysteria has grown and suspicion has pointed its ugly finger at loyal Americans, we have realized that many of the accusations have gained the credibilities of people who in more sane times would never lend an ear.[16]

As a guide to assist teachers and administrators to identify the techniques, tactics, and patterns of attack Skaife offered readers of the journal a 15-point hypothetical "destructive formula" that included:

1. Flood newspapers with letters attacking the schools...
3. Distribute vicious propaganda put out by such organizations as the National Council for American Education.
4. If a school board election or a school bond issue arises, make the schools a political issue...
8. Correspond with anti-school groups in other communities...
10. Challenge the board to defend the philosophy of the school program. Keep the board occupied with answering questions about the school...
12. Use the "big lie" technique — label the superintendent as a "progressivist" and repeat the phrase again and again...
14. Spread rumors that the school staff is loaded with subversives.
15. Keep the fires of controversy burning.[17]

Skaife concluded his intriguing exposé of red scare attackers by offering educators suggestions for positive action to counteract unwarranted criticism. In addition, in an appendix to the article, Skaife catalogued a list of "right-wing front organizations" and warned educators to be alert for their materials and vigilant of their influence at the local level.

During the early 1950s, the Defense Commission collected information on more than 500 groups plus other individuals who attacked education.[18] Understandably, the leadership of the commission was eager to inform educators of the existence of many of these red scare organizations and of the potential damage that they might wreak to public education. In repeated meetings and conferences attended by teachers and administrators, Robert Skaife informed audiences of red scare methods and exposed the organizations behind them. For example, in an "Open Meeting" for educators held in conjunction with the 1954 NEA annual meeting in New York, the commission's field secretary provided a detailed report that exposed many of the most powerful red scare groups. In his report, Skaife not only dealt with traditional red scare critics like Zoll, Crain, and Hoiles, but also exposed the activities of "new faces which have appeared among the anti-school propagandists."[19] Furthermore, in an interesting addition to his study, Skaife graphically illustrated the interrelationship and mutual association of groups, such as the National Council for American Education, CASBO, Operation America, Inc., the Minute Women, the Foundation for Economic Freedom, the Freedom Club of Chicago, and the Liberty Belles.[20]

The Defense Commission often used its regular mouthpiece, the *Defense Bulletin,* as a vehicle to expose red scare organizations. Frequent editions of the *Bulletin* allocated considerable copy space for this purpose. The way in which the commission revealed, monitored, and challenged Allen A. Zoll's organization in the pages of the *Defense Bulletin* perfectly illustrated the use of the *Bulletin* to expose red scare critics to teachers and administrators.[21]

Attention to Zoll's activities first appeared in the *Bulletin* in January 1949 under the banner heading, "What is the Truth About the National Council for American Education?" The analysis devoted the front page and over three subsequent pages to the exposé and informed readers that the NCAE's leader, Allen A. Zoll, "has been denounced as a 'very strong anti-Semite' and was reportedly at the back of the now defunct American Patriots, Inc., an organization listed as fascist and subversive by Attorney General Tom C. Clark."[22]

As a *bête noire* of the Defense Commission, Zoll's influences and activities regularly were reported in the *Defense Bulletin* in the years that followed. Indeed, the Defense Commission hounded Zoll to his very end. In May 1953, for example, not long before Zoll's organization became defunct, the *Defense Bulletin* gleefully printed a photograph of Temple Hall, McNabb, Illinois, an isolated, decrepit two-story building. Under the heading "a picture out of Mr. Zoll's past," the caption informed readers that the building depicted the "college" from which Zoll received his Ph.D. degree. Triumphantly, the *Bulletin* declared, that Zoll had not, as he claimed, earned his doctorate from Harvard, but from "a one man diploma mill operated by a man named Dr. Scott Swain." The *Bulletin* revealed "Swain's qualifications as an educator included the serving of a six-year prison term on six charges, including running a confidence game, obtaining a property under false pretenses, and passing bad checks."[23] Unquestionably, the Defense Commission keenly revealed this information in order that educators who encountered Zoll's propaganda and influence in their communities could use the material to undermine its credibility.

Officers of the Defense Commission realized that the machinations of red scare organizations not only had to be exposed to educators, but also to other groups within the community at large. As a consequence, Robert Skaife and other key individuals in the commission often spoke in communities troubled by growing criticism of the schools. In some cases, the Defense Commission took its arguments directly to organizations initially who appeared to support red scare groups. The officers of the commission believed that, if erstwhile supporters learned more about the beliefs and practices of the attackers, they would be likely to withdraw their support. Consequently, after the Defense Commission and local education associations effectively revealed the foundation of red scare attacks, many business interests and community figures revoked their support.[24] A classic example of this situation occurred in 1951.

On May 31, 1951, Allen A. Zoll wrote a strongly worded letter to members of the American Medical Association (AMA). Essentially, the letter argued that educators and textbooks throughout the United States advocated socialized medicine and attempted to indoctrinate students in the desirability of a socialist society. "At the root of the trouble," according to Zoll, was "the NEA — the super-bureaucracy which leads around by the nose the nation's school administrators and teachers — most of whom are good Americans, but who are powerless in the hands of this entrenched socialist autocracy."[25] Zoll asked AMA members for financial contributions and promised a complete report on the "socialist" and "un-American leanings" of the nation's educators. Largely as a result of Zoll's vigorous campaign, the association, at its Atlantic City meeting on June 13, 1951, passed a series of resolutions. They denounced "subversive textbooks" and school indoctrination in the "insidious and destructive tenets of the welfare state." Significantly, the AMA resolved to "endorse the principle of requesting Congress to make a thorough investigation of our entire schools system."

Alarmed by the AMA's precipitous and, in their view, ill-considered action, members of the NEA and the Defense Commission protested the resolution. After Zoll's background and methods were exposed by the commission and following a process of consultation, the AMA revised its position. At its Los Angeles meeting in December 1951, the house of delegates of the American Medical Association expressed faith in "the patriotism and Americanism of the vast majority of educators and of bona fide educational organizations." In addition, the AMA reaffirmed its "support of the American public school system as a bulwark of our constitutional republic...."[26] The AMA incident typified many of the Defense Commission's actions during this period. In order to extinguish red scare attack, its officers increasingly realized the need actively to confront and to challenge the attackers and to expose their perceived flaws and irrational assertions.

The Defense Commission both as Source and Collector of Information on Red Scare Attack

Throughout its existence, the Defense Commission operated as an information conduit for members of the teaching profession. By the late 1940s, much of the intelligence and information it gathered from, and distributed to, educators increasingly dealt with issues related to red scare attack. Harold Benjamin, Chairman of the Defense Commission, fully understood the importance of providing educators with reliable information on the enemies of public schools. Revealingly, Benjamin often described the commission as an "educational reconnaissance troop" with a mission to gather "combat intelligence" for the educators in the field. In his address to the NEA delegation in St. Louis in July 1950, for example, he reasoned:

> In warfare the main job of a reconnaissance troop is to get information on the enemy, to tell who he is, to discover where he is, to learn as much about his weapons and his tactics as possible, to find out where he is weak and where he is strong, and to pass out information quickly and accurately to the fighting outfit the troop represents — the combat team — which in turn passes it on to the division, the corps, and the army.[27]

Benjamin and other officers in the Defense Commission firmly believed that a central function of the commission was to provide educators with reliable, incisive, and regular information on those who sought to damage public education. Significantly, the leadership explicitly understood the additional need both to cultivate and to utilize existing relationships within the NEA at local, state, and national levels.

The commission urged local associations to use the "services of the Defense Commission as a clearinghouse for information on attacks." It also implored local NEA members to use the "material to acquaint boards of education and community groups with the nature of the propaganda put forth by 'pressure' and 'front' organizations."[28] The commission, therefore, regarded the dissemination of information to educators across the country as a vital task in the profession's fight against unjust attack. As a consequence, the Defense Commission devoted considerable resources to this goal. Hundreds and thousands of reprints of articles and leaflets concerning attacks on education were distributed to teachers and laymen throughout the United States. The commission also supplied background material and provided information to stimulate supporters of education to write articles in prominent national magazines. Furthermore, the Defense Commission, in its report to the NEA assembly in the summer of 1952, proudly boasted,

> Among the services that have been most appreciated have been (a) the provision of kits of materials to leaders who are studying the nature and methods of the attackers, and (b) the procuring of copies of reprints of newspaper and magazine articles, statements in the *Congressional Record* and other printed materials of

value for distribution in quantity to educators and other citizens in areas where
the schools might be subject to unjust attack.[29]

Routinely, the commission advertised the availability of these important
materials in the *Defense Bulletin*.

Many issues of the *Defense Bulletin* also recommended to members of
the NEA selected articles or books that constructively dealt with the attacks
on the schools. For example, the February 1951 issue prompted educators
to read such articles as "The Enemy in Pasadena," by Carey McWilliams
published in the *Christian Century*, "Zoll in Virginia" by Robert F. Williams
published in the *Virginia Journal of Education*, and "They Sow Distrust"
and "They Oppose Progress," two articles by Robert Skaife featured in the
Nation's Schools.[30] The *Bulletin* also urged teachers and administrators to
read books that treated attacks on the schools with perceived intelligence
and insight. The May 1954 edition of the *Bulletin* typified this approach. It
recommended members read Henry Steele Commager's *On Education and
Freedom* and V. T. Thayer *Public Education and Its Critics*. In addition, the
Bulletin informed its readers that "the Defense Commission maintains a
bibliography on attacks on schools which is revised at frequent intervals."
This bibliography was made available to NEA members on request free of
charge.[31]

The widespread provision of materials free or at nominal cost was an
important aim of the Defense Commission. Regularly, the commission
offered educators, without cost, reprints of articles that favorably treated
education.[32] On the occasions when members were required to make
payments, the reprints proved relatively inexpensive. For example, "Who's
Trying to Ruin Our Schools?" by Arthur D. Morse originally published in
McCall's was available for two and one half cents a copy. In addition, "The
Public School Crisis," an extensive report on six educational communities
that confronted red scare attacks, published in *The Saturday Review of
Literature,* was offered at a similarly reasonable seven cents a reprint.[33]
Undoubtedly, "Danger! They're After Our Schools" appeared as one the
Defense Commission's most requested publications. Co-sponsored by the
NEA, this hard-hitting pamphlet vigorously opposing the methods and
practices of the attackers of schools, was made widely available at the price
of one dollar per hundred. The reprint service proved immensely popular
with educators and offered teachers and administrators at the local level
valuable information and material with which to counteract attack and
criticism emergent in their communities.

The information services of the Defense Commission were not limited solely to the dissemination of writings in academic publications or popular journals. Throughout the late 1940s and early 1950s, the commission offered a range of information sources both to educators and to the public at large. The Defense Commission also popularized the availability of records, movies, novels, sound recordings, and information kits, all of which focused attention directly on the attacks on public schools.[34] These information kits appeared particularly popular. Indeed, according to the Defense Commission's 1953 annual report, the "Information Kit Concerning Destructive Criticism of Public Education" proved one of its most successful projects. Prepared in co-operation with the American Association of School Administrators, the Association for Supervision and Curriculum Development, the National Council for the Social Studies, the National Association of Secondary School Principals, and the NEA Department of Elementary School Principals, the kits provided a range of materials and information on the attacks on public education. In keeping with the commission's policy of keeping cost to members to a minimum, it offered the kits at $1.50 each, which represented "slightly less than the actual cost."[35]

The provision of reliable and detailed information by the Defense Commission effectively served many purposes. First, the information on attacks alerted educators to the methods and tactics of red scare provocateurs. It warned teachers to be constantly vigilant of criticism that surfaced in their communities, and it suggested that no school district was safe or immune from attack. For example, Ernest Melby, mindful of the dismissal of School Superintendent Willard Goslin in Pasadena, warned educators in 1951,

> You may say this hasn't happened to my school — to me. Maybe not yet. But it has happened in California, in New Jersey, in Louisiana, in Massachusetts...And your school may be next. Particularly if you are in a large school system where new buildings and increased tax support are needed.[36]

In addition to this first function, the Defense Commission also provided educators with information as a means to help teachers and administrators clarify their own personal views and policies on burning educational issues. For example, the commission both produced and recommended a collection of materials devoted to the issue of academic freedom. The April 1949 edition of the *Defense Bulletin* focused exclusively on this issue. It provided educators with extracts on the subject of academic freedom drawn from the

Red Alert!

pronouncements of Socrates and Epictetus to more contemporary writings in the *Phi Delta Kappa* and the *New Yorker*.[37] Fundamentally, officers of the Defense Commission adopted the position that Americans should place their faith in the "unbridled freedom of thought and speech" and reject "the iron hand of censorship." Accordingly, one excerpt cited in the *Defense Bulletin* contended,

> Faith in freedom of thought is democracy's weapon against those who would destroy it. Man's freedom to think is essential to his survival. Free thinking is his means of survival. Free public education is our great democratic invention to insure freedom of thought.[38]

Through argument and literature, therefore, leaders of the Defense Commission used information as a means to help educators "clear their thoughts" and adopt a positive position on academic freedom.[39]

Although the Defense Commission often targeted educators, it also offered information to other citizens. For example, the commission readily responded to requests for information from several sources including the media, Congressmen, parents, and community leaders. It actively provided mimeographed sheets, information bulletins, article reprints, and leaflets on the attacks, and it devoted considerable energy to answering phone calls and writing letters to those concerned by, or interested in, the attacks on public education.[40]

Arguably, one of the most important functions of the commission's information service was to raise the morale of the teaching profession; another was to develop unity of purpose. For example, in the early 1950s, the commission began a policy of conducting questionnaire surveys that reported "The State of the Nation with Regard to Attacks on Education."[41] The responses of over 6,000 educators nationwide were analyzed, and the conclusions reported to educators at local, state, and national levels. These detailed studies portrayed the national picture and clearly illustrated to teachers and administrators that attacks on education, far from constituting a local aberration, occurred in communities throughout the nation. Skillfully, the commission used the reports both to unify the profession in their shared troubles and to urge all educators to involve themselves in the fight against the critics.

In an effort to help educators to intelligently respond to critics and to raise the morale of teachers, the Defense Commission also offered information that illustrated the accomplishments of modern education. For example, the commission advertised and promoted an April 1951 study conducted by the NEA Research Division "The Three R's Hold Their Own at Mid-century," which catalogued "factual evidence" that schools taught "the basics" more successfully than in previous generations.[42] Other studies and reports adopted a similar position. For example, the widely read and widely distributed pamphlet, "Danger! They're After Our Schools," keenly pointed out that the commonly held belief that schools were somehow better in "the good old days" was a fallacy. It noted that schools of previous generations were burdened by serious problems:

> The buildings were frequently dark and bleak; sanitary facilities were meager or non-existent.
> Fifty or more children were sometimes crowded into a single class chafing under rigid discipline.
> The ideal child was one who memorized his textbooks, asked no questions, and managed to stay awake during long hours of enforced silence.[43]

In contrast, the pamphlet suggested that successful modern schools featured "light airy classrooms," "small classes which give teacher and children a chance to know and enjoy one another, a calm relaxed atmosphere where children feel free to ask questions," and "a curriculum that teaches the 3 R's, but also develops cultural and social interests and acknowledges individual differences."[44] Undoubtedly, information such as this not only allowed educators to respond to individuals or groups critical of education, but also it raised the spirit and confidence of many within the teaching profession.

Typically, the Defense Commission offered educators information with which to define their own personal view of educational principles and practice. In addition, it used information with regard to attacks on education explicitly to implore educators actively to confront or deal with unwarranted criticism. Repeatedly, Defense Commission publications encouraged teachers to act. Information of the "What *You* Can Do to Defend The Schools" nature appeared common in the early 1950s.[45] For example, educators were stirred by the Defense Commission to:

> Keep informed of the unjustifiable attacks made by groups and individuals against public education.
> Combat vicious propaganda by locating its source, the group sponsoring it and its motive in doing so.
> Challenge unfair statements made by local groups.
> Inform school board members and local citizens of the purposes and motives of interest organizations attacking the schools.
> Contact the Defense Commission for information or help.[46]

Officers of the commission, such as Harold C. Hand, published articles in educational journals that offered teachers and administrators positive suggestions both to prevent and to overcome attacks.[47] Similar publications urged teachers to be "on the alert," to "be vocal," and to "talk up the schools," and still others suggested small, but important, contributions individual teachers could make to the cause. Significantly, as the red scare era reached its peak in the late 1940s and early 1950s, articles on how educators might best deal with attacks on the schools also featured prominently in many educational journals.[48]

Above all, the Defense Commission both collected and provided information as a means to alert and to unite the teaching profession at local, state, and national levels. Corma Mowrey, President of the NEA, emphasized the importance of this professional solidarity at the 1951 annual meeting in San Francisco, at which she stated, "where teachers are alert and united the local attacks on schools are seldom successful," and further noted, "Professional unity throws a mantle of protection around every teacher, assuring him the right to breathe and speak as a free man."[49] As the teaching profession's only true national agency charged to monitor and expose attacks and to defend teachers in troubled times, the Defense Commission starkly understood its responsibility to be both a beacon and a vanguard for educators throughout the nation.

In order to establish an informative national picture of attacks on the schools, the commission heavily relied upon information from local community sources. Through the *Defense Bulletin*, for example, the commission often requested information, reports, newspaper cuttings, and post cards that reported areas where,

> Teacher leaders are threatened with loss of position.
> Special legislation is directed against teachers.
> Unfair practices and discrimination occur.
> Speeches...attack public education and public support for education.
> Articles or editorials...reflect on the importance of public education or the integrity of the teaching profession.[50]

Additionally, the commission wished to instill in each member of the NEA the conviction that every educator had a role to play in the defeat of the many forces that attacked education in this period. Harold Benjamin emphatically announced this position in his report to the NEA delegation in 1949,

The Defense Commission not only recommends, but urges that each delegate accept as a personal responsibility the task of watching the developments in his, or her, local region and alerting not only the Defense Commission, but the local and state educational organizations as well, to the important developments directly and seriously affecting education and the members of our profession.[51]

The creation of a national defense network was foremost in the minds of the officers of the Defense Commission in the red scare era. Indeed, it firmly believed that unless educators across the country were united in their determination to defeat undue criticism, the attackers would continue to enjoy a destructive influence on educational policy and practice.

Throughout the late 1940s and early 1950s, therefore, the commission implored local and state associations to "designate an advisor...who will serve as a contact person to alert the commission in important developments in the local situation."[52] The advisor also was charged to inform the local association of significant developments throughout the nation.[53] The commission proved very successful in this regard. By 1950, for example, 27 states and the U. S. territory of Hawaii reported the establishment of a committee or commission with officers to perform at the state level the same or similar function as the National Defense Commission. Furthermore, in the commission's summary of achievements at the end of its first decade of existence in 1951, it listed the creation of local and state defense officers as one of its major accomplishments.[54]

The commission encouraged local officers to be active in their duties. In the January 1954 *Defense Bulletin*, for example, they urged undertaking a number of responsibilities that included maintaining "active contact with the National Commission," posting and circulating on the bulletin board copies of the *Defense Bulletin*, collecting and sending to the national office "newspaper articles, cartoons, editorials, or any other relevant information," and acting as "an initiator of ideas...criticisms, and comments for the improvement of the work of the National Commission."[55] Of great significance, the editors of *Defense Bulletin* contended that:

In each of these endeavors, you and your association will be sharing in an enterprise of great mission. The nobleness of the conception of schools, free, universal, non-partisan, non-sectarian, publicly supported, and publicly controlled, is shared by all of those who work unselfishly for them. Your local association is an important link in insuring democracy's defense through education.[56]

The unity of national, state, and local organizations clearly strengthened the power and influence of the Defense Commission on the American educational scene and vigorously assisted the NEA's desire to undermine concerted red scare attack.

In its efforts both to acquire and to convey valuable information on attacks on education, the Defense Commission proved particularly successful. Assiduously, it gathered and distributed a vast array of documentary material on individuals and groups seeking to discredit public schools. Effectively, it garnered the support and commitment of educators throughout the nation, and, impressively, it helped to unify and strengthen the American teaching profession in the teeth of troubled times. Most important of all, the Defense Commission kept educators alert, informed, and aware of damaging criticism on a national scale. As the attacks grew in intensity, so the commission became more familiar with the tactics of national perpetrators and the complaints of local critics. This familiarity allowed the commission to develop and put into effect a vigorous and coherent campaign of defense. In many respects, therefore, by operating both as a source and as a distributor of information on red scare attack, the Defense Commission performed some of its most effective and important work.

The regular publication of its *Defense Bulletin*, a newsletter for NEA members, proved an important element in the Defense Commission's drive to protect teachers from vitriolic attack. Early issues of the *Defense Bulletin*, mimeographed on letter-sized paper, were confidential in general content and were distributed to no more than 300 select individuals. By mid-century, however, the *Bulletin,* which was published five or six times each year, boasted a national circulation of more than 20,000 educators, and it quickly became an important and valuable mouthpiece for the Defense Commission.

The *Defense Bulletin* reported on a wide range of topics, including issues such as intercultural education, UNESCO, federal aid to education, universal military training, and education for American citizenship. From the mid-1940s to the mid-1950s, however, the *Defense Bulletin* most notably reflected the Defense Commission's mounting concern with the impact of the red scare on public school education in the United States. Significantly, in all of the issues of the *Bulletin* between December 1941 and May 1945, only two notes refer to attacks using red scare rhetoric. From 1945 to 1955, however, scarcely an issue of the *Defense Bulletin* appeared without direct, and often dramatic and prolonged, reference to red scare propaganda. Accordingly, as a measure of the focus of the Defense Commission, as a window on the socio-political climate of the age, and as a barometer to the rising intensity of red scare criticism of the schools, the contents of the *Defense Bulletins* offer a rich and fascinating insight into American education in the post-war era.

As a central component in the Defense Commission's quest to blunt red scare attacks, the *Defense Bulletin* performed several important functions. Three, in particular, appear salient.

First, the *Defense Bulletin* acted as a national source of information for educators at the local level. It provided teachers across the country with a central forum for information, opinion, and support. A key feature of the *Defense Bulletin*, therefore, was its relentless drive to monitor, to investigate, and to expose red scare groups that attacked public education. Accordingly, many issues of the *Defense Bulletin* devoted considerable attention to exposing such organizations as the National Council for American Education and the Conference of American Small Businessmen.[57] The editors of the *Defense Bulletin* were eager to bring these national organizations to the attention of local educators. It emphasized to teachers and administrators that local red scare attacks were not isolated and atypical acts, but elements of a sinister and damaging national picture. The *Defense Bulletin* argued that in order to defeat attackers, educators must learn more about their methods and practices.

Second, armed with up-to-date information on red scare attackers, the *Defense Bulletin* frequently suggested to local educators ways they might challenge their accusers. Under such banner headlines as, "Let's Nip this Propaganda in the Bud," "Let's Keep the Witch Hunters Out of the Schools," and "What You Can Do To Stop the Attacks," the Defense Commission published information that advocated that local groups take positive steps to confront red scare propaganda.[58] To add credence to its advice, the *Bulletin* often proudly reported local examples of the withdrawal by powerful business organizations, prominent politicians, and influential pressure groups of their accusations against the public schools as a direct consequence of bold and assertive challenges from local NEA affiliates.[59]

The *Bulletin* also reflected the Defense Commission's pride in the production of a plethora of information for local educators to use in the fight against red scare attacks. Significantly, in the 1951 celebration of the commission's tenth anniversary, the *Defense Bulletin* heralded that one of its most important achievements was "the development of programs and materials to meet widespread attacks on the public schools and to win increased support for America's schools and their teachers."[60]

Issue after issue of the *Defense Bulletin* offered educators, often at no cost, an enormous range of information sheets, books, leaflets, and articles that set out arguments in support of such notable causes as academic freedom, federal aid to education, , and freedom of inquiry. By the late 1940s and early 1950s, therefore, the *Defense Bulletin* routinely provided local and state education associations with a wealth of information to support the cause of public education, highlighted and championed cases where red scare attacks successfully had been challenged, and offered practical advice and action plans for NEA members who sought to confront red scare practices in school districts throughout the United States.

Third, in an effort to elevate the status of educators and to raise the confidence of the teaching profession, the *Defense Bulletin* reminded teachers of the enormously important work they were undertaking. At a time when some teachers and administrators encountered personal accusations of "subversion" and many faced threats of dismissal, the morale of the nation's teaching force sank to low and, in some systems, to desperate levels. In this context, it was important to revive morale.

At every opportunity, the *Defense Bulletin* published accounts of prominent individuals and organizations who publicly supported American education. In many issues, the *Defense Bulletin*, therefore, reported the supportive words of individuals, such as Henry Steele and President Truman, and the fortifying declarations of organizations, such as the Congress of Industrial Organizations and the National Association of Manufacturers.[61]

The *Defense Bulletin* also reported on a range of successful conferences that focused on major educational issues that included academic freedom, civil liberties, and the increasing threat of the red scare. The overarching purpose of these conferences clearly was to induce a feeling of collective unity within the teaching profession. Indeed, inured by the shared experience of confronting red scare attacks, many educators, the *Defense Bulletin* claimed, grew more confident in their ability both to deal with and to confront the rising tide of venomous attack.

In many respects, therefore, much of the information in the *Defense Bulletin* was intended to comfort and to support America's teachers. For example, it published summaries of research studies that revealed that "modern schools" significantly were superior to schools of the pre-war era. In addition, teachers learned through the pages of the *Defense Bulletin* that fights over textbooks, the imposition of loyalty oaths, and the persistence of red scare attack were not peculiar to their local situation. Rather, they discovered that other teachers throughout the United States encountered similar opposition and endured similar attacks.

The *Defense Bulletin* reassured teachers throughout the nation that hundreds of thousands of NEA members and a significant portion of the general public supported the American system of public education. Furthermore, as the *Defense Bulletin* revealed, the NEA acted vigorously on their behalf by cajoling politicians and influential figures publicly to support education, by investigating areas in which educational controversies emerged, and by directly, and often successfully, confronting red scare propagandists. In these respects, the *Defense Bulletin,* undoubtedly, played a valuable role in boosting the confidence and morale of American educators and proved one of the Defense Commission's most successful ventures in the red scare era.

The extent to which the Defense Commission's support of educators and exposure of red scare critics blunted the effectiveness of attacks in the post-war period remains open to conjecture. Certainly, despite the commission's work, many groups continued successfully to undermine public education and to influence educational policy and practice in school districts throughout the nation. Nevertheless, the Defense Commission accomplished some notable achievements. It garnered the support of many community leaders and parental organizations; it influenced the actions of some business groups; it exposed to the undecided and concerned citizen the political extremism of many of the attackers, and, importantly, it boosted the morale of teachers. Furthermore, at a time when few professional education organizations appeared prepared to respond to attacks, the Defense Commission often stood resolute and defiant. As a consequence, even if the Defense Commission's exposure of red scare organizations ultimately only enjoyed limited success, in the eyes of many within the teaching profession its efforts proved both commendable and worthwhile.

A Question of Loyalty: The Commission's Response to Loyalty Oaths and Loyalty Investigations

As anti-communist rhetoric and activity intensified in the immediate post-war period, calls for Congressional investigations, loyalty oaths, and the scrutiny of public education burgeoned. Consequently, officers of the Defense Commission appeared concerned that educators throughout the nation be provided with reliable and up-to-date information on these seemingly intrusive measures. Through a steady stream of bulletins, reports, surveys, and articles, the commission helped teachers to articulate a response to the teacher oaths and investigations, to keep them fully informed of new developments, and, above all, to comfort professional educators that the commission was on hand to protect and defend their interests.

Loyalty oaths were not new to America's educators. The state of California, for example, passed loyalty oath legislation as early as 1863, and states such as Colorado, Oklahoma, Oregon, and Rhode Island introduced loyalty oaths in the years surrounding .[62] In addition, in a flurry of nationalistic fervor following the First World War, 25 states enacted legislation prohibiting the advocacy of acts of sedition. Despite the long-standing nature of much loyalty legislation, members of the NEA appeared alarmed by the renewed zeal for teachers' oaths that surfaced in the late 1940s and early 1950s.

In June 1949, the NEA's Committee on Tenure and Academic Freedom published a nationwide study that reported on teachers' oaths and related state requirements. The comprehensive study revealed that 28 states required public school teachers to take an oath of loyalty, 38 states passed general sedition laws, 31 states prohibited membership in subversive groups, 13 states barred public employment to disloyal persons, and 15 outlawed certain political parties.[63] Of concern to the NEA was the recent proliferation of loyalty legislation. For example, in 1949 alone, eight states authorized legislation that either called for the immediate dismissal of teachers considered subversive or required adherence to loyalty oaths. A further NEA report published in 1952 noted that an additional five states — Louisiana, Texas, Nebraska, Oklahoma, and Pennsylvania — passed loyalty oath legislation that year and that other states introduced bills with similar intentions.[64]

Loyalty legislation enacted in the immediate post-World War II period followed no standardized format. A curious assortment of legislative acts were in evidence, and loyalty requirements varied from state to state. Many states required teachers to swear their support and allegiance to the Constitution. Others, such as Texas and Arizona, additionally charged teachers to *defend* the Constitution. In 1949, eight states demanded that educators teach specific acts of patriotism. California, for example, required teachers to swear that they "will by precept and example, promote respect for the flag and the statutes of the United States and of the State of California, reverence for law and order, and undivided allegiance to the government of the United States of America."[65] Other states specifically prohibited teachers from teaching "alien" theories of government.

NEA officers seriously were concerned that legislation or oaths prohibiting teaching about certain topics explicitly threatened teachers' academic freedoms. "How could a social studies teacher in Georgia," a NEA report asked its readers,

> avoid 'teaching any theory of government or of social relations which is inconsistent with the fundamental principles of patriotism and high ideals of Americanism' as is required in the law prescribing the oath, if he discusses the causes which led to World War II?

In particular, NEA leaders appeared troubled that such legislation inevitably could lead to misinterpretation by pupils and parents and to "incompleteness of teaching which does not inform pupils of facts in world affairs."[66] Similar concerns also were expressed about oaths that focused on the "opinions" rather than the "actions" of teachers. The Rhode Island loyalty oath proved a case in point. Teachers in this state were required to swear,

> I affirm, in recognition of my official obligation, that though as a citizen I have the right of personal opinion, as a teacher of the public's children I have no right, either in school hours, or in the presence of my pupils out of school hours, to express opinions which conflict with honor to country, loyalty to American ideals, and obedience to and respect for the laws of Nation and State.

Increasingly, the commission's officers expressed concern that loyalty oaths and loyalty legislation were being used as a means further to discredit teachers, to place them under constant public suspicion, and to undermine their academic and personal freedoms. In the face of this menacing wave of restrictive loyalty requirements, the NEA and the Defense Commission eagerly leapt to the defense of teachers.

In the first place, the Defense Commission kept NEA members fully informed of the proliferation of loyalty legislation at state and national levels. It also helped educators to clarify their personal position with regard to teacher oaths.[67] Repeatedly, officers of the commission expressed their alarm that teachers were singled out for attack. They emphasized the steadfast conviction that teachers must enjoy the same democratic rights as any ordinary American citizen. This argument neatly was explicated by Willard Goslin in *Forces Affecting American Education*. Goslin asserted that "a citizen surrenders no rights as a citizen when he enters the teaching profession," and he warned of the danger of restricting the democratic rights of teachers, saying,

> Any society which permits those of its members who wish to manage freedom in terms of their own concepts or interests to cut away some of the citizenship rights of its teachers has taken a long step toward cutting the source of nourishment of its basic freedoms. We are opposed to all forms of limitations on the lawful and ethical actions of teacher citizens, including limitation through special loyalty oaths which are a different matter from the simple dignified oaths of office of the American tradition.[68]

Inexorably linked to this line of argument was the belief that teachers' academic freedoms further would be repressed by the passage of and strict adherence to loyal oath legislation.

Accordingly, in October 1949, The NEA's influential Educational Policies commission released a statement to the press declaring that "state laws requiring special oaths for teachers or establishing uniform tests of loyalty are harmful to educational freedom and local school autonomy."[69] Prominent individuals within the NEA, such as Martin Essex, Chairman of the Committee on Tenure and Academic Freedom argued that "loyalty checks" may lead to "potential abuses" that might "serve as deterrents to effective instruction." Essex, like many other NEA officers, believed that teachers should feel free to discuss a broad range of issues and to study "the relative merits of various social ideologies" with students. But, asked Essex "does any teacher dare discuss these current controversial issues when he may be branded as disloyal and dismissed from his position?"[70]

The concerns expressed by Essex were very real. In a 1951 study commissioned by the Committee on Tenure and Academic Freedom and conducted by the NEA Research Division, responses to a questionnaire revealed that the shadow of loyalty legislation caused many teachers to modify their teaching practices. Significantly, in the press conference held for the release of the report at the time of the 1951 NEA annual meeting in San Francisco, Martin Essex pointed out "that today's most critical danger to the right of students is the voluntary censorship imposed by the teachers themselves who submerge their own ideas to avoid controversy."[71] He noted the increasing reluctance of teachers to discuss controversial issues, such as "race relations" and "communism," in the classroom and argued that these limitations had serious consequences: "the injustice to the students if such conditions prevail, is that they will know nothing of the evils or dangers of communism, and will grow up in a 'hot house environment' that ill equips them to think for themselves."[72] Typically, therefore, prominent individuals within the NEA spoke out against the passage of loyalty oath legislation because they earnestly believed that such acts limited the academic freedom of educators. By repeatedly advancing this argument, the NEA not only hoped to convince the general public of the dubious value of loyalty legislation, but also to help educators articulate a considered response to it.

As part of its policy of questioning the efficacy of loyalty legislation the Defense Commission kept teachers fully informed of developments on the national scene. The May 1952 issue of the *Defense Bulletin*, for example, apprised teachers of the recent decision of the U. S. Supreme Court to uphold New York's Feinberg Law. Essentially, the Feinberg Law, adopted in 1949, required the state Board of Regents to list organizations found to be subversive and to disqualify from employment any teacher known to be a member of identified organizations. Members of the Defense Commission paid close attention to the law, chiefly, because they feared that it would encourage similar legislation in other states. In an institutional response to the Feinberg Law, NEA Executive Secretary Willard Givens specifically raised three objections,

> First, there is no valid basis for directing loyalty legislation solely to teachers as distinguished from certain other employees in public service. Second, there is a possible danger that in some communities unlisted organizations which are not subversive, but are committed to unpopular causes, may become suspect and teachers may therefore refrain from associating themselves with any group that arouses controversy. Third, the requirement that school authorities must file an annual report on each teacher indicating whether he has been engaged in subversive activities opens the door to abuses and can well develop in teachers the fear that their personal opinions and associations are being constantly checked by self-appointed spies or informers.[73]

Significantly, the Defense Commission also reported to NEA members the fears of Supreme Court Justice Douglas who ardently dissented from the ruling of his Supreme Court colleagues by stating,

> The law inevitably turns the school system into a spying project. Regular loyalty reports on the teachers must be made out. The principals become detectives; the students, the parents, the community become informers. Ears are cocked for tell-tale signs of disloyalty....The system of spying and surveillance with its accompanying reports and trials cannot go hand in hand with academic freedom. It produces standardized thought, not the pursuit of truth.[74]

These examples illustrate how the Defense Commission persuasively argued against loyalty legislation on the grounds that proposed loyalty measures repressed academic freedom, undermined the principle of free inquiry, and severely restricted how, what, and why many classroom teachers taught.

In their stand against loyalty acts, leaders of the Defense Commission also proved particularly eager to highlight occasional incidents in which teachers appeared bold enough personally to defend their democratic rights.[75] The *Defense Bulletin*, for example, proudly reported the refusal of two Maryland teachers, Mrs. Helen E. Baker and Miss Vera Shank, to sign the "Loyalty Pledge" in March 1950. The controversial "Ober Law" made it a crime for individuals to belong to "subversive organizations" and required all public employees (including teachers) to sign loyalty oaths.

As Quakers, the two teachers considered the Law to be an "infringement on thought and conscience" and elected not to sign the loyalty affidavit. Immediately they were dismissed. When asked to comment on her decision, Miss Shank said that she had discussed the loyalty oath the previous summer with German teachers while she was abroad and they told her "that sounds like the pledge we had to sign when Hitler came to power." Significantly, Mrs. Baker added,

> in our present situation, any criticism of the status quo is interpreted as subversive. As a member of a minority group, I have many criticisms of the status quo, so that to sign an oath, such as the Ober Pledge, would in effect gag myself.[76]

The leadership of the Defense Commission enthusiastically reported such incidents as these because they wished to demonstrate to other educators, and to the public at large, that some concerned educators rejected loyalty oaths not because they were subversive or disloyal, but because they valued the personal and academic freedoms guaranteed to them by the U. S. Constitution.

In this difficult period of scrutiny, repression, and intolerance, the Defense Commission sought to lift the spirits and raise the morale of the teaching profession. Part of that strategy involved the commission in highlighting those incidents where loyalty oath legislation successfully was challenged or renounced by political figures or boards of education. In May 1952, for example, the *Defense Bulletin* heralded, in a front-page banner headline, "CONNECTICUT STANDS FIRM FOR LOYALTY OF TEACHERS." The *Bulletin* proudly advertised the decision of the Connecticut State Board of Education, which voted not to recommend the use of loyalty oaths for teachers in the state despite calls for such legislation from the Connecticut Catholic War Veterans of America.[77] Triumphantly, the *Bulletin* reported the statement of Dr. Finis E. Engelman, secretary of the Connecticut Board, who claimed "that the citizens of Connecticut may depend upon its teachers, supervisors, and administrators to safeguard fundamental American principles in the schools of the state." Significantly, the leadership of the NEA and the Defense Commission claimed that the victory represented a "banner of wholesome logic for other states" and that the decision "should aid in the warding off of emotional and misplaced patriotism of super patriotic groups."[78]

Other successes followed and were accorded generous attention in Defense Commission reports and bulletins. The commission, for example, advertised the decision of Governor Adalai E. Stevenson of Illinois to veto a proposed state Seditious Activities Act in 1951. Stevenson ridiculed those who chose to intimidate and offend loyal citizens by repressive acts and further claimed that the "whole notion of loyalty inquisitions is a natural characteristic of the police state, not of democracy."[79] Additionally, the *Bulletin* reported the judgment of the Montgomery (Alabama) Circuit Court declaring "null and void" a previous legislative act that required "loyalty labels" in all textbooks.[80] The Defense Commission took solace in these important victories and, whenever possible, spoke out against loyalty oaths.

Above all, the officers of the commission argued the futility of loyalty oath legislation claiming that disloyal teachers would readily sign the oaths in order to avoid detection. However, they reasoned that loyal teachers, genuinely concerned about the suppression of academic freedom, might be subjected to persecution as a result of their passionate belief in the democratic rights of a American citizens. Repeatedly, the leadership of the commission articulated its loyalty to the basic principle of "unbiased and objective teaching of truth."[81] In this regard, at the commission's Chicago meeting in February 1949, it clearly explicated its position on loyalty oaths:

> Believing firmly in the strength of the profession in upholding the democratic ideals of our country, the Defense Commission deplores the constantly increasing legislation appearing in the various states which impugns the integrity of the teaching profession by requiring teachers to take oaths other than those required by all office holders.

The Commission's statement further excoriated the "totalitarian practices" of many state legislatures and claimed that they were "reminiscent of the witch hunting of the 20's."[82]

In the red scare era, therefore, the Defense Commission adopted a firm and positive stance against the imposition of loyalty oath legislation. Convinced that this form of legislation was repressive, ill-considered, and unlikely to uncover genuinely "disloyal" teachers, the commission questioned both their value and intention. Consequently, in the late 1940s and early 1950s, the commission articulated the teaching profession's most thoughtful response to loyalty oaths, informed teachers of their progress and imposition, championed incidents in which state legislatures or school boards rejected loyalty legislation, and above all, repeatedly emphasized to the public at large the importance of supporting academic liberty among educators and the freedom to inquire among students.

A Question of Loyalty: The Commission's
Response to Loyalty Investigations

In the early 1950s, state and national loyalty investigation of education also became a regular feature on the American political landscape. To some extent educators were divided on the question of whether or not to welcome or to deplore these state and Congressional investigations. For example, some organizations, such as the Association of American Colleges which represented 800 institutions and the American Council on Education, supported fair and impartial investigations. These organizations adopted the view that Congressional investigations would help to bring about an improved public understanding of the schools. In addition, they argued that educators who championed intellectual freedom for themselves could not be inconsistent and deny Congress the freedom to investigate. Above all, those who supported Congressional inquiries reasoned that loyal and dedicated teachers had nothing to fear from the investigative probes.[83]

Many educators, however, refused to place such faith in Congressional investigations. For example, prominent educational organizations, such as the American Association of School Administrators (AASA) and the Association for the Supervision and Curriculum Development (ASCD), passed resolutions at their 1953 national conferences that severely questioned the efficacy of Congressional educational probes.[84] The ASCD and the AASA both argued against national investigatory committees on the grounds that they usurped the function, responsibility and legal authority of local school boards. Furthermore, as the terms "communist," "subversive," and "disloyal" often were used without precise definition, many educators believed that teachers easily could become victims of political reprisal on the basis of rumor, smear, and innuendo and not on the strength of firm and well-documented evidence.

Other important leaders also warned of the danger of indiscriminate Congressional probes. For example, James Bryant Conant, U. S. High Commissioner for Germany, appeared troubled that the principles of dissent and free inquiry in the schools and colleges might be squashed if Congressional investigations became too powerful and repressive. Similarly, even conservative Senator Taft, who defended the right of Congress to conduct inquiries, decried "Congressional fishing expeditions" that sought to inquire into the personal beliefs of an individual. Representative Chet Holifield of California appeared more strident in his condemnation of Congressional investigations. Holifield claimed that the investigations into education would create an atmosphere of "coercion and intimidation" for educators. Furthermore, he noted,

> Congressional hearings, in the past, have often been marked by the use of unfair methods toward individual witnesses. They know that irresponsible charges against innocent people have been made public, although they have later been proved to be false. They know that their academic careers can easily be blasted and their reputations ruined through 'trial by publicity' by a Congressional committee.[85]

Unequivocally, the Defense Commission adopted the position of those individuals and organizations who understood the potential threat to education posed by state and Congressional investigations. Consequently, as political moves toward investigations into education quickened in the early 1950s, the Defense Commission became more supportive of public school teachers who appeared either directly or vicariously threatened by invasive state and Congressional probes.[86]

Among the Defense Commission's most cogent arguments against Congressional investigations was the contention that the rights and responsibilities of local school boards were more important than the intrusive claims of national politicians. Accordingly, the leadership of the Defense Commission argued that if "reds" really did exist in the schools, then the responsibility to identify and dismiss them should reside with locally elected school boards and not with authoritarian Congressional committees. This argument, repeatedly advanced by members of the Defense Commission, neatly was characterized by Walter F. Tunks, rector of St. Paul's Episcopal church, Akron, Ohio, in his address to the NEA delegation in Miami Beach, Florida, in 1953:

> Whatever screening is necessary, should be done locally by those to whom our schools and churches are responsible, rather than by Congressional committees too far removed from the facts and too often actuated by partisan politics. Far more to be feared than any radicalism in our schools is the tyranny that would force education into a straight jacket of regimented conformity.[87]

Significantly, the Defense Commission drew on the support of other members of the church to discredit Congressional investigations. For example, Robert Skaife, in an article published in the *Nation's Schools* in April 1953, eagerly reported the sermons of noted clergymen Dr. A. Powell Davies and the Very Reverend Francis B. Sayre who both claimed that McCarthy, Velde, and McCarran were "morally unfitted" to investigate schools and colleges. Indeed, on February 22, 1953, in a caustic attack on Congressional investigators, Dean Sayre poignantly asserted:

> It comes mighty close to tempting God when anyone operates on the assumption that he is the divinely constituted guardian of other men's consciences, other men's patriotism or thoughts.... What is this omnipotence that pretends it can ferret out all sin and purify all else? What revelation of righteousness do they claim for the all pervading power which they now propose to apply not only to public administration but to private education as well?[88]

Despite his brave opposition to the Congressional probes, implicit in Sayre's remarks was the recognition that investigators increasingly had assumed an extremely powerful position in American society. Indeed by 1952, McCarran, McCarthy, and Velde effectively used their influential positions to create the impression that schools throughout the country were riddled with communist infiltrators. The implications for the creation of this debilitating educational climate were both dramatic and profound.

In some cases, rather than face the publicity and tension implicit in Congressional investigations, some teachers chose to resign and not defend themselves. Probationary teachers appeared particularly vulnerable and often were forced to leave the profession because they were suspected of being communists. In Utah, for example, school Superintendent James Glove removed a local teacher because he had "seen Tremayne running around with Jews and niggers and he voted for Wallace and that's proof enough for me." Without tenure rights, many probationary teachers were automatically dismissed, often without a hearing.[89] Prompted by the political machinations of the radical right, many American citizens clearly became suspicious of public school teachers. In his powerful speech to the NEA assembly, for example, Walter Tunks alerted members of the threat to educators posed by these Congressional investigations. He warned,

> An overzealous brand of alleged patriotism has spread suspicion, mistrust, and fear across this country, reversing our traditional faith that a man is judged innocent until he is proven guilty, blasting reputations by smear and innuendo rather than established fact, and condemning any opinion other than his own as communistic.[90]

Increasingly, state and Congressional investigators, through a web of distortion, exaggeration, and falsehood, used their political influence to imply that schools were seedbeds for collectivism and subversion.

In New York, for example, despite evidence to the contrary, Senator McCarran's SISS report "Subversive Influences in the Educational Process" gave the distinct impression that scores of schools and colleges were littered with subversive influences. McCarran basked in the publicity and fueled newspaper headlines that exclaimed that "hundreds of reds" worked in the schools. Other examples of wildly exaggerated charges or instances where teachers were discharged for alleged subversive actions existed.

In Philadelphia, thirty of the forty teachers called before HUAC in the fall of 1953 were immediately suspended by the school superintendent Louis P. Hoyer. Hoyer claimed that, despite the superior ratings of the teachers and the fact that they had no opportunity to defend themselves, "their Communism had impaired their abilities as teachers."[91] Additionally, based upon the allegations of Bella Dodd in the SISS hearings in New York, 150 teachers in the Detroit school system were identified as communists. Despite the fact that Dodd appeared to conjure this figure out of thin air and that local investigations of the Detroit schools failed to substantiate the claim, the city's newspapers and national and local politicians religiously quoted the number.[92] As these examples illustrate, in many communities the use of grossly inflated calculations, damaging smear tactics, and explosive often effectively persuaded local citizens of the presence of subversive influences in the schools and blinded them to the reality of local situations.

Without question, Congressional investigations and red scare propaganda deeply affected the morale of teachers in the NEA. Marjorie Murphy claimed that "under the strain of the McCarthy era" teachers became isolated and intimidated and "the divorce of the professional teacher from the community appeared complete."[93] In the shadow of repressive investigations, teachers had only their professional associations for protection.

In many respects, the Defense Commission proved immensely active, if not entirely effective, in its defense of teachers. Throughout the late 1940s, and particularly in the early 1950s, the Defense Commission regularly kept its members informed of state and Congressional investigations, provided and articulated considered responses to them, and published an endless stream of materials that presented persuasive arguments denouncing loyalty probes.[94]

Robert Skaife encapsulated the essence of the Defense Commission's response to Congressional investigations in his article published in the *Nation's Schools*. In characteristic fashion he argued that the "educational profession has an obligation to resist indiscriminate inquiries into political beliefs, to insist upon fair hearings, to condemn loose accusations against the teaching profession as a whole, and to support the principle of 'local autonomy' for schools." Skaife, however, advised teachers that they must cooperate with investigations. "To refuse to cooperate," he warned, "might not only injure the professional status of the individual, but also arouse suspicion concerning the integrity of his colleagues."[95]

Skaife's attitude and policy typified that of the NEA, the Defense Commission, and many liberal commentators of the time. In the climate of intimidation and indiscriminate attack, they each shared the idealistic belief that reason would prevail. Accordingly, the Defense Commission continued both to take its argument to the people and to rely on a responsible and unsensational public relations policy.

To assess the overall impact of the work of the Defense Commission in challenging state and Congressional investigations appears problematic. On the one hand, the Defense Commission proved very active in providing members of the NEA with materials, arguments, and evidence to counter attacks at the local, state, and national levels. In addition, by recounting victories for academic freedom and by establishing the support of influential individuals, the commission boosted the morale of teachers under siege.

On the other hand, however, the Defense Commission's efforts to blunt attacks appeared limited, and, at times, flimsy. For, although the commission vocally denounced state and government investigations, it refused to overtly act against them. Significantly, it failed to support members who refused to cooperate with legislative inquisitions. Rhetoric often fell short of action. Furthermore, despite the commission's efforts to extinguish red scare attack, state and Congressional investigations, undoubtedly, took their toll on the profession. The numbers of teachers dismissed may have been relatively few, but the fear, intimidation, and distrust that investigations provoked severely impacted teachers throughout the United States.

Investigations were accorded generous treatment in the media and influential politicians, business interests, and right wing organizations effectively propagated among America's public a deep suspicion of the teaching profession. Educators typically withdrew into self-censorship, and educational policy and practice suffered as a result. Consequently, despite the earnest and committed work of the Defense Commission, its efforts to blunt red scare attack in the guise of state and Congressional investigations often proved disturbingly ineffective.

The Defense Commission's Work from National Headquarters

The leadership of the Defense Commission conducted a considerable portion of its work from its offices located within the NEA national headquarters in Washington, D.C. At its core, the commission acted as a focal point for tens of thousands of educators who faced red scare attack at local and state levels. In a perpetual two-way process, the commission gathered intelligence on red scare attacks from communities throughout the country and, simultaneously, distributed a plethora of information advising educators on how best to deal with the attacks.

The vigorous and substantial efforts of the NEA's Defense Commission to blunt red scare attack should not be overlooked. The Defense Commission was one of the first professional organizations in any occupational field established primarily for the purpose of defending its members against unwarranted red scare criticism. As the red scare intensified in the late 1940s, the NEA and the commission responded in kind. The leadership of the NEA, for example, re-enforced its commitment to the commission by substantially increasing both its budget allocation and its personnel. Moreover, some of the NEA's most dynamic and influential individuals were appointed to lead the Defense Commission in its increasingly vital work. As the red scare gathered momentum in the late 1940s and early 1950s, rather than shirk from the challenge, the Defense Commission intensified its own efforts and continued its attempts to defend the rights of educators.

In a fury of activity, the officers of the Defense Commission collected and distributed a galaxy of intelligence on red scare attacks. It offered educators throughout the country advice, information, and suggestions for positive action. It vigorously challenged the efficacy of loyalty oath legislation, and it questioned the political motivations behind state and Congressional probes into public education. It championed the causes of individual teachers who were unfairly dismissed, and, where appropriate, it exposed to the general public the unscrupulous political machinations of community leaders, local business interests, newspaper proprietors, and school board members. In addition, the Defense Commission gathered and disseminated an array of information on red scare organizations that sought to undermine public education. Through issues of the *Defense Bulletin*, journal articles, pamphlets, and information sheets, the Defense Commission monitored, challenged, and exposed the tactics, methods, propaganda, and sources of support of an estimated 500 red scare organizations.

Above all, the Defense Commission both alerted and united the teaching profession in particularly disturbing times. It comforted individual teachers that they were not alone in their personal defiance of harmful red scare rhetoric, propaganda, and activity. Moreover, on many occasions, the Defense Commission boosted the morale of teachers at local and state levels and offered them a source of advice, comfort, and support.

In sum, therefore, although the NEA's Defense Commission enjoyed only limited success in blunting red scare attacks and in diffusing the political motivations behind them, the leadership of the commission achieved some worthwhile accomplishments as a result of its activities from national headquarters. Significantly, as further testimony to its commitment to extinguish red scare attack, the intensification of anti-communist fervor in the late 1940s prompted the Defense Commission to focus more attention on conferences and investigations which directly impacted educators in communities across the country. These activities in the field are another intriguing aspect of the Defense Commission's efforts to suppress red scare attack during the late 1940s and early 1950s.

Chapter VIII

The Defense Commission's
Work In the Field, 1947-1954

Since the establishment of the Defense Commission in 1941, its leaders understood the need to take its message directly to the American people. Therefore, by the end of the 1940s, the Defense Commission rapidly accelerated this accepted, but underutilized, strategy. It aimed specifically to share with the American public the crucial issues and problems faced by educators during the red scare era. During the period from 1947 to 1954, therefore, the commission developed an extensive program to convey its educational philosophy and practical wisdom to citizens across the United States. Through a series of educator-lay conferences and public relations initiatives, the Defense Commission reached out to American communities and effectively influenced the opinions and attitudes of many citizens and community groups in school districts throughout the nation.

The Defense Commission's Program of
Educator-Lay Conferences, 1947-1954

The practice of using local, state, and regional conferences to elicit support for public education among American citizens was not new to the Defense Commission. In its inaugural year, 1941, the commission hosted a series of fifteen conferences in key cities throughout the United States that sought to strengthen the bonds between public schools and the business community. These conferences, entitled "Education and Industry," proved particularly successful, according to commission's claims, in the improvement of "the attitude of many of the antagonisms of business and industrial leaders toward financial support of the schools."[1]

The success of these early conferences prompted the officers of the Defense Commission to convene additional meetings during the Second World War. Beginning in 1944, for example, the Defense Commission conducted a series of 27 state conferences on "Post War Problems and Education." These conferences dealt with a range of issues, which included the responsibility of education in helping to create full employment, to maintain a national income, to promote the conservation and development of natural resources, to reduce racial intolerance, and to contribute to the goal of intelligent participation on the part of all citizens in the affairs of government. The conferences were attended by business interests, community leaders, educators, and representatives from national organizations, agriculture, labor, and the media. By the end of the war, these educator-lay conferences involved approximately 12,000 individuals in over 40 states.[2] The success of these conferences in the encouragement of public support for education was recognized in a study of the work of the Defense Commission that reported,

> The positive efforts of the Defense Commission in the area of conferences interpreting the problems of the American public schools have shown positive results. Through joint study of common problems by lay groups and educators, misunderstandings and controversies are allayed, and doubts and suspicions planted by opponents of the public schools have been reduced.[3]

In many respects, therefore, the perceived success of these early educator-lay conferences encouraged the Defense Commission to organize future meetings to elicit widespread support for the public schools.

As the red scare gathered momentum in the late 1940s, the leadership of the Defense Commission increasingly used educator-lay conferences both to suppress and to counter attacks on the schools. The commission initially favored two types of conference format. In 1949, it conducted a series of meetings entitled "Democracy Through Education Conferences," which, according to Field Secretary Skaife, proved "vital instruments for getting support for public education and for educating the public in its responsibilities as citizens to see that fair educational practices are in operation in the community."[4] The second conference format involved twenty-two national organizations in a series of "Off The Record Conferences Concerning Attacks on Educators, Education, and Educational Publications."[5] These large national conferences were convened in 1949, 1950, and, again, in 1951. They represented an impressive attempt to quell increasing red scare attacks on the schools and to promote "the right of free inquiry and the basic value of public education." These conferences garnered the support and raised the awareness of many influential Americans. They also led to the establishment of a permanent committee of the Defense Commission charged with three primary functions: (1) to act as a clearinghouse for current materials covering the problem of the attacks against the schools, (2) to develop a handbook to aid local school systems that may be subject to future unjustified attacks, and (3) to develop a program that will win the participation of other groups in studying and meeting attacks on the schools.[6] The "Off The Record Conferences" formed part of the Defense Commission's renewed and determined strategy to challenge the mounting attacks on the schools, which appeared especially acute in the years from 1949 to 1954.

By the end of 1951, the already serious situation worsened. Political attacks on education mounted and anti-communist provocateurs appeared more venomous and more menacing in their actions and rhetoric toward public schooling. For example, in its annual report to the NEA delegation, Executive Secretary Kennan remarked with alarm that 1951 had "been notable for the acceleration of attacks against the schools."[7] Furthermore, a national questionnaire completed that year by educators revealed "that the number of attacks against education have more than doubled in the past two years." The Defense Commission responded through its advocacy of a series of regional conferences to be "held to plan and develop materials, programs, and technics for meeting the unwarranted attacks on the public schools." As a consequence of these deliberations, in the spring of 1953, a series of conferences, entitled "Public Education in a Dangerous Era," was inaugurated.[8]

The first of these meetings convened in Philadelphia in May 1953. It was called by the Defense Commission avowedly for the purpose of,

> bringing together leaders of national state and civic organizations and of professional education associations, as well as noted individual citizens, to discuss the problems that public education faces that are developing out of this dangerous era, and also the special contributions that public education may properly make to the strengthening of our nation during this period.[9]

In this and future conferences, leading officials within the NEA explained the meaning intended by the theme of the conference, "Public Education in a Dangerous Era." In Philadelphia, for example, Richard Barnes Kennan, the executive secretary of the Defense Commission, revealed that the theme evoked several meanings, of which three appeared prominent. First, he noted the danger associated with "the physical threat of Communism within and without our nation." Second, he noted the danger from unprecedented attacks on the schools and wished to "emphasize the fact that public education itself is being threatened during this period." Third, Kennan argued that in these troubled times, the Defense Commission "wanted to get the best possible consideration and advice as to how the public schools might best contribute to the strengthening of our nation during this critical period."[10]

Typically, the Defense Commission and a state education association sponsored the conferences. Invited individuals included prominent leaders of the local community, business organizations, taxer groups, the media, citizens' committees, patriotic organizations, and educators. Attendees of the conference in Philadelphia, for example, included representatives from the Boy Scouts of America, the National Association of Manufacturers, the U. S. Steel Corporation, the American Legion Auxiliary, the Baptist Joint Committee on Public Affairs, the National Federation of Independent Business, the American Association of University Women, the Freedoms Foundation, the American Civil Liberties Union, and the *New York Times.*[11] The success of the first conference in Philadelphia prompted the commission to organize additional conferences during 1953 and 1954 in cities such as Denver, San Francisco, Oklahoma City, and New York.

At each conference, the Defense Commission appeared particularly eager to ensure that lay leaders worked in an atmosphere in which they felt free "to offer frank advice in helping schools to meet critical problems." As such, the commission took pride in the fact that "the proportion of lay leaders to education leaders in the conferences has run as high as five to one." "A preponderance of laymen rather than educators," the *Defense Bulletin* boasted, "insures free discussion from the laymen who cannot thus feel that the conference is 'stacked' against them."[12] Despite this genuine attempt to elicit the advice and opinions of influential citizens, attendees were unable to escape from direct and explicit Defense Commission propaganda and conviction.

Often, in an introductory session, members of the Defense Commission informed conference participants of the attackers and their methods. Richard Barnes Kennan for example, in his standard address, "Public Education in a Dangerous Era from the Viewpoint of a Member of the Teaching Profession," informed audiences that "public schools have been subject to destructive attacks of great intensity by a strange coalition of forces with strong financial support."[13] In his remarks, Kennan illustrated in considerable detail the nature, source, and deleterious impact of concerted red scare attack. Other Defense Commission members followed suit. In characteristic fashion, Robert Skaife alerted conference participants to the dangers of "self-anointed, self-appointed superpatriots" who "have succeeded in creating a climate of hysteria bearing many of the weathermarks of an incipient stage of ism."[14] In other similar addresses, many leading figures from the world of education further testified to the substantial threat posed by unscrupulous attacks on American public schools.

After the opening address by a Defense Commission member, conference attendees routinely separated into four discussion groups in order to consider many of the vital issues faced by public education. Each member of the discussion groups was provided with a kit of materials that outlined a "hypothetical case intended as a possible basis for starting the discussion in each group." Discussion groups varied in size. In Philadelphia, for example, the smallest group constituted 17 members whereas, in Denver, one group included 52 participants.[15] Four topic areas consistently were selected for deliberation. Typically, group one was asked to consider issues related to curriculum matters. Primarily, discussion focused on educational issues, such as the teaching of controversial subjects, the place of religion in the schools, and the arguments for and against the social studies. Significantly, group two typically concentrated its attention on the growing attacks on education and on how communities might best deal with them. In an effort to raise public awareness of the serious plight of public education, group three discussed how best to address such pressing educational problems as acute teacher shortages, classroom overcrowding, and dilapidated school buildings. The group four was charged to determine the positive attributes that sound public education brought to American society.

After a lengthy deliberative process, the designated discussion chairman, always a non-educator, presented a feedback report to the conference. The "Chairman's Report" varied in both detail and substance. Commonly, however, each report listed a set of recommendations that addressed the problem(s) considered. For example, at the conference at the Hotel Bellevue-Stratford in Philadelphia, the organizers charged group two to address "How should the schools deal with criticism? Honest criticism, whether informed or prejudiced? Attacks on textbooks, methods of teaching etc.?" Chaired by Joseph A. Brunton of the Boy Scouts of America, the group responded with a set of seven recommendations:

1. The schools need to concentrate on improving the quality of teaching.
2. Much more effort must be put forth to interpret what the schools are doing. The more we take our community into the planning, the less we have to interpret.
3. Better relations with the press must be developed.
4. Conferences like this one should be held throughout the country.
5. National organizations should come together to build understandings by "pooling their differences."
6. The Defense Commission should carry on research studies on what the public think about the schools and publicize the results.
7. The Defense Commission's program should be strengthened financially in order that "6" may be carried forward vigorously and that a central agency to combat unwarranted criticism may be available to the profession and the public. Professional and lay groups, such as represented in the Philadelphia conference, should be asked to contribute to the budget of the commission, thus building a wider base of concern throughout the culture for the maintenance of an education devoted to the ways of life of free men.[16]

By directly challenging educators and lay people both to appreciate the problems faced by public education and to ask for constructive suggestions positively to address these problems, the Defense Commission made undeniable progress in its efforts to enlist the support of many influential American citizens.

Officers of the commission undoubtedly believed that the conferences were major successes. The commission's annual report to the NEA in 1954, for example, noted that "the newly developed conferences on 'Public Education in a Dangerous Era' have been tried and proved valuable in several states and regions." Further, the report contended, "the results of the conferences are mutually valuable to the local as well as the state and national associations."[17] In a similar vein, the May 1954 issue of the *Defense Bulletin* proudly boasted the comments of two participants who claimed that the commission's conference appeared as "the most stimulating and satisfactory conference I ever attended," and "one of the best things that happened to me." Likely, the "Public Education in a Dangerous Era" conference series proved somewhat effective in harnessing public support for the schools. Scores of influential citizens participated in meetings held in cities and regions throughout the United States. In most cases, they responded sympathetically to the complex problems which confronted American education in the early 1950s.

Yet, despite these worthwhile achievements, the discussion group reports and recommendations revealed a rather timid response to the proliferation of menacing contemporary red scare attacks. In most cases, for example, groups which discussed how to respond to vigorous attacks argued for "improved public relations," "more information," and "more detailed explanation of school policy."[18] Almost without exception, the groups failed to consider policies which aimed to investigate and to challenge red scare organizations and the political forces that supported and motivated them. Significantly, no discussion group directly explored the relationship between the climate of anti-communism that pervaded American culture in this period and the political motivations behind red scare attacks. Accordingly, the conferences further fueled the belief that schools endured scolding criticism not because they represented a battleground for competing ideological forces, but, primarily, because educators neglected sufficiently to explain to the American people the achievements and importance of public education. This implicit failure to appreciate the source and nature of red scare criticism, undoubtedly, throws into question the overarching effectiveness of the conferences in blunting destructive red scare attacks on the schools.

Public Relations, Public Support, and
Defense Commission Policy

The period from 1949 to 1954 marked a peculiarly ambivalent time for American public education. On the one hand, educators in many communities throughout the United States suffered from the debilitating excesses of red scare attack. Some teachers lost their jobs. Others fled from the profession. Many more engaged in vigorous self-censorship in their daily classroom practices. Frequently, vicious red scare propaganda and accusations created a deep sense of alienation and suspicion between the teaching profession and the community at large.

Nevertheless educators in many other communities throughout the nation enjoyed an unprecedented burst of support for public schools among the American citizenry. Indeed, by the early 1950s, many leading educators marveled at the positive attention accorded public education. "There is more interest in public education today than ever before in the history of our country," Andrew Holt joyously informed NEA delegates in his presidential address to the national conference in St. Louis in June 1950. "From Sitka Switch to New York City," he continued, newspapers throughout the past year have been filled with news columns, editorials, and feature stories about education. All the leading radio programs have emphasized the problems of the schools. Movies have been prepared showing the important function schools perform in a democracy. Organizations of every description from the Chamber of Commerce to the Saturday night Canasta Club have had active education committees.[19]

Three years later, Robert Skaife similarly noted, "Perhaps never before have citizens been so actively interested in public schools as they are at the present time." This apparent and unparalleled perception of zeal for public education arose for a complexity of reasons and derived from an assortment of citizens' committees, commissions, and associations.

Prominent among the many organizations that impressively burst on to the educational scene in the late 1940s and early 1950s was the National Citizens commission for the Public Schools (NCCPS). The genesis of the NCCPS stemmed from a 1946 conference attended by a group of influential lay people and educators at the invitation of James B. Conant, President of Harvard University. Three years later, in 1949, the National Commission was formed. Roy E. Larsen, President of Time, Inc., served as chairman of the non-profit NCCPS, which was financially supported by the Rockefeller and Carnegie Foundations and the General Education Board.[20] In all respects, the NCCPS was a lay organization headed by many distinguished American citizens not professionally associated with education, politics, or religion.

According to Larsen, the commission was formed to achieve two fundamental goals: "to help Americans realize how important our public schools are to our expanding democracy, and to arouse in each community the intelligence and the will to improve our public schools."[21] For its first goal, the commission began a cooperative campaign with the Advertising Council to draw public attention to the problems of the nation's public schools. In newspapers, in magazines, on outdoor posters, on radio, on television, and on license plates, breadwrappers, and matchbooks, the commission's message, "Better Schools Make Better Communities," was trumpeted across the United States. In 1951 alone, some 10,257 advertisements appeared in newspapers in every state of the nation; five thousand large outdoor posters, proclaiming "Our Schools Are What *We* Make Them — Good Citizens Everywhere Are Helping," were displayed the length and breadth of the country, and approximately 90,000 display cards spread the message in buses and subway trolley cars across the United States.

Although the NCCPS was a national organization with a centralized structure, its leaders fully appreciated the importance of devolving responsibility for the improvement of community schools to local citizens. To achieve its second goal, therefore, the commission poured enormous energy into providing extensive support of individuals in local communities to establish and effectively operate local citizens' groups. The phenomenal increase in the formation of local citizens' committees under the NCCPS umbrella testified to the incredible effectiveness of the commission. Whereas, for example, in 1949, the National Citizens commission supported only 50 citizens' committees working at the local and state level, by the end of 1953, that figure had soared to more than 8,000.[22]

To support local groups, the NCCPS constructed an extensive and ever-expanding program. For example, it gathered laymen and educators together at local workshops and invited hundreds of citizens from all walks of life to its national conferences. It published two well-received and widely used handbooks for local citizens' committees, "What Do We Know About Our Schools?" and "How Can We Help Get Better Schools?" It also produced an array of pamphlets, information sheets, booklets, and film strips intended to help local communities in their quest for better schools. Roy Larsen's media expertise also was devoted to the cause. His Time/Life Films, for example, dedicated two "March of Time" films to the subject of public education, and a series of radio broadcasts further spread the message of the NCCPS.[23] In addition, in an impressively effective contribution to the improvement of American schools, the commission created a national clearinghouse library that amassed a rich store of material that illustrated actual school improvement practices at the local level.

The burgeoning interest in public education in the early 1950s similarly was indicated by the rapid rise in the membership of the National Congress of Parents and Teachers (NCPT). Always a loyal supporter of the schools, in the late 1940s and early 1950s, the National Congress witnessed an explosion of interest in its long-standing efforts to improve public education. Indeed, between 1946 and 1953, membership of the NCPT doubled to a staggering 7,953,000 and boasted 37,000 local PTAs in 50 state branches.[24]

Other leading national organizations also actively championed the cause of public education in this period. In 1953, for example, Robert Skaife, identified the Congress of Industrial Organizations (CIO), the American Federation of Labor (AFL), the National Association of Manufacturers, the Anti-Defamation League, the American-Jewish Committee, the American

Association of University Women, and the United States Chamber of Commerce as organizations that proved particularly stolid defenders of public schools in this period.[25] In addition, in November 1953, Lucile Ellison, editor of the *Defense Bulletin*, detailed seven groups that emphasized in their programs "support for public education and defense of the schools against attack."[26] Those organizations included the United Church Women, the National Conference of Christians and Jews, the American Library Association, the American Textbook Publishers Institute, the John Dewey Society, the Anti-Defamation League of B'Nai B'rith, and the American Jewish Committee.

Increased citizen involvement in the schools did not always lead to harmonious relations between professional educators and community activists. Teachers and educational bureaucrats often resented over-zealous lay involvement. Many firmly believed that citizens' committees frequently proved too attentive to, and too demanding of, the public schools to be of value to them. Consequently, some school officials treated community groups with grave suspicion: school people believed them to be yet another unwelcome agency interfering in school affairs.

For the most part, however, informed citizens and professional educators soon realized the mutually advantageous value of establishing sound working relationships. Increasingly, organizations, such as the NCCPS and the NCPT, joined with teachers and administrators. In scores of communities throughout the nation, this combination proved immensely effective in the elevation of the status of public education.

The intensification of profuse and widespread support for the schools appeared most prominently in the early 1950s. It was explained by a complex of interrelated factors. Three causes particularly dominated the development. First, public concern for the plight of the public schools, almost without exception, was based upon a genuine desire to see American public schooling prosper. Influential lay leaders continually emphasized the relationship between a sound public school system and the cherished ideals of a democratic society. Accordingly, in an article published in *The Educational Forum* in May 1952, Roy Larsen, Chairman of NCCPS, carefully detailed the correlation between the rise of America as a powerful democratic nation and the ascendancy of its national system of public education. Larsen described the American public school system as "one of the greatest social triumphs in history," and in rationalizing the work of the NCCPS, he argued, "There are two compelling reasons for pressing our efforts for better education: One is that this work is far from finished. The second is that this work tests and measures the integrity of the democratic purpose."[27] Larsen's sincere commitment to the schools and their importance for the advancement of American society was shared by countless prominent figures and national organizations.

From 1949 to 1954, in particular, thousands of citizens at the local, state, and national level recognized the dangers to American society of schools systems burdened by rapidly increasing enrollments, poor school facilities, acute teacher shortages, and inadequate financial support. As a consequence, the dramatic rise in public support for the schools in this period largely may be attributed to the genuine and sincere concern of citizens to support public schools as a fundamental bastion of American society and as a quintessential symbol of the American community.

The second reason for increased support for the schools stemmed from the determination of many citizens' groups to quell the burgeoning, outrageous, and unprincipled attacks on public education. Clearly, not every lay organization which supported the schools was formed exclusively to blunt mounting red scare criticism. Nevertheless, many communities stirred to action primarily as a result of these venomous attacks. Indeed, the Defense Commission's Executive Secretary, Richard Barnes Kennan, argued, "Vitriolic and unreasonable attacks may have some useful value if they will arouse men and women of good will to...endeavor to find means and procedures for improving conditions that affect the children of our communities."[28] Unquestionably, many citizens of good will were aroused in scores of communities throughout the country. For example, Robert Skaife identified six communities in which citizens' organizations chiefly were formed to counteract "destructive activities." In his contribution to Van Til's *Forces Affecting American Education*, Skaife catalogued in impressive detail the work of local organizations, such as the Committee on Public Education, the Citizens Action Committee, and the Friends of Public Education who vigorously opposed attacks in Scarsdale (New York), Ferndale (Michigan), Pasadena (California), Port Washington (New York), Monterey (California), and McAllen (Texas).[29]

In other instances, concerned citizens' groups combined to counter attacks on public education. For example, under the striking headline "New Threats to Schools Offset by Co-operative Efforts: Friends of the Schools Rally to Their Support," the March 1953 *Defense Bulletin* reported the collaborative efforts of local groups in Colorado to oppose loyalty investigations "designed to check textbooks, teaching, and other phases of Colorado schools."[30] In keeping with the enthusiasm for loyalty probes at the national level, on February 11, 1953, the Colorado State Senate voted to carry out an extensive investigation of public education in the state. However, within 24 hours the decision was overturned. The abrupt about-face undoubtedly was prompted by the intense, rapid, and ultimately effective combined activities of the Colorado Education Association, the State Board of Education, the State Department of Education, the Denver Citizens' Committee for the Public Schools, the PTA, the League of Womens' Voters, the American Association of University Women, the American Federation of Teachers, the Congress of Industrial Organizations, the local branch of the National Association of Manufacturers, and the Denver Chamber of Commerce.

Rejoicing in the triumph of these community forces, the *Defense Bulletin* reported the comments of one Denver citizen who claimed that "the real feature" of the event "was the united front by all groups interested in the schools." The Colorado situation appeared typical of many other communities across the United States. Indeed, as attacks on the schools grew in strength in the early 1950s, local organizations, which often feared that education was being unjustly attacked by meddling extremists, impressively and effectively rallied to the defense of education.

The third and, arguably, most important reason for the dramatic rise in public support for American education in the late 1940s and early 1950s stemmed from the growing realization by many educators of the need to solicit lay support actively and determinedly. Indeed, a significant feature of this period was the increasingly popular notion among educators and their professional associations that the active involvement of local citizens was vital to the future success of the American public school system.

Many leading professional figures vigorously urged fellow educators to involve themselves in activities designed to improve public relations. Harold Benjamin, for example, emphasized to teachers and administrators the importance not only of communicating their views and ideas within educational circles, but also of reaching out to the public at large,

> In writing as in speaking, school men and women talk to themselves. This, of course, is very necessary for any professional group. Public educators, however, are also under a peculiar necessity to talk to all their people. The school teacher is not the same kind of professional worker as the physician, the attorney, or the engineer. He is a public servant, and he forgets that fact at peril to his community's children. He has to live with his people, work with them, and talk with them or, if he does not, his living, work, and talk will not be well done.[31]

Other luminaries in the educational world also reasoned that the only way for education to counter vehement criticism was to embrace the support of American citizenry.

William Van Til convincingly argued that, although research supported claims that "modern," or "progressive," education was an overwhelming success, educators had not conveyed effectively this important message to the American public.[32] Van Til cited Pasadena as a classic example of this perceived failure. He noted that "despite research facts" showing the educational standards of Pasadena's children to be superior to national averages in reading, arithmetic, and language usage, "the general public continually heard charges by critics that Pasadena's achievement was inferior to national standards." Consequently, Van Til implored educators not only to conduct research comparing "modern" and "traditional" education, but also to broadcast the positive results to the American people.

Deeply conscious of his own painful personal experience in Pasadena, Willard Goslin also urged American educators to solicit the "great human resources of the people." As he believed schools were embroiled in a series of divisive cultural issues, Goslin vigorously underscored the importance of public support. In 1953, he wrote,

> The schools are at the center of nearly all the bitterly contested issues in American culture — race relations, politics, religion, international relations, and others. This nation and its freedoms will stand or fall by what happens to the education of its people. What happens to education will depend on how much of the power of the people is brought to its support. That is the challenge to educational leadership in our times.[33]

The views of Van Til, Benjamin, and Goslin did not appear in isolation. Indeed, the drive toward improved public relations was illustrative of sentiments expressed in many of the leading educational journals of the period. Articles such as Isaac Kandel's, "We Must Educate Our Masters," Harry Fosdick's "The Counterattack Starts in the Classroom," and H. Gordon Hullfish's "The Profession and the Public Face a Common Problem" appeared characteristic of the time.[34] Fundamentally, these and similar scholarly contributions asserted the common belief that education's best possible defense against attack was the enlistment of widespread public support for the schools.

Determined efforts to reach out to lay people and to citizens' groups increasingly became a central policy of the NEA and the Defense

Commission during the early 1950s. In no small measure, events in Pasadena rapidly jolted the profession into action. Significantly, in 1950, the NEA conferred departmental status upon the National School Public Relations Association (NSPRA) and aggressive public relations measures resulted.

Although the NEA's public relations program clearly flourished in the early 1950s, the association appeared aware of the importance of better communication with the public during the late 1940s. For example, in August 1949, in a workshop conference co-sponsored by the Defense Commission, Lyle W. Ashby informed his audience of the impressive work of the NEA to reach the American public. He noted the extensive activity of the Press and Radio Relations Division of the NEA which maintained "an active program of public relations through releases to newspapers, through radio programs — including a monthly script service to local educational associations — and other activities."[35] Ashby also celebrated the undoubted success of the NEA-sponsored "American Education Week," which resulted in the visit of an estimated 10 million citizens to local schools. Additionally, he boasted the association's five-year motion picture program, which aimed to produce a 20-minute movie each year for five years. Above all, Ashby heralded the undoubted success both of the NEA's regular four-page periodical "The Public and Education," which was distributed eight times each year to more than 40,000 local, state, and national "leaders," and of the association's "Annual Report of the Profession to the Public," which principally was designed to enlist the support of "newspaper editors, columnists, radio editors, and commentators." In many respects, therefore, the NEA's public relations program originated in the late 1940s. Significantly, in the decade that followed, the NEA rapidly built upon these strong foundations in public relations.

The NEA's most impressive agency for the promotion of the schools, unquestionably, was the National School Public Relations Association (NSPRA). At the 1951 NEA annual meeting, Frederick L. Hipp, President of the NSPRA reported the staggering success of the association in affecting improved educator-lay relations. He noted,

> A few years ago anyone in school public relations work had to fumble along on his own making costly and time-consuming errors while acquiring the fundamentals of this field. Today, through the National School Public Relations Association, which became a department of the NEA in 1950, more than 2,000 members of the profession are organized to share and pool their ideas on public relations.[36]

Spurred by the early effectiveness of the NSPRA, the following year, in 1952, Hipp argued that through a concerted policy of public relations, attacks on the schools could be blunted. "We have heard a great deal lately about attacks on education," he commented. "Once such attacks are made, it is a public relations function of the profession to meet them....We must *sell* education, as if it were the product and responsibility of teachers alone, who must, by various tricks, make it attractive to the rest of the community."[37] Hipp's emphasis on the ability of a robust public relations policy effectively to crush critical attacks explained the NEA's enormous attention to community relations in the early 1950s.

From 1950 to 1955, a period in which the red scare appeared particularly acute, the NEA and the Defense Commission devoted considerable attention to improved relations between educators and the community at large. For example, largely through the NSPRA, it continued actively to support "American Education Week," which, in 1955, encouraged an estimated 20 million Americans to visit the schools. It offered a plethora of information to educators, such as the enormously popular "It Starts in the Classroom: A Public Relations Handbook for Classroom Teachers," "88 Techniques in School Public Relations for Teachers and Administrators," and the 1954 publication, "Let's Go To Press," a handbook designed to "help classroom teachers and other school press representatives to channel more and better school news to the local press and to build better working relations with editors and reporters."[38] Handbooks also were made available to parents. For example, in 1951, more than 300,000 copies of the NSPRA 12-page booklet "Our Schools Have Kept Us Free," a reprinted version of comments by Henry Steele Commager, were distributed. From 1953 to 1955, the NEA also produced more than 850,000 information handbooks to help parents further appreciate and understand the work of the schools.

During the 1950s, the NEA also produced a series of radio broadcasts and motion pictures, of which the 1954 film, "The Freedom to Learn" and the nationally acclaimed "Skippy and the 3 Rs" proved particularly successful. "The Public Relations Tool Kit" proved another enormously popular feature of the NEA public relations policy. It contained "six current NSPRA handbooks, plus pamphlets, leaflets, and newsletters covering many phases of school public relations." In addition, the NSPRA, in joint association with the NEA Division of Press and Radio Relations, produced a PR Guide for 1953-54 which included a "where to look list of public relations reference books, pamphlets, motion pictures, filmstrips, radio transcripts, and other special aids.[39]

Co-sponsored by the American Association of School Superintendents (AASA) and the NSPRA, the NEA-supported public relations conferences for educators in cities throughout the nation. For example, in 1952 alone, over 2,800 educators talked public relations in regional gatherings in St. Louis, Boston, and Los Angeles. NEA public relations conferences were not solely aimed at educators, though. In 1953, for instance, the NSPRA pioneered a series of meetings in which educational leaders collaborated with hundreds of representatives from the business world and the media to address "key basic concerns to school public relations."[40]

Although NEA departments, like the NSPRA, agencies, such as the Press and Radio Relations Division, and joint committees, like the NEA and the National Congress of Parents and Teachers singularly, focused on improved public relations, many other departments, commissions, and committees actively contributed to the cause. Indeed, as early as 1949, Lyle Ashby pointed out that "there are aspects of public relations in the work of practically all of the headquarters divisions, the commissions, committees, and departments."[41] The NEA's Defense Commission was no exception in this regard. In its efforts both to counter attacks on the schools and to promote public education in the eyes of the public, the Defense Commission proved one of the NEA's most effective agencies.

To a large extent, leaders of the Defense Commission realized the importance of building positive educator-lay relationships long before the NEA's dramatic conversion to the policy in the early 1950s. Of note, two of the seven reasons which justified its creation in 1941 explicitly emphasized the need to secure widespread "public understanding and support." As attacks on the schools mounted in the late 1940s and early 1950s, the Defense Commission, much like other agencies in the NEA, paid increased attention to its public relations policy.

Fundamentally, leaders of the commission firmly believed that attacks on the schools could only achieve success in areas where the public appeared ill-informed. "When thinking individuals have access to facts," reasoned Robert Skaife, "they will reject the distorted argument, the half truth and the phony logic characteristic of the literature circulated by organizations endangering freedom of education."[42] Officers of the commission, therefore, placed tremendous faith in the argument that once citizens knew the facts and were brought into close association with the schools, then attacks would be thwarted. In characteristic fashion, the October 1951 issue of the *Defense Bulletin* purposely informed educators,

> Schools generally need to take the public more into their confidence regarding school programs and objectives. Where parents and patrons are familiar with the work teachers are doing, they are not gullible to the charges of sinister activities in the classroom.[43]

Repeatedly, through issues of the *Defense Bulletin*, through regional conferences, through information sheets, and through pamphlets and booklets, the Defense Commission emphasized the importance of capturing public support for the schools.

The Defense Commission provided NEA members and influential lay leaders with an enormous amount of practical information on how to respond to fierce criticism of the schools. Robert Skaife, for example, argued that the "best preventative against highly publicized irresponsible charges" involved the development of a long term "two-way channel of communication between school and community." Accordingly, he offered local citizens five suggestions for communities facing a school crisis,

1. Start with organizations already established rather than set up a new group immediately. If the need for an entirely new organization becomes apparent, existing groups should take steps to form it.
2. Staff members in the school system should not take an active part in a citizens organization, but should have a representative at meetings.
3. If a new organization is established, it should draw up a set of principles which any open-minded supporter of public education may accept. These principles should not be stated in such a way as to commit members to a particular philosophy of education.
4. Every effort should be made at meetings to provide opportunity for expression of criticism and to search for facts in studying charges against the schools.
5. The organization should build support for schools by publicizing what it is doing.[44]

In addition to providing advice for community groups and local citizens, the Defense Commission also offered educators an array of information on how to deal with attacks through a policy of positive public relations.

The Defense Commission organized a series of workshops exclusively intended for educators that focused to a significant degree on public relations. Routinely, workshop participants were asked to consider three central questions in small discussion groups:

1. What are the agencies of a community which may be utilized to inform the public about school problems?
2. What is the function of the school, faculty, staff, students, in utilizing these agencies to promote a good public relations program?
3. How can each individual in the school system contribute most to a good public relations program?

Subsequent to a lengthy discussion, each group of educators was required to summarize its discussion and draw up a list of recommendations for an improved policy of public relations. One group, meeting in Shawnee, Oklahoma, in August 1949, for example, drew up a list of 18 recommendations, five of which included these suggestions:

1. Satisfied children are the most effective agents for public relations.
2. The press should be invited to school functions.
3. Preparation for radio speaking should be included in all school programs.
4. The school should have a public relations director or committee to keep an even flow of school information going to all agencies which disseminate news to the public.
5. Teachers should be aware that they are the first element in a public relations program: How they look, how they talk, how they meet people, and how and when they work in their social contacts [sic].[45]

Likely, these workshop conferences performed an important function in drawing to the attention of educators the value of sound public relations. The Defense Commission, however, appeared aware that, no matter how successful these conferences proved, ultimately, they could only impact a relatively small number of communities. Accordingly, the Defense Commission devoted considerable attention to providing information through the *Defense Bulletin*, information sheets, and pamphlets.

The *Defense Bulletin* usefully conveyed a significant amount of information to educators intended to assist them in their campaigns against concerted attacks. For example, a popular and widely issued criticism of the schools during the red scare era was the contention that educators focused on socialistic activities at the expense of teaching the "3 R's" and the "fundamentals." In response, the *Defense Bulletin* frequently provided educators with considerable ammunition and counter argument. Typically, issues of the *Defense Bulletin* published studies that demonstrated the effectiveness of modern education. Also, they urged educators to communicate this information to the public. The May 1955 issues of the *Bulletin*, for example, detailed the progress that educators had made in elevating literacy standards in the United States. It offered statistics that demonstrated the tremendous decline in the rates of illiteracy in the country, the dramatically increased use of public libraries, and the soaring circulation figures for newspapers and magazines. Furthermore, the *Bulletin* informed NEA members that "in answering charges of too slight emphasis on the 3R's in today's schools you will want to be familiar with" a selection of listed NEA materials.[46]

The Defense Commission also made effective use of pamphlets and information sheets in its efforts to build supportive school-community relations and, by extension, to blunt the red scare attacks. The widely read "American Education Under Fire" pamphlet written by Ernest Melby illustrated this type of activity. Published in 1951, Melby wrote that "during the past year or two America has experienced one of its most shameful periods of character assassination." Melby continued, "Name-calling, insinuation, misinformation, partial truth, hysteria, have been characteristic of our approaches to problems. We have been plagued by insecurity." Set against this background the pamphlet used its central section, "Good Education Answers the Attacks," to offer evidence that modern schools and progressive methods were very successful in raising educational standards. Melby addressed each of the charges against the schools: they failed to teach the 3R's, they usurped the function of the family, they lacked discipline, they were godless, and their teachers were subversive.[47] Impressively, he provided reports, arguments, research findings, and statistical evidence with which to counter the charges, and, importantly, he urged educators to communicate this information to local citizens.

Through a range of public relations initiatives, therefore, the NEA and the Defense Commission made progress in increasing widespread community support for the schools. Indeed, during the red scare era when attacks on the schools appeared ubiquitous, the positive impact of the association's public relations program proved a notable achievement. As a result of this progress, Robert Skaife remarked in 1952, that, "although communities have had some rugged experiences, there are healthy signs appearing. More people are interested in the schools. More people are actively participating in community groups concerned with school programs."[48] Many other positive indicators of increased public support for the schools existed.

For example, according to a Roper poll conducted in 1950, fewer than 17% of respondents claimed dissatisfaction with the schools, and two-thirds of those polled thought that the current curriculum was more worthwhile than the curriculum twenty years earlier.[49] That same year, NEA President

Andrew Holt told delegates at the national meeting that "largely as a result of increased lay interest in education, every state in our nation has increased its support of education." Significantly, more schools were constructed in 1954-55 than in any previous year, and research reports, such as Henderson and Hand's, "To What Extent Is the General Public in Sympathy with the Current Attacks on the Schools?" revealed widespread public approval of modern schools.[50]

Increased public support for the schools, however, did not eliminate damaging red scare attacks. Despite the NEA's many public relations accomplishments, it failed to diffuse explosive attacks in dozens of communities throughout the United States. The NEA may have achieved a great deal in forging new partnerships between schools and their communities, but the climate of anti-communist repression was larger than that focused just on schools. Throughout the early 1950s, teachers remained wary of teaching sensitive subjects; loyalty investigations took their professional toll, and biting attacks often caused teachers and administrators dire problems.

Accordingly, although Robert Skaife appeared optimistic that increased support for the schools portended a brighter future, he also understood the debilitating impact of the red scare on the schools during the early 1950s. "Evidence of this climate of fear," he wrote in 1952, "is all around us — removal of controversial textbooks, banning of speakers, labeling of books, dismissal of loyal educators, legislating of negative-type loyalty oaths." More alarming to Skaife than these "visible examples of curtailment of freedom," however, appeared the more subtle and less explicit manifestations of the red scare. "Think of the many unseen examples of restraint," Skaife implored an audience of educators and citizens. "Individuals who practice self-repression and, thereby, help to perpetuate this climate of fear! How many times have teachers held back from expressing their sincere beliefs for fear of being identified with what some people call subversive views?"[51] Ultimately, therefore, Skaife realized that, although relations between educators and the broader community significantly improved in this period, they frequently failed to prevent harmful and at times destructive red scare attacks on public education.

Chapter IX

Defense Commission Investigations

In addition to the Defense Commission's popular sequence of educator-lay conferences and its prodigious public relations program, its field work also involved an important series of Defense Commission investigations. During the twenty years between 1941 and 1961, the commission conducted 29 full-scale investigations in towns and cities throughout the United States. Specifically, in the period of heightened red scare activity between 1949 and 1954, the commission investigated 11 major cases.[1] These investigations occurred for a variety of reasons and took place in vastly different locations. For example, some focused on educational controversies in large population centers such as Miami (Florida) and Kansas City (Missouri), whereas others focused attention on small communities such as Polson (Montana) and Mars Hill (North Carolina).

Explicit evidence of red scare activity in the 11 investigations held between 1949 and 1954 was not always obvious. Indeed, in some cases it was markedly absent. For example, although investigations in Newport (New Hampshire), Twin Falls (Idaho), and Ogelsby (Illinois), dealt with the unfair dismissals of teachers, no proof surfaced that the firings were motivated by anti-communist sentiment. Similarly, little overt red scare activity was identified in the Defense Commission investigations in Salt Lake City (Utah), and in Kelso (Washington).

The apparent absence of anti-communist involvement in these communities, however, did not mean that red scare attacks were exceptional. Likely in Mars Hill (North Carolina), and in Miami (Florida), in which deep political controversy lay behind educational unrest, ideological motivations associated with the red scare existed. Moreover, in Polson (Montana), the dismissal of school superintendent W. L. Emmert was prompted to some extent by accusations from individuals in the community that teachers under his supervision were "communists or communistic in their activities."[2]

Without question the two most dramatic and explicit examples of red scare activity encountered by Defense Commission investigators occurred in Pasadena (California), and Houston (Texas). Of significance, the Defense Commission's decision to conduct thorough and detailed investigations in these two cities reflected the concern that attacks motivated by red scare agitators proved typical of other school districts throughout the country. In keeping with its policy, which directed that investigations give "priority attention to those cases which appear to have the greatest significance for the national welfare of the profession," the Defense Commission targeted Pasadena and Houston. Events in both cities were recognized as cases representative of deeper educational problems in the country at large.[3] From a historical perspective, therefore, the commission's decisions to investigate the Houston and Pasadena school settings should not be viewed as two isolated examples of red scare activity, but rather as symptomatic of a much broader problem facing American educators in the late 1940s and 1950s.

Of the two investigations Pasadena undoubtedly attracted the greatest amount of attention.[4] The reasons for this concentration on Pasadena are not difficult to understand. Simply, the Pasadena situation was the first major red scare incident to invite widespread national notoriety. The commission's investigation principally focused on events from the summer of 1949 to the summer of 1951 and, as such, it alerted educators at a relatively early stage to the chilling dangers of organized red scare tactics and propaganda. Moreover, the attacks in Pasadena brought down an educational "king." The dismissal of School Superintendent Willard Goslin sent shock waves throughout the educational community. As president of the American Association of School Administrators, as an experienced professional, and as a close associate of many influential leaders within the progressive education movement, Superintendent Goslin symbolized the sensitive, efficient, forward-thinking educator *par excellence*. His forced resignation on November 21, 1950, therefore, appeared as a dramatic warning sign to educators in school districts throughout the nation.[5]

Consequently, the portentous events in Pasadena — and the Defense Commission's reaction to them — are worthy of serious review. Despite the importance of Pasadena, however, the situation in Houston and the Defense Commission's investigation of that city's educational problems should not be overlooked. Indeed, the situation which surrounded the Defense Commission's investigation in Houston merits attention, chiefly, for three reasons.

First, in many respects, Houston typified the post-war boom in metropolitan America. In the summer of 1954, the city and its environs housed an estimated population of one million people. Between 1940 and 1950, the population of Harris county (the Houston metropolitan area) increased 52.5%. More remarkable, however, the number of children in the city's school district dramatically increased. In just one decade, the number of children aged five through nine years of age rose by 80.5%, while the numbers of children under five years of age soared by a staggering 123.7%. By March 1954, the Houston Independent School District reported an enrollment of 121,702 students. Its nine senior high schools, 18 junior high schools, and 114 elementary schools made Houston the seventh largest school district in the nation at the time.[6]

The rapid rise in the Houston school population placed the issue of public education at the center of the city's post-war political struggles. The schools quickly became a sensitive issue in which Houston's rival political factions had an important stake for two principal reasons. First, the dramatic increase in school enrollments called for an attendant rise in the financial resources allocated to education. In the post-war era, Houston schools, like hundreds of other school districts throughout the nation, received insufficient finding. Teacher shortages, inadequate facilities, and classroom overcrowding appeared common. In opposition to the city's liberal supporters who favored increased tax support for the schools and the infusion of federal funds, the conservative faction that controlled public education in the city proved reluctant to allocate desperately needed funds to education. As a consequence, school board elections in the late 1940s and early 1950s reflected arguments between conservative leaders, who refused to support federal aid and local tax increases, and liberal supporters, who advocated a significant rise in the amount of money expended on public education.[7]

Because educational arguments in Houston also became both emotionally and politically charged events, they typified the ideological schism in post-war American society. As with other school districts throughout the nation at the time, the Houston public schools wrestled with burning educational issues, such as federal aid to education, racial integration of schools, the use of UNESCO materials, the efficacy of progressive methods, and the perceived infiltration into the classroom of "subversive" materials.[8] The simultaneous existence of these deeply divisive issues pitted liberals against conservatives and thrust public education into a maelstrom of political activity. In their efforts to exact ideological control over the schools, liberals and conservatives appeared at each other's throats. School board elections became bruising, dramatic, and at times, vicious events, and intense political battles characterized the period.

As historian Don E. Carleton has shown, a significant feature of these political battles was the reflexive and extremely effective use of red scare tactics and methods by Houston's power elite, patriotic organizations, and conservative media. In a concerted campaign to discredit educators and liberal opponents, right wing groups frequently alleged charges of subversion and "socialist infiltration" of the schools. Unfortunately for George Ebey, the newly appointed deputy superintendent of the schools, he stepped into this highly charged and intensely politicized educational environment. As a supporter of racial integration, as former president of the American Veterans Committee, as a member of the Urban League, and as a denouncer of teacher loyalty oaths, Ebey conveniently was portrayed as a controversial figure, and his liberal beliefs made him an easy target for red scare attack.[9] Accordingly, following the political right's lengthy, vocal, and often unscrupulous attack on his character and suitability, the Houston school board decided on July 15, 1953, not to renew his contract. The board's decision reflected another important victory for the city's reactionary forces and, more important, demonstrated the enormous power of the red scare on the American political scene in the early 1950s.

The second reason why the Defense Commission's investigation in Houston appeared important related to its historical timing. Significantly, in the summer of 1953, at a time when several contemporary commentators, including officers of the Defense Commission, believed that the worst of the red scare to be over, the Ebey affair surfaced as a dramatic and shocking slap in the face. Published in December 1954, the Defense Commission investigation of Houston starkly illustrated that the red scare was very much alive. The Houston investigation report demonstrated how a devoted and highly regarded educational professional effectively could be overthrown by anti-communist forces. Indeed, the situation in Houston graphically emphasized to educators throughout the nation the profound and continuing menace of the red scare.

Finally, the Defense Commission's investigation of Houston remains noteworthy because it revealed striking parallels with the situation that occurred in Pasadena two years earlier. Both communities became embroiled in ideological conflicts that surrounded the use of identified instructional materials and teaching methods. Both communities became deeply affected by aggressive red scare campaigns principally mounted by right wing organizations, such as the Committee for Sound American Education and the Minute Women in Houston and Pro-America, and by the School Development Council in . Moreover, citizens in both communities appeared persuaded by the propaganda of national red scare organizations, such as Allen A. Zoll's National Council for American Education.

In Houston, as in Pasadena, powerful right-wing business interests and conservative newspapers manipulated and fueled the crisis mentality of the red scare. Decisive political elements in the two cities also shared a reactionary loathing of moves toward the racial integration of the schools or the re-zoning of the school district to ensure a more racially integrated society.[10] In addition, the red scare in Houston and in Pasadena drove educators to self-censorship, restricted the creative energies of many teachers, and profoundly impacted classroom practice.[11] Finally, despite evidence that no subversive activity existed in either school district, in both cities the promising careers of two prominent school administrators, George Ebey and Willard Goslin, abruptly were ended.[12]

The situation as uncovered and portrayed by the Defense Commission in its investigations of both Houston and Pasadena also revealed remarkable similarities. In both cases, the commission became alerted to the crises through appeals from educator and teacher associations at the local and state level. In both cases, the commission established a committee of investigators to explore the local situation first hand. In both cases, following a detailed examination, the commission prepared an objective report, which both identified the cause of local discontentment and established a set of firm recommendations for the improvement of the school environment in the two trouble spots. Close examination of the Defense Commission's investigative work in Pasadena, therefore, not only serves as a useful model for analyzing the commission's treatment of the red scare in the two cities specifically investigated by the commission, but it also offers insight into other communities in which red scare activity likely occurred.

The Pasadena Investigation

"Goslin Out!" screamed the headline of *The Pasadena Independent* on Wednesday, November 22, 1950. This newspaper's unsympathetic treatment revealed the forced resignation of the city's school superintendent, Willard Goslin, and marked it as one of the most significant educational events of the red scare era. It sent shock waves throughout the education profession, and it "provided headline copy all over the nation."[13] To activists on the political right, Goslin's sensational removal signaled victory against the perceived evils of liberalism and progressivism and further represented the ascendancy of conservative forces in American culture at mid-century. To liberal educators, Goslin's fateful demise signified the awesome power of the red scare and portended nervous and intimidating times ahead.

In the summer of 1948, when Goslin arrived in Pasadena to take up his new post as the superintendent of schools little sign of the impending crisis existed. Goslin went to California with an impressive reputation and a proven track record. He had been a principal when he was only twenty-two. He had served as an effective superintendent in St. Louis and Minneapolis. Additionally, as president of the American Association of School Administrators, he enjoyed national prestige. Accordingly, in their search to replace the departing superintendent, John Sexson, members of the Pasadena Board of Education recognized Goslin as the ideal candidate and aggressively recruited him for the position. His appointment to the highly desirable superintendency was greeted with much enthusiasm and widespread approval. Indeed, the Defense Commission report on Pasadena noted, "Few superintendents have enjoyed a more hearty welcome than that which Pasadena gave to Dr. Goslin."[14]

Goslin's honeymoon period, however, proved short lived. In less than a year his actions raised eyebrows of suspicion among some community factions. By the spring of 1950, the politically charged climate in Pasadena propelled the superintendent into a storm of controversy that ultimately led to his downfall.

Goslin was appointed superintendent of schools in Pasadena in the summer of 1948. Over the next two years, he tackled many of the school district's pressing problems. In the fall and summer of 1949-50, he introduced a gradual program of in-service education for teachers and organized a well-supported teacher summer workshop. In April 1950, he published plans to build new school facilities and to re-zone the existing school attendance areas. In June 1950, he attempted to address the serious financial underfunding of Pasadena's schools through a local tax election. However, as Goslin's design for Pasadena's schools unfolded, he deeply offended the political and racial sensibilities of many influential Pasadenans. Specifically, his attempts both to re-zone the district and, thereby, racially integrate community schools and to raise local taxes to support public education met with a storm of criticism from powerful business interests and patriotic groups. Throughout the spring and summer of 1950, the Goslin administration endured bitter attack. Consequently, on June 2, 1950, it suffered an alarming defeat in the local school-tax election. Buoyed by their election success, Pasadena's right-wing forces then targeted Goslin and repeatedly called for his dismissal. On November 15 and 16, the California Senate Committee on Education investigated alleged subversive infiltration in Pasadena's schools and further damned Goslin's leadership. This investigation substantially added to the mounting chorus of red scare criticism. The school board asked him to resign, and, on November 21, 1950, he duly acceded to the demand.

The reasons for Goslin's downfall became the subject of contemporary debate. On one side of the argument stood a clutch of individuals who contended that the Pasadena controversy had more to do with politics than pedagogy. Archibald Anderson, for example, noted that the Pasadena school district's "excellent testing program showed a record of solid achievement over a period of 19 years." He believed that attacks on the schools were not motivated by genuine concerns about educational standards, but by the exigencies of unscrupulous political forces.[15] The most famous contemporary exposure of red scare attack was authored by journalist David Hulburd. His book, *This Happened in Pasadena*, appeared shortly after the debacle and unreservedly pointed an accusatorial finger at "certain forces vicious, well organized, and coldly calculating" who "would like to change the face of education in the United States."[16] James B. Conant, former President of Harvard University agreed. In an article published in April 1951, he noted that "certain reactionary forces...hostile to public education seem clearly to have been at work."[17]

On the other side of the debate appeared individuals who contended that Goslin's removal simply underscored the determination of Pasadenans to rid their schools of an unacceptable educational philosophy. These critics concluded that, troubled by the perceived excesses of progressive education, concerned parents rose up to dismiss an unwelcome influence. Frank Chodorov's article, "Educators Should Be Warned by the Pasadena Revolt," which appeared in the *Saturday Evening Post,* forcefully advanced this line of argument. He noted the undeniable "socialistic character" of progressive education that, he alleged, prepared pupils merely to be a "cog for the social machine." "These ideas" Chodorov asserted, "did not set too well with many parents; they held the notion that schools were for the teaching of the three R's and some other subjects which their children might find more helpful."[18] In a similar vein, John B. Sheerin argued that Goslin's fate resulted not from any red scare conspiracy, but from widespread parental disaffection and a "swelling chorus of genuine criticism." Sheerin's argument was further corroborated by Hugh Russell Fraser. Fraser claimed that educators who argued that attacks were motivated by red scare propagandists like Allen A. Zoll amounted to "drivel."[19] Confidently he asserted that "Zoll had no more to do with what happened in Pasadena than the flowers that bloom in May" and reasoned that educators should take the criticism seriously and not attempt "to shift the blame elsewhere."

Several educational historians also have sought to explain the reasons behind Goslin's denouement. Scholars, such as John Beineke and Arthur Zilversmit, persuasively argue that political, and not educational, motivations lay behind the attacks on his administration. In contrast, Diane Ravitch and, to some extent, Lawrence Cremin attribute Goslin's downfall to the seemingly growing chasm between progressive educators and the general public. "What happened in Pasadena," Ravitch claims, "revealed an extraordinary lack of understanding between professional educators and a significant number of the lay public."[20]

Unquestionably, the reasons for Goslin's forced resignation are complex. The Defense Commission's detailed analysis of the controversy, for example, concluded that the "Pasadena crisis was not the result of any one, two, or three causes; but the result of a concatenation of events, personalities, and pressures that seemed to lead inexorably to the tragic conclusions." In truth, some blame reasonably may be attributed to the Goslin administration. The Defense Commission's investigation, for example, questioned the discretion of some of Goslin's key appointments, his apparent aloofness from the press, his lack of "personal contact with the influential people in the community,"[21] and the timing of some of his most critical decisions.[22] Yet, despite these apparent shortcomings in Goslin's administrative style and actions, overwhelming evidence existed to conclude that the controversy occurred not as the result of deep public disaffection with the schools, but rather as the result of intense and destructive red scare activity.

When Goslin first arrived in Pasadena, he stepped into one of the nation's most attractive and prosperous communities. According to David Hulburd, the three key characteristics of this "city on the Arroyo" essentially were that it was "rich, reactionary, and Republican."[23] For many citizens, any change appeared both unnecessary and unwelcome. Unfortunately for Goslin, he inherited significant educational problems that required immediate attention and, thereby, made some change inevitable.

In the immediate post-war years, the population of Pasadena soared from 80,000 to 112,000. The community experienced a period of rapid transformation. War-time industrial development in the area led to an influx of thousands of "people from other parts of the country, including Negroes, Mexicans, Chinese, and Japanese, all of lower economic status." The Defense Commission report noted that this change that "had all occurred in about six or eight years...seemed to constitute a serious threat to the status quo."[24] The dramatic rise and shift in population presented the Goslin school administration with serious problems in need of resolution.

First and foremost, new school buildings urgently were required to meet the escalating demand for school places. Initially, Goslin succeeded in securing a $5 million bond issue from Pasadena's citizens. However, as time passed, and as school leaders recognized that more money would be required, many community leaders proved exceedingly reluctant to support school-tax increases.

The problem further was exacerbated by Goslin's April 1950 proposal to coordinate the school building program with the re-structuring of existing school attendance zones. The plan disallowed white parents from enrolling their children in schools in "neutral zones" with predominantly white students. Instead, school districts were determined by geography, and not race. Neutral zones were eliminated and, irrespective of race, children were to attend their local schools. In essence, the plan called for the racial integration of Pasadena's schools. This decision both offended and outraged the racial proclivities of many white Pasadenans.[25] Throughout the spring of 1950, therefore, influential community leaders and right wing organizations rallied to defeat the school-tax increases and, by extension, the desegregation of city schools. Significantly, their vicious campaign to defeat the Goslin proposal bore all the hallmarks of classic red scare attack.

Vocal, well-organized, and generously financed opposition to Goslin stemmed chiefly from three organizations: the School Development Council (SDC), the Real Estate Board, and the Pasadena chapter of Pro-America. These groups attacked the superintendent with familiar red scare charges. Goslin's interest in camping, the United Nations, and better human relations, for example, maliciously were interpreted as subversive attempts to indoctrinate children in communism. Moreover, these right-wing groups further described the schools as godless institutions that failed to teach the 3 R's, lacked discipline, and actively sought to undermine parental influence.

The fog of red scare rhetoric and activity conveniently allowed to be forgotten the Real Estate Board's actual concern that property values might tumble as a result of re-zoning. Similarly, the unsubstantiated allegations of Pro-America and the SDC proved remarkably effective in undermining public confidence in the Goslin administration and thereby maintaining the ascendancy of Pasadena's well-organized, well-financed, and well-established reactionary elite.

Progressive education appeared as a particularly obvious target for concerted red scare attack. Right wing critics argued that Goslin's support for the "pernicious educational philosophy of progressivism" amounted to nothing more than an attempt to indoctrinate students in the evils of socialism. As evidence, they pointed to Pasadena's invitation to renowned progressive educator William Heard Kilpatrick to attend a workshop in the summer of 1949.[26] Despite overwhelming historical evidence to the contrary, critics widely publicized the allegation that Kilpatrick was a "known communist sympathizer" and a danger to Pasadena's children.[27] Significantly, during Kilpatrick's visit, and in the months immediately thereafter, little public criticism of him surfaced. Not without coincidence, however, once ideological swords were drawn in the spring of 1950, red scare critics made dramatic reference to Kilpatrick's allegedly destructive influence. Not for the first time anti-communist forces made effective use of past events to advance current political arguments.

Considerable evidence also existed to suggest that anti-Goslin forces impressively were aided by national red scare organizations.[28] The SDC, for example, used materials produced by the Sons of the American Revolution and pamphlets published by extremists, such as Augustin J. Rudd and Allen A. Zoll. Zoll's propaganda leaflets, "Progressive Education Increases Delinquency" and "They Want Your Child," were widely circulated. One representative of the SDC, who stated that she also was a member of Zoll's national organization, "cited the NCAE as the source of most of the information concerning 'progressive' education and its proponents in America."[29] The most conclusive evidence of Zoll's influence in Pasadena was Ernest Brower's admission to the California Senate Investigating Committee that the SDC had used Zoll materials in the June tax election. Unashamedly, Brower, President of the SDC, further added that "we thoroughly agreed with the contents of the pamphlet [Progressive Education Increases Delinquency], and we felt that it would be proper literature for us to use at our meetings, and I think we still think so."[30]

In a fashion characteristic of red scare attacks in other American communities, conservative political leaders and right wing groups in Pasadena also enjoyed extensive support from the local press. Although, of the city's two principal newspapers, *The Pasadena Independent* appeared more aggressive in its animus toward the Goslin administration, the traditional *Pasadena Star News* also assisted powerful conservative groups in effectively attacking the schools. Significantly, fierce criticism of education in Pasadena reached its peak in the few weeks preceding the tax levy election of June 2, 1950. At this time the *Independent* became almost a mouthpiece of the SDC, and the *Pasadena Star News* similarly began to accord increased attention to those who vilified the schools.[31]

Local confidence in public schools also was undermined by a collection of articles featured in the *Los Angeles Herald Express* entitled "What's Wrong with the Schools?" and by a biting and intensely critical six-part series written in the *Los Angeles Times* by journalist John Copeland in May 1950.[32] Likely these newspapers proved an extremely significant factor in destroying public support for the schools in the June tax election. As their primary source of information, citizens of Pasadena depended on the local press for reliable and intelligent news and comment. Thus, despite the fact that Pasadena's newspapers appeared as servants of a conservative elite who repeatedly leveled red scare charges against the schools, their charges often were treated as fact. In the spring and summer of 1950, therefore, red scare accusations reported in the press proved immensely influential both in discrediting the public schools and in irrevocably tarnishing the reputation of superintendent Willard Goslin.

Not without coincidence, on November 15, 1950, six days before Goslin resigned his position, the California Senate Committee on Education convened in to investigate alleged subversive infiltration of the schools. Chaired by redoubtable anti-communist Nelson Dilworth, the committee seriously questioned the subversive nature of the Goslin administration and further fueled public suspicion. The committee was far from neutral in its political agenda. It arrived in Pasadena at the behest of Bruce A. Reagan, a known member of SDC, and Louise Hawkes Padelford, founder of the local chapter of Pro-America and daughter of rabid anti-communist ex-Senator Albert Hawkes of New Jersey.[33] Significantly, the evening before the hearings began, Dilworth Committee members allegedly "were dined and entertained by School Development Council and Pro-America members."[34]

Held in the Pasadena City Hall, with members of the SDC occupying the first three rows, the investigation appeared far from objective in its procedures. One member of the School Development Council, who also was a member of the state legislature, even freely interrogated witnesses. In contrast, thirty teachers subpoenaed to attend the investigation were forced to sit in silence while attacks on the schools poured forth.[35] The investigation proved a perfect platform to castigate the school superintendent. Goslin was branded a communist because of his connections with UNESCO and the National Conference of Christians and Jews.[36] In addition, the committee claimed that "the communists were attempting to use the controversy to their own advantage," and pointedly objected to "the subjection of teachers" to "the doctrines of visiting lecturers who have long communist affiliations."[37]

The Dilworth Committee's unforgiving red scare attack marked the final chapter in Goslin's dramatic fall from power. Despite the fact that Pasadena the school curriculum had not significantly changed since 1931, that no evidence of subversive acts in the schools was uncovered, that the vast majority of parents and teachers supported the superintendent, and that educational standards had improved under Goslin's leadership, the relentless red scare campaign against the superintendent proved devastatingly effective.[38] resigned his position on November 21, 1950.

The Pasadena Investigation: An Evaluation

The Defense Commission's stance on the Pasadena controversy reflected its profound concern over the deepening crisis, its active and determined response to it, and its ultimate failure significantly to alter its dramatic outcome. However, to employ the benefit of historical hindsight to judge the Defense Commission's actions too harshly perhaps is unfair. Indeed, in many respects, the Defense Commission achieved a great deal by its investigation.

When telegram requests flooded the NEA from leaders of prominent education associations in California for an urgent investigation of the Pasadena school conflict, the Defense Commission acted expeditiously. The first telegram requests reached the desk of Willard Givens, NEA

Executive Secretary, on November 16, 1950. After securing the cooperation and approval of the American Association of School Administrators, quickly informed Arthur F. Corey, Executive Secretary of the California Teachers' Association, Herbert C. Clish, Chairman of the Professional Standards Committee in California, Harold B. Brooks, Executive Secretary of the California Association of Secondary School Administrators, and Superintendent Willard Goslin of the decision immediately to send Defense Commission Field Secretary Robert Skaife to Pasadena.[39] Skaife arrived on Monday, November 20, 1950.

Upon arrival, Skaife urgently attempted to persuade Goslin not to resign. He failed. The following day, from his hotel room in Pasadena, Skaife wrote to Richard Barnes Kennan at the NEA headquarters in Washington, D.C.:

> resigned this afternoon — made a wonderful statement and exhibited a professional spirit and grandeur which few men in such a position could do. I attended the board meeting — there was quite a crowd and very few dry eyes.[40]

Skaife's letter and his subsequent correspondence indicated his grave concern with the situation in Pasadena. Skaife noted that the Pasadena school board had "been under terrific pressure from the School Development Council and Pro-America to 'purge' Dr. Goslin," that at the heart of the situation lay "subversiveness from the right," and that an "investigation should be made."

To the Defense Commission's credit, its officers acted promptly. Within days, an experienced investigating committee of educators was established to analyze the Pasadena situation. The team comprised of W. Howard Pillsbury, former superintendent of schools, Schenctady, New York, and former President of the AASA; George Roudebush, former superintendent of schools, Columbus, Ohio; and Alice Latta, representative of the and high school teacher from Couer d'Alene, Idaho. The committee flew to California on December 10, 1950, and joined Skaife in Pasadena's Hotel Constance.

The three members of the investigating committee agreed with Robert Skaife that the case constituted educational importance beyond Pasadena. Kennan wrote to Skaife, "You are certainly handling one of the most important cases that has come up for the Defense Commission since its inception. There's a lot at stake, and I have full confidence that you will do a swell job."[41] Similarly NEA Executive Secretary Givens wrote to the chairman of the committee, W. Howard Pillsbury:

I appreciate your willingness to serve as chairman of a committee to study and report upon the present public school situation in Pasadena, California....We believe that this report will serve public education well throughout the United States. The same forces that are at work in Pasadena are at work in many other communities throughout our nation.[42]

In their investigation, Pillsbury, Roudebush, and Latta remained in Pasadena for a little over a week. During their stay, they worked feverishly both to analyze and to evaluate the situation in the school district. Their actions principally were guided by a series of ten questions posed by Willard Givens in his letter to Pillsbury:

1. Is it true that two of the Board members yielded to the pressure of outside organized groups in requesting Goslin's resignation? If so, what were the groups, and why did they want Goslin to resign?
2. Is there evidence of collaboration with groups unfriendly to education in other cities?
3. Was there evidence of participation in the Pasadena affair by anti-Semitic, anti-Negro, and anti-public school zealots?
4. Had the racial issue been openly injected, or was it the basis of a whispering campaign?
5. Was any teaching in the Pasadena schools actually un-American?
6. Was Communism being taught? Was socialism being taught? Was the teaching of the three R's and other so-called fundamentals being done effectively?
7. Was there a serious rift in the school system as alleged?
8. Was the opposition in the Goslin affair inspired by mistaken attitudes and errors of judgment by the superintendent, or is there evidence that these groups have been active in opposition to the school program before?
9. To what extent did agencies with printed materials and propaganda services to sell enter the situation in Pasadena following Goslin's arrival?
10. Does it appear that the organized opposition was merely interested in the discharge of Superintendent Goslin or was the attack on the superintendent merely a cloak for the hidden objective of controlling the Pasadena public school program?

To understand more fully the local situation, the committee met with school teachers, members of the press, educational administrators, community leaders, parents, and representatives of local citizens' organizations.

Field Secretary Skaife assisted them throughout this period and stayed in Pasadena until December 21, 1950. Skaife worked in difficult circumstances. In interviews, some members of the community were openly hostile to him, candidly objecting to the NEA's apparent interference in local affairs.[43] As a result of the sensitive political climate, other citizens and educators appeared cautious in the amount of information they were prepared to reveal to the field secretary. Skaife's personal situation also was far from ideal. He worked out of a hotel room for more than a month and, sometimes, grew frustrated by his predicament. His wife also appeared "upset" by his "long absence." Indeed, in December, Kennan wrote to Skaife, that "I hope she won't influence you to leave the Defense Commission for it seems to me you're doing an exceptionally good job...."[44]

In the first months of 1951, Skaife regularly corresponded with members of the committee as the Pasadena report gradually took shape. A draft document was discussed in February 1951, and, in the months which followed, many prominent individuals in the NEA read and commented upon the original draft, which principally was written by Pillsbury.[45] The final 40-page report, "The Pasadena Story: An Analysis of Some Forces and Factors That Injured a Superior School System," was published in June 1951.

Although some citizens and commentators objected to the final report, it was generally well received in educational circles. For example, Ole Lilleland, the NEA's Director for California, wrote to Skaife that he sincerely hoped,

> ...you Kennan and Snow realize how much we in Pasadena feel the grave debt we owe to the Defense staff and the commission as a whole for not only the excellent job on the Pasadena story, but for your continued support and interest. You have served as an excellent 'safety valve.'[46]

Similarly, George A. Bowman, President of Kent State University, wrote to Pillsbury that he and his committee had "rendered a service to the public schools." He continued,

> The Pasadena story becomes an anchorage for those who have been confused by the many conflicting currents of expression. Your committee has reported to the nation in a most statesman like way and always with high integrity and unemotionally.[47]

Essentially, the report identified the principal factors that impacted the educational climate in Pasadena: the city's changing demographics, the pressures brought about by the urgent need for increased financial support for education, the influence of politically right-wing forces, the role of the media, the administrative success and failures of Goslin's leadership, the involvement of outside organizations, and the actions of the school board.

It concluded that Goslin's dismissal and the deterioration of harmonious relations in the school district resulted from a combination of these factors and not from a singular cause.[48]

Unquestionably, however, the investigating committee both sympathized and empathized with Goslin and his administration. It understood the many problems the superintendent faced when he assumed responsibility for the city's schools in 1948, and it acknowledged the enormous pressures placed upon him by "unreasonable" community forces. Thus, despite the fact that many American educators remained unnerved by the Goslin episode, they appreciated the way in which the Defense Commission revealed the destructive influences of politically motivated forces within the community.

The Defense Commission investigation also served three other important functions. First, it raised the spirits and morale of some American teachers and administrators. For example, from 1950 to 1951, a steady stream of correspondence between members of the teaching profession and Defense Commission staff revealed the appreciation of local educators for the commission's involvement in Pasadena. In excessively difficult and repressive times, the commission acted as a great source of defense and comfort to many professional educators.[49] Second, *The Pasadena Story* offered educators throughout the country an example of how local attacks, if unchecked, easily could result in highly destructive consequences. The report, therefore, alerted American teachers and administrators to the importance of responding effectively to reactionary forces in the community, to improved public relations, and to greater administrative competency.

Significantly, the Defense Commission's investigation pointed the way forward. It urged educators to become more directly involved in forging positive community relations. Also, it implored reasonable citizens to take greater interest in public education. The final page of *The Pasadena Story* noted the early progress made in this regard. It reported the union of Pasadena's Citizens' Action Committee and the Committee on Public Education (COPE) and optimistically remarked,

> If these forces are widely used, if a lively public interest in the schools can be consistently maintained under strong leadership, the schools cannot only recover the lost ground, but even advance to further heights. They will then be in a truly stronger position with their program based on widespread public understanding and support.[50]

To the Defense Commission's credit, it played an important role in advising and liaising with these citizens' groups. COPE's Executive Secretary, Elizabeth Purcell, and the Defense Commission's Robert Skaife regularly corresponded and shared considerable information on local and national developments.[51] The Pasadena schools gradually recuperated from the excesses of the Goslin debacle. In 1951, a local tax election passed by a vote of 16,288 to 7,097, and the considerable influence of red scare groups appeared to diminish. More than a year after Goslin's departure Henry Troy Jr., director of the NCCPS, visited Pasadena and reported,

> The new spirit in Pasadena was a genuine feeling of community pride and community responsibility. The citizens were starting to work out their problems, and they were sitting down with the school personnel, looking at the facts and working for a mutually satisfactory school program.[52]

The Defense Commission's work in Pasadena likely had some unacknowledged impact on the community's improved educational situation. It provided local citizen's groups with literature and advice on how best to organize an effective force to support the schools. It identified serious problems in the community, and it somewhat helped to calm a potentially explosive situation. It stood by local teachers in difficult times, and it held out the possibility of a brighter future. Above all, it shone the spotlight on a community troubled by excessive criticism and illuminated to educators throughout the nation the political motivations behind the attacks. In many respects, therefore, the Defense Commission's work in Pasadena deserves considerable credit and attention.

Still, despite these positive accomplishments, the Defense Commission proved deficient in many important areas. Of note, the commission's Robert Skaife clearly misread and misunderstood the signs of an impending crisis when he undertook his preliminary investigation of Pasadena in late June 1950. At the request of local educational leaders, Skaife visited Pasadena soon after the stunning tax election defeat of June 2, 1950.[53] The field secretary spent a week in the city examining the local situation.

Although Skaife noted with concern that some individuals appeared politically motivated and demonstrated "a closed mind and an antagonistic attitude," he underestimated the influence of other salient red scare forces in Pasadena. For example, on June 26, in a letter to Superintendent Goslin, he observed that the failed tax-election resulted from a combination of factors most important of which was the administration's failure effectively to convey the importance of the tax increase to the success of local schools. Revealingly, Skaife further noted that, although he was at first troubled by "anti-school propaganda," he reached the conclusion that he "was unduly troubled by it."[54] As a result, Skaife did not believe the situation in Pasadena in June 1950 to be serious or important enough to recommend a full Defense Commission investigation.

In contrast, when Skaife returned to Pasadena six months later he was so disturbed by the local situation that he immediately recommended a full investigation. In correspondence to other NEA members, he noted the dramatic and destructive impact of right wing political forces.[55] By the time Skaife arrived in Pasadena for the second time, however, the damage already had been done. Four days before his arrival, the board requested Goslin's resignation. The Defense Commission's subsequent attention to Pasadena during the winter of 1950-51, therefore, obscures its failure to act decisively in the crucial months between the tax election in June and Goslin's removal in November.

Legitimate questions also may be asked of the Defense Commission's apparent failure to uncover the core of the educational crisis in Pasadena. The committee's conclusion that a concatenation of events and causes combined to create the school controversy submerged the important and dramatic impact of red scare attack. Its conclusions, which apportioned part of the blame to the Goslin administration and to a multiplicity of other causes, significantly diluted the very real impact of and activities in .

The Defense Commission firmly, and somewhat naively, believed that it could comment objectively on educational events in Pasadena. As such, the officers of the commission frequently paid more attention to the creation of an image of neutrality than on an attempt to exorcise the truth. For example, while compiling its final report, the committee appeared conscious of the need not to offend overtly some community interests and to avoid contentious statements or viewpoints that "might be considered libelous."[56] Simply, the commission's officers appeared substantially more concerned about the red scare menace than the final report suggested.[57]

From its inception in 1941, the Defense Commission claimed that investigations were designed for two purposes. First, they perform a preventative function and, thereby, served to quell an identified local crisis. Second, they performed a curative function and, accordingly, "suggest constructive measures for improving the local situation and remedying irritating or bad conditions."[58] The actions of the Defense Commission in

Pasadena reveal that it certainly failed to prevent an educational crisis from building in the city. It also failed to dampen the burning problems that already existed.

True, by 1951 the immediate problems that brought down the administration appeared to abate as local citizens' groups became more active in their support of public schools. However, red scare activities, unquestionably, left deep and lasting wounds: Goslin lost his job. One administrator, demoted as a result of the Pasadena affair, collapsed and died, probably as a result of the strain he was put under by the relentless attacks on his character.[59] Other administrators and teachers nervously feared the end of their professional careers as a result of political reprisals. Pasadena teachers also engaged in widespread self-censorship, and the school curriculum, undoubtedly, was affected.

An evaluation of the overall effectiveness of the Defense Commission in Pasadena remains problematic. Certainly, the commission may be faulted for underestimating the influence of red scare activity in the city in the summer of 1950. It also may be criticized for concentrating enormous attention on Pasadena only after Goslin's dismissal in November, at a time when much damage to education already had been done. However, whether or not the Defense Commission, through educator-lay conferences, through vigorous public relations activities, or through an earlier investigation, could have prevented the fury of red scare attack remains open to conjecture. At best, the commission enjoyed only scarce resources and limited personnel. In reality, in the rarefied political climate of the early 1950s, the commission's ability significantly to blunt organized red scare attack appeared minimal. Ultimately, what happened in Pasadena revealed more about the irresistible power of the red scare than it did about the apparent ineffectiveness of the Defense Commission.

Chapter X

The Defense Commission
Versus the Educational Red Scare

By the mid-1950s, the worst days of the post-World War II red scare appeared over. McCarthy had been censured by the U. S. Senate, the Korean War had ended, the Rosenbergs had been executed, the Republicans controlled the White House, and Stalin was dead. Not without coincidence, once the flames of red scare frenzy diminished on the national and international scenes, so too they abated in the theater of American education. "We do know," remembered William Van Til, "that by the mid-1950s McCarthy was stripped of power and the educational McCarthyites disappeared locally into obscurity, at least for the time being."[1] The Defense Commission increasingly became optimistic that the reactionary storm had been weathered. In its 1954 report to the NEA, for example, it proudly boasted,

> Some of the individuals who seemed to be most active in developing, inciting, and encouraging destructive criticism of public education became less active and less effective during the 1953-54 academic year. Lucille C. Crain, who edited a leaflet of 'purported' reviews of textbooks, announced that her periodical has ceased publication. Amos A. Fries, one of the first to issue bitter tirades against the leadership of the teaching profession in his bulletin, 'Friends of the Public Schools,' has not been heard of for more than eight months. Allan Zoll [sic] has not interfered in a school trouble spot in nearly a year.[2]

However, although the Defense Commission took comfort in the apparent calm in the red scare storm, the tranquillity offered little cause for celebration. The red scare, which proved a particularly virulent force between 1947 and 1954, already had inflicted deep and serious wounds on American public education. Assessing the overall impact of the red scare on education in American schools is fraught with historical problems. Although explicit evidence indicates that as a result of political reprisal, educators were dismissed, curriculum materials were suppressed, educational policy was altered, the red scare, undoubtedly, possessed a hidden dimension. Essentially, the anti-communist ferment of the post-war period created a climate of repression. This climate, was an amorphous, intangible atmosphere; it often resulted in subtle, but no less dramatic, damage to public education. Unquestionably, teachers were dismissed as a result of red scare attack, but how many were fired is open to conjecture. Some teachers, frequently vulnerable for lack of tenure security, likely were released by school boards for political, not educational, reasons. However, because these actions received little publicity and remain undocumented, the real impact of the red scare on school employment practices is difficult to assess.[3] That even a few teachers were dismissed, on the other hand, contributed a deadening aspect to the educational climate of the period.

Similar problems exist in attempting to discern the nature and extent of teacher self-censorship. Certainly, evidence exists to suggest that some teachers consciously decided to eliminate controversial topics, to prune course syllabi, and to avoid the use of certain instructional materials. Documentary evidence that informs precisely how many teachers succumbed to the political pressures of the period, how frequently, and to what extent, routinely remain elusive. Furthermore, to gauge the extent to which educators unconsciously yielded to the prevailing anti-communist mindset is impossible to quantify. Ellen Schrecker encountered this same historical problem in her study of McCarthyism in higher education. Revealingly, she noted,

> Anecdotes abound, but the full extent to which American scholars censored themselves is hard to gauge. There is no sure way to measure the books that were not written, the courses that were not taught, and the research that was never undertaken.[4]

Uncovering evidence that details the personal wounds inflicted by the red scare on American educators poses additional problems for historians.

Certainly, evidence does exist that portrays the crushing experience and profound anguish of some individuals. However, how many teachers left the profession as a result of attack, how frequently educators retreated to their homes frustrated by unwarranted criticism and accusation, and how deeply affected teachers were by the political situation remains open to speculation. As historian John Beineke contended, "the personal and professional toll suffered by academics and the nation's schools from assaults at this time may never be known."[5]

Despite these apparent historical deficiencies, a body of evidence exists to suggest that the red scare had a profound influence on many elements of American public school education in the immediate post-war era. Most important, the red scare explicitly claimed the dismissal of hundreds of educators in communities across the nation. Historian David Caute, for example, calculates that more than 600 educators lost their jobs as a result of anti-communist political purges, 380 in New York City alone.[6] Furthermore, in cities, like Houston and Pasadena, where the Defense Commission shone its investigative spotlight, graphic evidence of the use of red scare methods to remove liberal educators starkly was apparent. Political purges impacted all sectors of the profession. From prominent educational leaders, such as Willard Goslin and George Ebey, to dedicated classroom teachers, such as Frances Eisenberg and Blanche Bettington, the red scare claimed many victims.[7] Although the circumstances of the many documented and undocumented teacher dismissals certainly remain tragic, arguably the most troublesome aspect of the period was the political and educational climate they induced. As Robert Hutchins noted in 1954, "The question is not how many teachers have been fired, but how many think they might be...You don't have to fire many teachers to intimidate them all. The entire teaching profession of the U. S. is intimidated."[8]

The red scare clearly stimulated fear and anxiety among thousands of educators throughout the United States. In an emotionally charged political climate fueled by state and Congressional investigations, loyalty oaths, and extremist propaganda, teachers increasingly became intimidated. Although scores of teachers lost their jobs directly as a result of investigative probes, the indirect and broader consequences of these inquisitions arguably was more significant. Fear of being called before a state or Congressional committee, or of arbitrarily being labeled a communist in the press, or of being targeted for attack by reactionary groups exacted a heavy personal and professional toll on many educators throughout the nation.[9]

In Houston, for example, an independent survey of the city's teachers initiated by the Defense Commission illustrated an alarming atmosphere of fear and intimidation among the teaching profession. According to a survey analysis, 58% of the Houston teachers revealed,

> one or more persons or groups had exerted pressures on them to (a) support a political candidate, (b) slant some courses toward a certain political belief, (c) present only one side in discussing current events, (d) participate or refrain from participating in political, professional, or social activities.[10]

The debilitating impact on education as a result of such concerted political pressure further was illustrated by teachers' responses to other questions. For example, Houston's educators were asked to assess the consequences of expressing their personal "social or political actions or beliefs regardless of their skill or ability as teachers." In response, a staggering 48% feared that they would be transferred to a less desirable position, 44% expected to lose their job, 42% believed that they would be subject to "attack from non-school groups," and 42% envisaged facing "loss of reputation" as a result of "false charges."[11] Thus, although Deputy Superintendent George W. Ebey appeared as the sole victim of Houston's political reprisals, in reality the wounds from the educational controversy cut deeply and caused considerable damage to the confidence and freedom of a significant proportion of the city's teachers.

Even in those towns and cities in which red scare attacks seemingly were thwarted, the impact of attack left a telling and destructive legacy. For example, in Scarsdale, New York, in which right-wing political extremists ultimately suffered a humiliating election defeat, a considerable educational price was paid. "The morale of the whole school staff has been sharply lowered," remarked *McCall's* reporter John Bainbridge.

> Teachers are genuinely frightened lest they say or do something, not only in the classroom but in their social contacts, that might be interpreted by the critics' watchmen. On many occasions the teachers have found the very fact that they work in the Scarsdale schools makes them suspect in the eyes of certain new acquaintances. The infiltration of fear is bound to have a bad effect on the quality of instruction and, in addition, may well cause a newly graduated teacher to think twice before accepting a post in Scarsdale.[12]

The Scarsdale example, undoubtedly, was replicated in countless other communities throughout the United States. Some of the most dramatic examples of red scare intimidation, however, appeared in large urban areas such as Los Angeles, Philadelphia, Detroit, Houston, and New York.

David Caute's attention to the red scare's impact on New York City schools, for example, graphically illustrated the profound direct and indirect consequences of the anti-communist purges. Caute noted the acute and "contagious fear" experienced by many of the 58,000 employees of the Board of Education, the 447 teachers who experienced investigative trials first hand, and the dozens of suspended teachers who, because the Board of Education published their addresses, "suffered the miseries of obscene or threatening phone calls in the middle of night."[13] Not surprisingly, the red scare also affected important aspects of educational policy, practice, and philosophy.

Unequivocally, the wave of anti-communism that swept across American schools in the immediate post-war era seriously wounded progressive education and the progressive education movement. Whatever the merits or deficiencies of progressive education, two convictions appear certain. First, progressivism as expounded by liberal educators of the 1940s and 1950s, emphatically bore little resemblance to communism. Second, progressive education did not dominate the American educational scene in the immediate post-war era.[14]

Yet, despite this stark reality, critics effectively convinced many American citizens (a) that most schools were riddled with the capricious and anti-intellectual excesses of progressivism and (b) that progressivism was tantamount to collectivism and/or communism. Indeed, a salient feature of the period was the way in which virulent, relentless, and unforgiving attacks on progressive education so seriously undermined public confidence in the schools.[15] Educational historian Robert Iversen noted with considerable insight that red scare critics appreciated the simple genius of shifting attacks from particular individuals to the less specific realm of educational philosophy:

> The main targets for attack shifted from individuals with front records, who increasingly became hard to find, to the more general and intangible area of educational philosophy and 'atmosphere' about which almost anything could be said with some justification.[16]

The response of liberal educators to the avalanche of criticism that suffocated progressive education in this period also was very revealing.

Significantly, rather than to defend their progressive instincts, many educators chose to disassociate themselves with what they increasingly perceived to be at best a controversial, and at worst an explicitly un-American, educational philosophy. Routinely, educators went on the defensive. Teachers and administrators elected to use the term "modern" rather than "progressive" to reflect their educational position. Even the Progressive Education Association changed its name to the New Education Fellowship and then in 1955, "quietly disbanded."[17] Above all, red scare attacks on progressive education impacted school curriculum policy throughout the nation. Acutely aware that progressive education frequently aroused vigorous emotional opposition, teachers and administrators avoided invoking the term and adopted a more conservative, cautious, and traditional guise.

Accordingly, rather than devote energy to seemingly contentious issues such as "life adjustment education" and the "child centered curriculum," educators chose instead to champion publicly the 3 R's and what the NEA commonly referred to as the "fundamentals of instruction." For example, in his 1949 address to the public, Willard Givens, NEA Executive Secretary, informed citizens that,

> the amount of time spent in today's schools on the 3 R's is more than four times as great as it was a hundred years ago...The 3 R's are still the foundation of the school studies. Schools are teaching them better than they ever were taught.[18]

Throughout the early 1950s, therefore, in order to deflect criticism or not to offend parents, the NEA continued to attention to the "fundamentals of education," to patriotic sentiments, and to traditional subject disciplines.[19] This apparent shift toward a more conservative approach to schooling was simultaneously motivated by economic considerations. As a consequence of burgeoning financial pressures on American schools during the post-war era, many teachers and administrators additionally realized the need to appear innocent of controversial, and, thus, by extension, progressive methods.

At a time when thousands of schools suffered from dilapidated buildings, inadequate facilities, and overcrowded classrooms, educators could not afford to alienate tax-paying citizens.[20] As a consequence, in extensive public relations initiatives, educators frequently played down features of progressive education lest they be construed subversive, and vigorously emphasized the "3 R's," the "fundamentals," and loyalty to American traditions.[21] In no small measure, therefore, red scare critics consistently proved influential in undermining the progressive education movement, in shifting the school curriculum to the political right, and in placing teachers and administrators across the land squarely on the defensive.[22]

The red scare also seriously affected how, what, and why individual teachers elected to teach. Typically, anti-communist ferment induced widespread teacher self-censorship and profoundly affected educators' academic freedoms.[23] For example, according to the April 1954 issue of the *Defense Bulletin*, a NEA study of 522 school systems reported that, "American teachers are finding it increasingly difficult to consider controversial issues."[24] The following year a comprehensive study of thousands of educators in every state of the nation bar Rhode Island revealed that 13% of secondary school teachers and 15% of social studies teachers were subject to "increased pressures against freedom to learn" and, as a result, tended "to avoid discussion of controversial issues."[25]

Wary of being reported to the authorities for teaching issues considered subversive, educators the length and breadth of the country considered their choice of classroom subject matter very carefully.[26] Teachers' extreme caution was understandable considering that the range of topics considered controversial sometimes included consumer education, family life education, the brotherhood of man, peaceful solutions to international matters, the dignity of labor, and democratic human relations.[27] The experience of teachers in Englewood, New Jersey, exemplified those of scores of other communities.[28] As a result of concerted political pressure that bore all the hallmarks of classic red scare attack, journalist Arthur Morse noted a "subtle and distressing change creeping over Englewood." He reported, "Teachers [are] jittery." "They [are] afraid the open healthy discussion that had previously characterized their classes [will] somehow be misconstrued."[29]

In the climate of the red scare, teaching about the Soviet Union and communism appeared particularly risky, and many teachers chose to avoid the subject altogether. At the 1952 NEA assembly in Detroit, James Cullen, NEA delegate from New York, lamented, "the tendency on the part of some teachers to 'play safe' because of the fear of criticisms." He also remarked that "to avoid discussing Communism's dangerous goals is a disservice to the public schools and to this nation....I think that we should give every encouragement...to see that controversial issues are fairly and adequately discussed in every classroom in this nation."[30] His comments drew applause from the conference delegates, and the resolution was adopted without dissent by the association. In reality, however, teachers all over the country shunned topics considered controversial and often taught about the Soviet Union from a distinctly pro-Western and anti-communist perspective.

The prevailing anti-communist mood not only impacted how and what teachers taught, but it also affected the contents of the textbooks with which they taught. As a competitor in a multi-million dollar business, textbook publishers proved exceedingly cautious in their treatment of certain controversial topics. Fear of losing their stake in a profitable market drove publishers to appease red scare critics and to avoid subjects that might invite undue criticism. The result of such pressure, revealed William Spaulding, past President of the American Textbook Publishers Institute, "can be an enforced moratorium on all real progress in textbooks and in teaching, a demand only for what is considered 'safe,' and a colorless, conformist, watered-down brand of education that may bring us to disaster in a time of national crisis."[31]

The crucial need for administrators, school boards, and textbook committees to expend enormous amounts of time and considerable energy scrutinizing school textbooks illuminates another hidden, but very real consequence of red scare attack. At a time when administrators and school boards faced acute educational problems that required urgent attention, too often their focus needlessly was diverted to refuting unfounded and illegitimate criticism.[32]

Essentially, therefore, the red scare had a profound, dramatic, and persisting impact on American education. It affected how teachers taught, what they taught, why they taught, and, in some cases, if they taught. It affected the shape of the school curriculum, the use of instructional materials, and the content of school textbooks. In addition, it seriously impacted the efficacy of progressive education and the future direction of educational policy and practice. Accordingly, given the unquestionable influence of the red scare on American public schooling and given that the Defense Commission appeared as the teaching profession's principal defender, legitimately one may ask what affect, if any, did the commission have in blunting red scare attack in the immediate post-war period.

The Defense Commission: A Creature
of the Red Scare Age

A revealing feature of Defense Commission policy and activity was its frequent tendency to accept many of the "red scare's" underlying assumptions. To be sure, the Defense Commission was not an agency of counter-culture. It internalized the prevailing belief that a very real and dangerous communist threat existed both within and outside the United States. As such, it proved both a product and a fixture of the red scare era. The most graphic illustration of the stance of the Defense Commission and the National Education Association stemmed from the 1949 NEA conference resolution to exclude Communist Party members from the teaching profession.[33]

The question of whether or not a person could be both a member of the Communist Party and a responsible educator surfaced as one of the burning issues of the red scare. Conflicting opinions on the subject neatly were encapsulated in a debate in the *New York Times Magazine* between Sidney Hook and Alexander Meiklejohn following the dismissal of scholars at the University of Washington in 1949. Fundamentally, Hook took the position that any individual who declared allegiance to the Communist Party automatically renounced his right to academic freedoms. Being a communist, Hook reasoned, implied following the party line and prohibited academics from thinking for themselves. Accordingly, party membership was tantamount to the acceptance of thought control and served as *prima facie* evidence of academic incompetence.[34] In contrast, civil libertarian Alexander Meiklejohn argued that dismissals purely on the strength of Communist Party membership amounted to a serious violation of academic freedom. Moreover, he questioned the extent to which any academic truly was brainwashed and programmed by forces within the Kremlin.[35]

Despite Meiklejohn's inherent eloquence, support for his convictions proved exceptional. In the climate of the red scare most Americans, including most liberal academics, adopted Hook's position that an avowed communist had no place in the nation's schools or colleges. The NEA and the Defense Commission explicitly shared this argument. In July 1949, at the NEA annual conference in , the association passed a resolution specifying,

> Members of the Communist Party shall not be employed in the American schools. Such membership involves adherence to doctrines and disciplines completely inconsistent with the principles of freedom on which American education depends. Such membership and the accompanying surrender of intellectual integrity render an individual unfit to discharge the duties of a teacher in this country.[36]

The resolution stemmed from a comprehensive 54-page report drafted by the NEA's Educational Policies Commission. The report, entitled "American Education and International Tensions," was produced by a twenty-person commission chaired by John K. Norton of Teachers College, Columbia University and included James B. Conant, President of Harvard University, and Dwight D. Eisenhower, President of Columbia University.[37]
Norton's explanation of the main conclusions of the report drew enthusiastic support from the NEA delegation.[38] His address frequently was greeted with applause and at the point in which he spoke out against Communist Party members having the right to instruct "your child, my child, and the children of other local citizens,"[39] the convention accorded him a standing ovation.

The NEA leadership was particularly eager to use the report as a means to convince American citizens that the teaching profession was a fiercely loyal and patriotic group. Significantly, Norton remarked that "after most careful deliberation" the commission concluded,

> That a statement should be made which would leave no doubts in the minds of the public that American teachers have no sympathy with the ruthless, immoral, and anti-democratic movement — Russian communism — and that American teachers believe that a person who officially allies himself with this movement, representing as it does a challenge to everything which a free man holds dear, is not qualified to teach the children of a democracy.[40]

The NEA delighted in the popular approval that the report received in the media. More than 300 newspaper articles revealed overwhelming support from the policy statement with only the *Daily Worker* of New York City, an organ of the Communist Party, renunciating the resolution. Norton eagerly noted that the *Daily Worker*'s "rejection is perhaps our highest praise."[41]

The overwhelming acceptance of the 1949 resolution demonstrated the extent to which NEA members embraced the orthodoxy of anti-communism. In a revealing moment, at the 1953 annual meeting of the NEA in Miami Beach, a guest speaker, Walter F. Tunks, told a joke about the two rabbits in which one rabbit said to the other, "'I'm scared that McCarthy's going to investigate antelopes.' 'What are you afraid of?' said the other rabbit. 'You're not an antelope!' 'No,' said the first rabbit, 'but how can I prove it?'"[42] The joke drew laughter from the audience. The laughter, however, hid a stark and telling reality. By opposing communist teachers, the NEA and the Defense Commission embraced a paradoxical situation. On the one hand, the Defense Commission vowed to defend teachers. However, on the other hand, its adopted policy made extremely difficult the support of those accused of being a communist, often whether or not they were innocent.

In addition, the NEA's resolution to exclude Communist Party members from the teaching profession proved a mouthwatering invitation for the radical right. Simply, arch-conservatives realized that if progressive or liberal educators could be tainted with current or previous Communist Party affiliation, then they could be dismissed with ease. In this regard, Rose Russell, NEA delegate from New York recognized the resolution's potential danger to educators. As one of only a few NEA members openly to dissent from the association's adopted position, she argued that every teacher should be judged on his or her actions, not on his or her opinions or political beliefs. "We do know that there have been many dismissals," she asserted, on other political grounds and that is the danger that I wish to point out. Because once we open the door to this, we set a trap into which everybody may fall. Many have been dismissed for supporting Wallace, and the people at Olivet College in Michigan had no taint of Communism about them, but large numbers were dismissed. You cannot aim this bullet into a single bulls-eye and hit it, because as this gun is fired at alleged Communist Party members, it is going to intimidate large numbers of teachers and is going to put a weapon into the hands of every reactionary legislature, every reactionary chamber of commerce....You are going to give a weapon to those school officials who like to use the subterfuge of disloyalty when they want to get rid of active teachers who fight for better schools and higher salaries.[43]

Russell's warnings went unheeded. Amid the strident anti-communist fervor of the late 1940s, NEA members ardently believed that ridding the profession of communists was more important than protecting a seminal principle of academic freedom.

Red scare concerns also prompted many educators to teach about the Soviet Union in an extremely cautious manner. In fact, some teachers even avoided speaking about the Soviet Union in the classroom lest they be accused of favoring the communist foe. Those teachers who elected to inform students about Russia frequently did so in an explicitly prejudiced way. Certainly, many teachers throughout the United States tackled this sensitive subject with a considerable degree of unease. The Educational Policies commission aimed to clarify the NEA's position on this issue. It argued that teachers should teach about the Soviet Union and communism. However, "Teaching about communism," the commission's report asserted, "does not mean advocacy of these doctrines. Such advocacy should not be permitted in American schools."[44] Underpinning the argument of the Educational Policies commission was the belief that if students learned about communism "as a result of an objective exposure to the facts" America's youth would firmly reject the alien ideology. "We want, in other words, no behind the barn learning about this thing [Communism], we want it to be handled by loyal, competent, conscientious teachers."[45]

Despite the claim of NEA policy makers to teach about communism and the Soviet Union in an "objective" manner, members of the association clearly promoted the need to present the facts in a decidedly pro-American and anti-communist way. Typically, little or no attempt was made to understand the Cold War or historical or cultural events from a Russian perspective. Rather, as far as the NEA leadership was concerned, teaching about the Soviet Union meant exposing its inherent evils. Officers of the Defense Commission shared this conventional wisdom.[46] Ernest O. Melby, for example, argued that students needed to learn about communism in order to be alert to its corrupt propaganda:

> Communist propaganda is insidious, unscrupulous, and crafty. It cannot be met through ignorance, through naive dogmatism, or fallacious reasoning. Only people who have clear understanding, who are in possession of the facts, and who know the process of reasoning characteristic of both free society and communist societies can cope with propaganda. It is important to equip boys and girls as fully as possible to meet the argument and withstand the propaganda.[47]

Consciously or unconsciously, therefore, members of the Defense Commission and the NEA abandoned one of the underlying precepts of free and objective inquiry. Courses and curriculum materials explicitly were to be both anti-communist and slanted in favor of American democracy. Accordingly, the 1949 resolution to bar communists from the profession was bolstered by a further resolution that asserted that "the responsibility of the schools is to teach the superiority of the American way of life."[48] Andrew Holt, NEA President, additionally noted that teachers are duty bound to inspire "our children with a love of democracy that will be inoculated against the false ideology of Communism."[49]

An overarching feature of NEA deliberation, policy, and practice through the red scare era was the repeated inclination to portray American education as a weapon in the ideological battle against communism. In an era in which schools eagerly sought public support, the NEA understood the value of asserting education's loyalty to American culture and tradition. In his 1951 "Annual Report of the Profession to the Public," Willard Givens, NEA Executive Secretary, noted with alarm that the communist foe, "almost a billion strong," waged "a constant war of ideals against the nations which uphold individual human freedoms." Consequently, he pronounced that "the school has a special assignment in any war of ideals" and that education had a purposeful role in "the defense of America against the encroachment of totalitarianism."[50]

At every opportunity, the Defense Commission and the NEA affirmed its loyalty to America and its distrust of the Soviet Union. For example, "We Pledge Allegiance," appeared as the selected theme for 1953 NEA annual meeting in Miami Beach. "In choosing the theme of this convention," Sarah C. Caldwell, NEA President, informed delegates, "we have emphasized the rededication of ourselves in greater service to the ideals of our country and our profession."[51] Significantly, at the 1953 NEA conference, the association's executive committee also announced its intention to give high priority to three activities, one of which included the promotion of "Public Appreciation for the Schools' Work for Loyal Citizenship."[52] Executive Secretary William G. Carr[53] forcefully remarked that through "a nationwide program, using all publicity media," the NEA would "hammer on the simple truth that the American teacher is a loyal defender and exponent of democracy."[54]

The Defense Commission played a crucial role in heralding the devotion and loyalty of the American teaching profession. For example, in conjunction with the U. S. Department of Justice and the NEA Citizenship Committee, the Defense Commission organized a series of annual national conferences on citizenship.[55] Attended by thousands of delegates from several hundred national organizations, these conferences typically convened in major American cities. They brought educator-lay leaders together to discuss the influential role of education in encouraging the development of responsible, loyal, and patriotic citizens. The conferences provided the NEA and the Defense Commission with a perfect vehicle to demonstrate the passionate and unquestioned loyalty of American teachers to the traditions and principles of the United States.

In many respects, the NEA's decision to exclude communists from the profession, its determination to teach about the Soviet Union from a pro-American stance, and its fixation with loyalty issues, illustrated the extent to which the NEA leadership accepted the post-war gospel of anti-communism. A further indication of the NEA's political conservatism also was demonstrated by the association's repeated flirtation with the practices and opinions of the fiercely anti-communist American Legion.

Ironically, despite the fact that a national survey of educators revealed that the American Legion frequently proved one of education's fiercest critics,[56] and despite the fact that its magazine launched a caustic attack on teachers,[57] the NEA and the American Legion collaborated on a number of important projects. The partnership between the NEA and the American Legion, of course, was not new. The two organizations had declared common interests in 1921, and a joint committee of the NEA and the American Legion appeared as an annual fixture in NEA proceedings for many decades.[58] In the post-World War II years, the relationship continued to develop. Erle Cocke, Jr., national commander of the American Legion, proudly boasted the strength of the bond in his address to educators at the NEA's annual meeting in 1951,

You of the National Education Association and we of the American Legion have many interests in common. We have formed and are maintaining a close working alliance in numerous constructively patriotic youth programs, designed to dramatize America and built on lofty objectives which foster a 100 per cent Americanism, inculcate a sense of individual obligation to serve America, and create a will to perpetuate the great gains in liberty and justice which America has made.[59]

Many examples of this "close working alliance" existed. Co-sponsored by the NEA and the legion, American Education Week went from strength to strength. Guest speakers were exchanged at the organizations' respective annual meetings, Legionnaire-School Masters clubs were formed, and both organizations shared common ground on textbook adoption procedures.[60]

A significant characteristic of the NEA-American Legion relationship during the red scare era increasingly centered on a blatantly anti-communist stance. The most graphic illustration of this shift in focus was the NEA's decision to participate with 60 other national organizations in a series of annual conferences sponsored by the American Legion entitled the "All American Conference to Combat Communism."[61] The conference series, as the title suggested, explicitly focused on ways in which the domestic communist threat could be thwarted by concerted activities on the part of national organizations. As a result of the conference, the joint NEA and the American Legion committee adopted a broad policy platform that included the expansion of American Education Week, the denial of any form of public employment to members of the Communist Party, the widespread establishment of Legionnaire-Schoolmaster Clubs, and "increased emphasis on the promotion of programs that create greater loyalty to American democracy." In particular, the joint committee advocated, "active cooperation...to meet the challenge of communism and to pledge our support...as a safeguard against the invasion of this alien ideology in the various areas of American life."[62]

In the context of the Korean War, the loss of China to the communists, and the rapid deterioration in Soviet-American relations, the NEA's acute fear of communism was somewhat understandable. However, what was so revealing about the position the NEA leadership adopted was that unreservedly they accepted the red scare's underlying assumption that a serious internal communist threat existed.[63] Accordingly, in a period in which countless individuals in education desperately needed an agency to stand against the rhetorical and practical excesses of the red scare, the Defense

Commission and the NEA often embraced many of its fundamental convictions.

The essential conservatism of the NEA and the Defense Commission was further illustrated by its position on teacher strikes, loyalty oaths, and state and Congressional investigations. During the existence of the Defense Commission, from 1941 to 1961, 105 teacher strikes were reported in school districts throughout the United States. In fourteen cases alone substantial data indicated the loss of 7,691,400 pupil days of school.[64] The cause of these strikes was not difficult to understand. Between 1939 and 1946 the average industrial worker's income rose 80% in real terms, while the average income for a classroom teacher fell 20%. Teachers' economic futures looked bleak, and their anxieties further were exacerbated by the poor working conditions many of them continued to endure.[65] Consequently, following months of fruitless negotiations with their employers, thousands of teachers took to the picket lines.[66] The leadership of the NEA and the Defense Commission clearly understood and sympathized with the plight of discontented teachers. Occasionally, they supported industrial action euphemistically referring to strikes as "professional group action by professional methods."[67] As a general rule, however, the commission refused to support teacher strikes and warned teachers of the dangers of using them for short term gain. In December 1946, for example, the *Defense Bulletin*, after detailing a series of strikes throughout the country asserted,

> The Defense Commission believes that after teachers have signed contracts they should live up to them, that in the long run teachers will not gain by striking, but will lose a good deal of the public backing and support they have been building up for the past four or five years. The temporary advantage which a few teachers may secure from the strikes will be more than offset by the black eye which the profession as a whole will suffer through the disapproval of such methods.[68]

As the red scare intensified in the late 1940s and early 1950s, the Defense Commission increasingly sought to disassociate itself from the whiff of militancy. Labor activism and strikes, the commission's leadership reasoned, smacked too much of socialism. To support such action in an age dominated by anti-communist fervor appeared tantamount to professional suicide. As a consequence, in May 1951, at the height of the red scare, a Defense Commission investigation in Oglesby, Illinois, revealingly concluded that "it is unprofessional for teachers, through striking and picketing, to disrupt a school system."[69]

The red scare also led the NEA and the Defense Commission to surrender the teaching profession to the imposition of loyalty oaths and state and Congressional investigations. Despite the passage of NEA resolutions that objected to loyalty measures, the association failed to advise educators to refuse to sign loyalty oaths or to shun cooperation with legislative investigations.[70] Repeatedly, NEA members endorsed a resolution that stated, "The National Education Association recognizes the right of legislative bodies to conduct investigations....Educators called upon to testify in such investigations should do so fully and frankly."[71]

Essentially, therefore, a gulf appeared between the rhetoric and actions of the NEA leadership. Although NEA officers, including members of the Defense Commission, frequently and vociferously spoke out against the dangers of loyalty probes, in the final analysis few members of the association were prepared explicitly to act against these measures. Thus, unlike educators, such as Robert Hutchins of Chicago University who were prepared defend the academic rights of every educator without exception, the NEA and the Defense Commission were only prepared to offer teachers cautious protection.[72] For example, not once did the Defense Commission and the NEA earnestly discuss the practical possibility of encouraging teachers to refuse to sign loyalty oaths or to shun participation in loyalty investigations. At not time did the Defense Commission entertain the thought of resolutely supporting the right of any educator identified as a communist to teach, and on no occasion did the commission seriously question the reflexive anti-communist mindset of the period. Reasonably, one may conjecture that, if the Defense Commission had persuaded hundreds of thousands of teachers to stand against loyalty measures, and if it had not passed its 1949 resolution to exclude communists from the teaching profession, some of the red scare frenzy which surrounded public education seriously may have been challenged. The Defense Commission's explicit failure even to explore the possibility of taking such a stand undoubtedly casts a gloomy shadow over its claim to be the teaching profession's most resolute defender and champion.

To a large degree, the actions of the Defense Commission were governed by the political expedience of the red scare. The commission's involvement with and unapologetic acceptance of NEA policy in the immediate post-war period reflected the power of the anti-communist crusade. The Defense Commission's refusal to allow communists in the teaching profession, its brittle reaction to loyalty oaths and legislative investigations, its disapproval of teacher strikes, its appeasement of the American Legion, its incessant quest to demonstrate the commission's unerring loyalty to America, and its ardently anti-Soviet stance illustrated the extent to which the commission fell victim to red scare passions. As an agency devoted to the protection of teachers from red scare attack, the Defense Commission capitulated on many fronts. Rather than stand as a perpetual and comforting lighthouse for educators in a vicious and unrelenting storm, its presence frequently appeared dim and indistinct.

Any condemnation of the activities of the Defense Commission, however, must take into consideration the practical alternatives available to the commission at mid-century. The ubiquitous, all-consuming, and repressive force of the red scare in this period casts serious doubt on whether or not the Defense Commission effectively could have encouraged teachers to refuse to sign loyalty oaths or to refuse to participate in loyalty investigations. Furthermore, in the delicate political atmosphere of the red scare, few institutions or individuals in American society saw the practical wisdom of challenging the dominant anti-communist orthodoxy. Undoubtedly, therefore, the Defense Commission's leadership reasoned that to renounce allegiance to the American Legion, or to support the right of a communist to teach, or to condone and support teachers' strikes, or to advise teachers to stand against loyalty probes, was certain to invite damaging political reprisal. As such, the Defense Commission refused to go out on a precarious political limb and suffer humiliating public criticism.

In some respects, in the exceedingly demanding and difficult climate of the red scare, the commission offered a way forward. Cautiously, it plotted a middle course between, on the one hand, assiduously protecting the teaching profession from the excesses of red scare criticism and, on the other, from appearing too radical or too un-American to the general public. Fundamentally, the commission kept its eyes on the prize: greater public support for American schooling, increased financial funding for education, and improved professional conditions and security for teachers. In its hunger to accomplish these goals, the commission undoubtedly surrendered some of its principles and integrity to the red scare. In many other respects, however, the Defense Commission accomplished some worthwhile successes.

Limits of Accomplishment

Reviewing two decades of Defense Commission activity, a 1961 NEA publication noted with pride,

> For more than twenty years the National Commission for the Defense of Democracy has been proud of the role assigned to it by the National Education Association. It has fearlessly defended the rights of those who serve in the nation's schools. It has honestly criticized those who deter the educative process. The commission has given conscientious and effective service not only to the NEA and its members, but to the cause of American education itself.[73]

To the Defense Commission's credit, it recognized at an extraordinarily early stage the danger to public education of sustained and unforgiving red scare attack. Established in 1941, the commission sought to defend the teaching profession throughout the turbulent years of the Second World War and continued in its efforts to protect and champion the rights of educators amid the fury and invective of the red scare years.

The importance of the Defense Commission's early arrival on the troubled educational scene and its sustained commitment to the teaching profession in the two decades thereafter should not be underestimated. Indeed, the Defense Commission's astute recognition of the destructive influence of concerted red scare attack in the early 1940s suggested that the leadership of the NEA acted with considerable foresight. Certainly, no other agency existed at this time to protect the interests of American public school teachers and administrators. The American Federation of Teachers (AFT), for example, had no equivalent group. In fact, during the 1940s and early 1950s, the AFT frequently shied away from the defense of teachers identified as socialist or subversive for fear of appearing un-American and disloyal. Thus, despite the AFT's long-established affiliation with organized labor, amid the frenzy of the red scare era, it lost its nerve and surrendered to the infectious tide of anti-communism.[74]

Unlike any other professional education association or educational publication during the 1940s, the Defense Commission eagerly monitored, tracked, and exposed the mounting agencies of red scare attack. From the commission's very beginning in 1941 and throughout the 1940s repeated issues of the *Defense Bulletin* illuminated the menace to education posed by right-wing extremists. The commission exposed the machinations of organizations such as General Amos A. Fries' Friends of the Public Schools, Allen A. Zoll's National Council for American Education, the Committee for Constitutional Government, and the Sons of the American Revolution. It noted the outspoken red scare attacks on educators perpetrated by business groups and tax-payers organizations, and it both reported and challenged those politicians who accused the teaching profession of subversion and disloyalty.

Even when many educational organizations awakened from their lethargic slumber following Willard Goslin's dramatic dismissal in the fall of 1950, their responses proved less vigorous and more anemic than that offered by the Defense Commission. The Progressive Education Association, for example, which literally was fighting for its life in the early 1950s, offered only limited resistance to attack. Similarly, the actions of other organizations, such as Phi Delta Kappa and the National Association of Secondary School Principals (NAASP) showed remarkable restraint in their individual response to the mounting criticism of public schools. With a few exceptions, articles which cogently answered red scare attack in educational journals, such as *School and Society, Teachers College Record*, and *Educational Leadership,* proved a distinct rarity before 1951 and only surfaced irregularly thereafter.[75]

In essence therefore, for almost two decades, the Defense Commission appeared as the teaching profession's principal shield from red scare attack. If teachers faced unfair dismissal, encountered criticism laced with anti-communist rhetoric, or stood accused of subversive actions, they turned to the Defense Commission for advice and support. In the red scare era, no other educational agency offered the range of resources and the breadth of experience to compare with those of the commission.

No better illustration of the commission's serious and unyielding commitment to the defense of educators existed than a consideration of the quality and nature of those individuals who were appointed to serve within it. From the outset, the Defense Commission boasted some of public education's most noted and influential individuals. Significantly, its first Executive Secretary, Donald DuShane, accepted the commission's leadership while he was president of the NEA. Throughout its twenty-year existence, the sitting NEA president served on the commission's national committee of ten. During the 1940s, the Defense Commission also was chaired by three of education's leading lights.

Alonzo B. Myers served as chair from 1942 to 1946. As a former visiting professor at Yale and George Peabody College for Teachers and as the Chairman of the Department of Higher Education at New York University, Myers earned a reputation as an astute and energetic leader. In addition to his distinguished career in higher education, he served as captain in the U. S. Infantry during World War I and subsequently devoted his considerable energies to the role of chairman of the Commission for International Education, the forerunner of UNESCO.[76] Myers was succeeded in 1947 by Ernest O. Melby. As Dean of the School of Education at New York University, Melby offered the commission a wealth of practical experience. As a sagacious adviser and a fearless practitioner, Melby produced some of the most biting rebuttals of red scare criticism. In books, such as *The Education of Free Men*, 1955, *Freedom and Public Education*, 1953, and *American Education Under Fire: The Story of the Phony Three-R Fight*, 1951, Melby vigorously challenged attacks that he perceived to be motivated by unhealthy political extremism.[77]

In 1949 and 1950, the commission enjoyed the chairmanship of Dean Harold Benjamin of the University of Maryland. Benjamin had established a national reputation as one of America's finest and most charismatic educational personalities. He had served as a member of the Defense Commission since 1947 and played a considerable part in the commission's determination to extinguish mounting red scare attack. In addition to these educational luminaries, the Defense Commission also was served by a host of other prominent educational leaders, including Frank Graham of the University of North Carolina and Harold C. Hand of the University of Illinois.

Importantly, therefore, assembled within the ranks of the Defense Commission appeared many of education's most distinguished individuals. Ably supported by the prudent advice of Willard Givens, NEA executive secretary from 1941 to 1952 and by the committed and energetic activities of Richard Barnes Kennan and Robert Skaife, the commission intended to shine as a beacon to educators throughout the land. The NEA leadership regarded the commission with pride. They lauded its achievements and considered it one of the NEA's most effective and influential agencies. Indeed, NEA historian Edgar B. Wesley boasted, "It would be difficult to cite a group that has moved with more wisdom, courage and success than the National Commission for the Defense of Democracy Through Education. Tactful, careful, judicious, it has...proved that the NEA can and does move with commendable courage and forthrightness."[78] In some respects, Wesley's positive judgment was justified. Under the stewardship of the commission's strident and capable officers, it proved a considerable source of support for teachers throughout the nation.

The Defense Commission's response to the red scare reasonably may be summarized by attention to three interrelated areas. First, the Defense Commission stood up to the most violent manifestations of red scare criticism. It selectively differentiated between honest criticism and "biased, hostile, or untruthful" attack and determined vigorously to challenge education's dishonest accusers. Like no other educational organization in the country, it vigorously pursued anti-communist extremists and exposed the apparent unfairness and irrationality of their propaganda to the American public. Above all, the commission alerted and prepared the teaching profession to the dangers of red scare attack.

Over a twenty-year period, the commission assembled a near-mountain of information on political extremists and, according to the NEA, housed the country's most complete collection of material on the known critics of education.[79] It gave teachers and administrators advanced warning of the poisonous influences of targeted red scare critics, provided intelligence on how they operated, and offered bountiful advice and information on how best to challenge their assault. The commission clearly could not prevent all of the damage perpetrated by these critics. Moreover, it could not thwart critical attacks in every community in the nation. The commission, however, did enjoy some notable success. Significantly, in the mid-1950s, when Zoll, Crain, Fries, and other vehement red baiters evaporated from the educational scene, the Defense Commission stood firm and continued to perform its influential activities.

Second, the Defense Commission enjoyed considerable success in its promotion of positive relations between educators and the general public. Firmly, it believed that red scare criticism of the schools more likely would be ignored by citizens if they understood and appreciated the difficulties public education faced in the post-war era. Mabel Studebaker, NEA President in 1949, appropriately described the Defense Commission as a "catalytic agent" intent in bringing about "a common meeting of the minds to solve the problems at hand."[80] In this regard, the Defense Commission became extremely influential. For twenty years it effectively employed an ongoing series of educator-lay conferences to communicate to lay leaders the importance of supporting public education. In addition, it used these fora both to ridicule and to expose the arguments of those extremists who sought to undermine the schools.

On a daily basis the commission's information service distributed to politicians, business representatives, and local and national organizations a vast array of reprints, articles, bulletins, and information sheets that both heralded the achievements of public schools and challenged those who attacked them. In concerted efforts to win over the general public to the cause of education, key individuals in the commission, such as Richard Barnes Kennan and Robert Skaife, also addressed citizens' groups and civic organizations in communities throughout the nation. Importantly, despite attacks on the agency from reactionary groups and individuals, the Defense Commission frequently enjoyed widespread credibility and support. Defense Commission investigations increasingly earned favorable national reputations, and the commission routinely was considered an honorable, eminently professional, and highly respected organization.

The commission's third achievement was its effective efforts to unify and bolster the teaching profession during the particularly harrowing years of the red scare. Few other educational bodies enjoyed as much success as the Defense Commission in linking together educators at the local, state, and national level. commission investigations often improved teacher employment rights and practices in dozens of school districts throughout the nation. As a result of a nationwide campaign sponsored by the commission, many educators in local school districts frequently were protected from capricious and arbitrary dismissal on the basis of their political beliefs or affiliation. Furthermore, the Defense Fund offered local teachers and administrators a source of financial security when faced with economic hardship as a result of losing their jobs to political reprisal.

During the red scare years, the commission also became the focal point of thousands of educators the length and breadth of the land. It demonstrated to local teacher associations and individual educators that political attacks were not confined to isolated school districts, but symbolized a much broader and geographically widespread problem. Teachers felt comforted that they were not alone in their personal battle against anti-communist attack. Above all, the commission's extensive connections at local, state, and national levels helped to protect and defend teachers who encountered harmful red scare attacks.

At the 1941 NEA annual meeting which established the commission, a number of speakers predicted that an effective commission devoted to the protection of educators, undoubtedly, would encourage more teachers and administrators to join the NEA.[81] In no small measure that prediction came true. In 1941 NEA membership stood at 211,191; fourteen years later it had soared to 612,716.[82] This dramatic increase in part may be attributed to the Defense Commission's success in reaching out to educators and boosting the profession's morale in school districts throughout the nation. Significantly, writing in 1957, Edgar B. Wesley noted,

> Thousands have joined the NEA because they have seen it as a mechanism for enhancing their welfare....The growth in the NEA can be attributed to its changed policies and to the revolution in the attitude of classroom teachers. They had at last found a defender....[83]

Unequivocally, therefore, many within the teaching profession deeply valued the work of the Defense Commission. Indeed, repeated expressions of gratitude from teachers stand as the most significant testimony to the commission's effectiveness during the red scare era.

Approval of Defense Commission activity was not confined to classroom teachers. Many academics lauded the commission's achievements. For example, two University of Chicago professors, William S. Gray and William J. Iverson, noted "the excellent work of the National Commission of Defense of Democracy Through Education" in exposing destructive critics. In September 1952, they argued that the commission served as an example of how "the profession must continue to respond with unity and courage" to prevent "school people" from becoming "intimidated and maligned."[84] In a similar fashion, the authors of *Public Education Under Criticism*, who candidly detailed the arguments for and against criticism of the public schools, observed, "the commission's record on answering criticism and meeting attacks clearly puts it in class by itself."[85] In addition, Benjamin Fine, education editor of the *New York Times*, impressed by the work of the commission, informed readers that "the counterattack against those who attack the schools dishonestly has been spearheaded by the National Commission for the Defense of Democracy Through Education."[86]

The effectiveness of the commission in blunting attacks on the schools, however, must not be overstated. Certainly, the commission did not eliminate the destructive influence of the red scare on the schools. Moreover, in dozens of communities, the commission appeared completely unable to prevent the damaging impact of concerted and organized anti-communist furor. However, any fair assessment of the achievements of the Defense Commission must consider that, throughout its twenty-year existence, it worked within considerable limitations.

Above all, the Defense Commission suffered from shortage of funds and personnel. For example, in its annual report to the NEA in 1952, the

Defense Commission urged the delegate assembly to "give careful consideration to the need for more nearly adequate facilities and staff to meet the critical and demanding needs of this day and the foreseeable future." The commission's report noted that apart from secretarial staff and two individual members who gave "attention to the work of related committees," only three full-time staff remained with "direct responsibility for action in defending the profession against unfair attack." At the height of the red scare, the commission reported with considerable alarm that, despite these severe restrictions, it was expected to "give aid and advice to 51 state and territorial associations, 4,500 local associations, and 480,000 individual members."[87] In addition, although the NEA's budgetary allocation for the Defense Commission had climbed steadily since 1941, it still remained poorly funded.

In 1952, for example, a year in which the NEA enjoyed revenues of $2,750,150, the Defense Commission was apportioned only a meager $72,249. Personnel and budgetary restrictions, therefore, severely limited the commission's ability to combat all red scare attacks. The commission recognized that it must be selective and give "priority attention to those cases which appear to have the greatest significance for the national welfare of the profession."[88] Accordingly, the leadership of the Defense Commission constantly worked under the explicit assumption that they could not battle every red scare attack in every community.

The Defense Commission also was aware that its actions were bounded by the broader economic climate that confronted educators in the immediate post-war period. Robert Skaife, for example, reported that a Defense Commission survey identified the "high cost of public education" as the general public's number one criticism of the schools in 1951.[89] Officers of the commission clearly understood that their actions should encourage citizens to support the schools. More important, however, they also understood that the commission's actions should not alienate or offend the general public. As a consequence, the commission's officers appreciated the need to appear non-controversial, to be sensitive to some critics, and to be inherently conservative in many of their activities. Certainly, in order to win over the support of the general public, the commission could not be perceived as a radical or un-American organization. Much of the commission's work in the red scare period, therefore, must be viewed within this larger context. To a considerable extent, it accepted the political and societal mood of the age because it believed this to be the most effective way to harness widespread approval of public education.

Arguably the Defense Commission's most significant achievement rested not in quelling contemporary red scare criticism, but in providing lessons for the future. In several respects it pointed the way forward. It was one of the few educational agencies fully to understand the importance of soliciting the support of the general public in the battle for control of the schools. In communities throughout the United States its presence was felt whether through commission investigations, educator-lay conferences, the perpetual dissemination of material and information, contact with the local press, and public addresses by commission officers. It understood the responsibility of educators to American citizens, and it embraced associations with many parental organizations, citizens' groups, and community leaders. To a considerable degree, therefore, the teaching profession's future coalition with important sections of the populace was guided by the actions of the Defense Commission in the post-war period.

Chiefly as a result of its investigations, the Defense Commission also proved influential in promoting the rights and responsibilities of educators. By exposing unfair administrative practices and acting decisively to rectify professional injustice, it continued to elevate the professional status of teachers.[90] In no small measure, the improved security of the teaching profession in the mid to late 1950s, the growth in state tenure provisions, and the removal of legislation that restricted the freedom of teachers may be attributed to the activities of the Defense Commission.

The Defense Commission also made future teachers and administrators acutely aware of the need both to be alert and responsive to attacks. It advised educators to establish policies and procedures to deal with criticism. It emphasized the importance of taking precautions to thwart attacks before they gathered momentum. In addition, it advised teachers continually to explain to the American public the importance to democracy of supporting academic liberty, freedom to inquire, and the right to explore controversial issues.

Throughout its existence, the commission was driven by three central purposes: (1) "to give the public more understanding of the importance of education for all our people," (2) to "defend the cause of education against unjust attack," and (3) to "work for educational conditions essential for the perpetuation of our democracy."[91] To some extent, the commission made advances toward accomplishing each of these three goals. However, despite the committed efforts of its officers, the commission could not stop the red scare from having a profound influence on educational policy and practice in the immediate post-war period. This failure was partially due to the fact that it never had the resources to deal with the enormity of the situation it encountered.

By the 1950s, the red scare, that had flickered in the early 1940s, soon flared into a raging inferno that engulfed American public education. The commission did not have the funds, the personnel, or the political or institutional allies effectively to respond to the crisis. Unquestionably, it did extinguish isolated fires. For example, it dampened the influence of individual critics like Allen A. Zoll, and it helped to diffuse attacks in selected communities. However, partly because the Defense Commission failed to appreciate the enormity of the red scare and the influential, political, business, and reactionary forces behind it, it alone could never eliminate all red scare attack.

Of greatest significance, because the Defense Commission accepted many of the underlying assumptions of the prevailing anti-communist mindset, it failed seriously to influence or to challenge the essence of the red scare that so dramatically shaped American culture in the late 1940s and early 1950s. Ultimately, communism was to have profoundly less of an impact on American education than the debilitating forces of anti-communism. In the final analysis, the red scare proved such a powerful and dominant force that the Defense Commission appeared unable, and at times unwilling, to prevent this ironic and disturbing reality.

Appendix A

NEA Defense Commission Members, 1941-1961

Mary D. Barnes, 1941-43
Harold Benjamin, 1947-50
Bertha P. Boyd, 1961
Mozelle Causey, 1947-51
Stephen M. Corey, 1959-60
Jennie L. Davis, 1951-56
John W. Davis, 1947-52
Elizabeth Dennis, 1958-60
John W. Dodd, 1945-48
Lois Edinger, 1959-61
John G. Fowlkes, 1951-53
Kate Frank, 1941-46
Mathilda A. Gilles, 1958-61
Inez Gingerich, 1953-58
George W. Gore, Jr., 1953-58
Frank P. Graham, 1941-43
Harold C. Hand, 1949-54
Theodore W. H. Irion, 1944-45

Nolan C. Kearney, 1961
Virginia Kinnaird, 1944-47
Frederick Houk Law, 1941-43
Eldridge T. McSwain, 1955-57
Ernest O. Melby, 1941-48
Winona Montgomery, 1947-52
Rose Muckley, 1947-50
Alonzo F. Myers, 1941-45
Raymond Ostrander, 1961
Orville C. Pratt, 1941-43
Leila Rawls, 1957-61
James T. Reiva, 1952-57
Virgil M. Rogers, 1949-54
Francis C. Rosecrance, 1960-61
Oscar E. Thompson, 1961
Mary E. Titus, 1944-46
Earle W. Wiltse, 1955-60
Ruth Winter, 1954-59

Defense Commission Chairs

Alonzo F. Myers, 1942-46
Ernest O. Melby, 1947-48
Harold Benjamin, 1949-50
John W. Davis, 1951-52
Jennie L. Davis, 1953-56

James T. Reiva, 1957
Inez Gingerich, 1958
Ruth Winter, 1959
Earle W. Wiltse, 1960
Mathilda Gilles, 1961

Appendix B

Professional Staff Members

Executive Secretary:	Donald DuShane, 1941-47
	Richard Barnes Kennan, 1947-61
Associate Secretary:	Richard Barnes Kennan, 1944-47
	Virginia Kinnaird, 1947-61
Legal Counsel:	Cyrus C. Perry, 1947-55
	Henry E. Butler, Jr., 1956-61
Associate Legal Counsel:	Robert Mukai, 1958-59
	Richard L. Morgan, 1959-61
Field Secretary:	Robert A. Skaife, 1949-55
Associate Secretary for Special Studies:	Edwin W. Davis, 1956-61
Assistant Secretary:	Lucile W. Ellison, 1949-61
Conference Director:	Ralph W. McDonald, 1944
Professional Assistant:	Glenn Archer, 1943-44
	Boyd Comstock, 1944
Assistant to Secretary:	Mildred Wharton, 1942-45
	Eleanor Fishburn, 1945-47
Administrative Assistant:	Lucile W. Ellison, 1947-49
	Geraldine M. Fitez, 1952-56
	Bernice C. Brigham, 1957-61

Appendix C

Defense Commission Investigations

New York City	February 1944
Chicago, Illinois	May 1945
McCook, Nebraska	March 1947
North College Hill, Ohio	November 1947
Chandler, Arizona	October 1948
Grand Prairie, Texas	September 1949
Kelso, Washington	June 1950
Newport, New Hampshire	August 1950
State Education Agency, Utah	August 1950
Twin Falls, Idaho	September 1950
Polson, Montana	April 1951
Oglesby, Illinois	May 1951
Pasadena, California	June 1951
Mars Hill, North Carolina	October 1951
Miami, Florida	October 1952
Houston, Texas	December 1954
Kansas City, Missouri	October 1955
Bridgewater Township, New Jersey	May 1956
Gary, Indiana	June 1957
Bethpage, New York	February 1958
Monroe, Michigan	March 1958
Hawthorne, New Jersey	April 1958
Missoula County High School, Montana	July 1958
Ambridge, Pennsylvania	May 1959
West Haven, Connecticut	September 1959
Hickman Mills, Missouri	January 1960
Indianapolis, Indiana	May 1960
Santa Fe, New Mexico	January 1961
Fullerton, California	May 1961

Endnotes

Chapter I: The Red Scare: Origins and Impact

1. These examples of anti-communist repression were drawn from David Caute, *The Great Fear* (New York, 1978), 406; Martha Kransdorf, *A Matter of Loyalty: The Los Angeles School Board vs Frances Eisenberg* (San Francisco, 1994), 33; Robert Iversen, *The Communists and the Schools* (New York, 1959), 257; Don E. Carleton, *Red Scare! Right Wing Hysteria, Fifties Fanaticism, and Their Legacy in Texas* (Austin, Texas, 1985), 156; *Defense Bulletin* 55 (April 1954): 3-4, 6-7; *Defense Bulletin* 54 (February 1954): 2-3, box 1026, National Education Association Archives, Washington, D.C. Hereafter cited as NEA archives.

2. Mary Ann Pesognelli, "The Erosion of Freedom," *NEA Journal* 40 (May 1951): 321-322.

3. The personal toll exacted by the educational red scare has been documented by a number of historians. See, for example, Iversen, *The Communists and the Schools*; Mary Ann Raywid, *The Ax-Grinders: Critics of Our Public School* (New York, 1962*)*; and Ellen Schrecker, *No Ivory Tower: McCarthyism and the Universities* (New York, 1986).

4. Ellen Schrecker, *No Ivory Tower*, 9.

5. See for example, Diane Ravitch, *The Troubled Crusade: American Education 1945-1980* (New York, 1983), Chapter 3, 81-113; Jack E. Nelson and Gene Roberts, Jr., *The Censors and the Schools* (Boston, 1963), 36-39; Iversen, *The Communists and the Schools*, 176-179, 186-222; Caute, *The Great Fear*, 20.

6. Skaife, Benjamin, and Melby were prominent figures in the National Commission for the Defense of Democracy Through Education. Ernest O. Melby was a member of the Defense Commission from 1941-1948 and was president of the commission in 1947 and 1948. Harold Benjamin was a member from 1947-1950 and was president in 1949 and 1950. Robert Skaife served the commission as field secretary from the time of its creation in 1949. Skaife actively worked for the commission throughout the red scare era.

7. Donald DuShane, Presidential Address, "A Challenge to the Teaching Profession." *National Education Association of the United States Journal of Proceedings and Addresses of the Annual Meeting* (Washington, D.C., 1941): 33. Hereafter cited as *Addresses and Proceedings*.

8. For the incredible rise in school enrollment in the first sixty years of the twentieth century, see David Tyack, *The One Best System: A History of American Urban Education* (Cambridge, Massachusetts, 1974), 66-71, 269.

9. Ravitch, *The Troubled Crusade,* 112.

10. Don E. Carleton, "McCarthyism in Local Elections: The Houston School Board Election of 1952," *Houston Review* 3 (Winter 1981): 169.

11. United Nations' Educational, Scientific, and Cultural Organization.

12. C. Winfield Scott and Clyde M. Hill, eds., *Public Education Under Criticism* (New York, 1954), 3.

13. Robert Skaife, "Groups Affecting Education," in *Forces Affecting American Education*, ed. William Van Til (Washington, D.C., 1953), 51.

14. See, for example, Robert Skaife, "Know the Enemy," *Connecticut Teacher* (December 1951): 68-71. Also, a series of articles written by Skaife and published in *Nation's Schools* reflected Skaife's passionate defense of education: "They Oppose Progress," *Nation's Schools* 47 (February 1951): 31-33; "They Sow Distrust," *Nation's Schools* 47 (January 1951): 27-30; and "They Want Tailored Schools," *Nation's Schools* 47 (May 1951): 35-37.

15. Extracts of Benjamin's speech, presented on July 3, 1950, proudly were reported in the Defense Commission's *Defense Bulletin* 35 (July 1950): 1-4. Benjamin was chairman of the Defense Commission during 1949 and 1950.

16. Ernest O. Melby, "American Education Under Fire," (New York, 1951): 7, box 1025, NEA Archives.

17. Robert A. Skaife, "An Evaluation of the Program of the National Commission for the Defense of Democracy Through Education," (Ph.D. diss., University of Maryland, 1951), 149.

18. See, for example, Robert Griffith, *Politics of Fear* (Lexington, Kentucky, 1970); Robert Griffith and Athan Theoharis, eds., *The Specter: Original Essays on the Cold War and the Origins of McCarthyism* (New York, 1974); Thomas C. Reeves, *The Life and Times of Joe McCarthy: A Biography* (New York, 1982); Caute, *The Great Fear*; and Richard M. Fried, *Nightmare in Red: The McCarthy Era in Perspective* (New York, 1990).

19. An engaging account of McCarthy's famous "Wheeling speech" may be found in J. Ronald Oakley, *God's Country: America in the Fifties* (New York, 1986), 26.

20. Oakley, *God's Country,* 27.

21. Godfrey Hodgson, *America in Our Time* (New York, 1978), 40-41.

22. Carleton, "McCarthyism in Local Elections," 168.

23. For extensive details of American prosperity in the 1950s see, for example, Oakley, *God's Country*.

24. Arthur Schlesinger, Jr., *The Vital Center: Politics of Freedom* (Boston, 1949), 1.

25. Robert M. Hutchins, "'Liberal' vs. 'Practical' Education — The Debate-of-the-Month" cited in Scott and Hill, eds. *Public Education Under Criticism*, 55-58.

26. Caute, *The Great Fear*, 21.

27. Hodgson, *America in Our Time*, 44.

28. Skaife, "Groups Affecting Education," in *Forces Affecting American Education*, ed. Van Til, 43.

29. Charles S. Johnson, "The Culture Affecting Education," in *Forces Affecting American Education*, ed. Van Til, 40.

30. Kransdorf, *A Matter of Loyalty*, 21.

31. *Defense Bulletin* 44 (May 1952): 1-7.

Chapter II: The Power and Ubiquity of the Red Scare in American Post-War Culture

1. Barbara Ehrenreich, *Fear of Falling: The Inner Life of the Middle Class* (New York, 1989), 33.

2. Schlesinger, *The Vital Center,* 183; Peter F. Drucker, *The New Society: The Anatomy of an Industrial Order* (New York, 1950), 1.

3. John Kenneth Galbraith, *American Capitalism: The Concept of Countervailing Power* (Boston, 1952), 1.

4. As cited in Michael Parenti, *Inventing Reality: The Politics of News Media* (New York, 1993), 117.

5. Howard Zinn, *A People's History of the United States* (New York, 1980), 429.

6. Howard Zinn, *Post War America 1945-1971* (New York, 1973), 73.

7. Leuchtenburg, *A Troubled Feast* (New York, 1979), 26.

8. Leuchtenburg, *A Troubled Feast*, 26.

9.   Parenti, *Inventing Reality*, 77.

10. Leuchtenburg, *A Troubled Feast*, 88.

11. Schrecker, *No Ivory Tower*, 8

12. Athan Theoharis, *Seeds of Repression: Harry S. Truman and the Origins of McCarthyism* (Chicago, 1971).

13. Michael Parenti, *The Anti-Communist Impulse* (New York, 1969), 99.

14. For the red scare's impact on the entertainment industry see, for example, Larry Ceplair and Steven Englund, *The Inquisition in Hollywood* (Garden City, NY, 1980); Victor Navasky, *Naming Names* (New York, 1980). For influences on the press, see, for example, James Aronson, *The Press and the Cold War* (Indianapolis, 1970); Edwin R. Bayley, *Joe McCarthy and the Press* (Madison, Wisconsin, 1981). Examples of studies on the relationship between McCarthyism and the labor unions include Harvey A. Levenstein, *Communism, Anti-Communism, and the CIO* (Westport, Conn., 1981); Bert Cochran, *Labor and Communism* (Princeton, New Jersey, 1977); Roger Keeran, *The Communist Party and the Auto Workers Union* (Urbana, Ill., 1980). Religion and the red scare also has received treatment in many works. See, for example, Donald F. Crosby, *God, Church, and Flag: Senator Joseph R. McCarthy and the Catholic Church, 1950-1957* (Chapel Hill, 1978); Douglas P. Seaton, *The Association of Catholic Trade Unionists and the American Labor Movement, from Depression to Cold War* (New York, 1981).

15. Parenti, *The Anti-Communist Impulse*, 130.

16. Oakley, *God's Country*, 6.

17. As cited in Caute, *The Great Fear*, 215.

18. The internal threat from Communist infiltration was minimal. For example, at its peak, during the US-Soviet military alliance during World War II, membership of the American Communist Party was fewer than 80,000. In 1950, party membership dropped to 43,000 and, by the end of the fifties, amounted to no more than 5,000 members.

19. Iversen, *The Communists and the Schools*, 332.

20. See, for example, Carleton, "McCarthyism in Local Elections," 173.

21. See Lewis C. Fay, "'Abolish Public Schools,' says owner of newspaper chain Robert Cyrus Hoiles," article reprint, box 1026, NEA Archives. Fay's article originally was published in *Nation's Schools* 50 (August 1952): 31-36. Hereafter cited as Fay, "Abolish Public Schools."

22. *Defense Bulletin* 48 (January 1953): 3.

23. See JoAnne Brown, "'A is for Atom, B is for Bomb': Civil Defense in American Education 1948-1963," *Journal of American History* 75 (June 1988): 68-90.

24. In New York City, $159,000 was spent on equipment and materials to produce two and a half million free dog tags for the city's school children.

25. See, for example, Ravitch, *The Troubled Crusade*, 84-105; Iversen, *The Communists and the Schools*, 176-203.

26. Richard Barnes Kennan, "Public Education in a Dangerous Era from the Viewpoint of a Member of the Teaching Profession," Proceedings of the First National Conference on Public Education in a Dangerous Era, Philadelphia, May 18, 1953, box 1021, NEA Archives. Hereafter cited as PEDE (Philadelphia).

27. Iversen, *The Communists and the Schools*, 360

28. Frances Eisenberg's story is told in Kransdorf, *A Matter of Loyalty*.

29. See Arthur Zilversmit, *Changing Schools: Progressive Education Theory and Practice, 1930-1960* (Chicago, 1993), Chapter 7.

30. National Commission for the Defense of Democracy Through Education, *The Pasadena Story: An Analysis of Some Forces and Factors that Injured a Superior School System* (Washington, D.C., 1951): 16. Hereafter cited as *Defense Commission Report: Pasadena.*

31. Zilversmit, Changing Schools, 118.

32. In both Houston and Pasadena, the NEA's Defense Commission produced detailed and exhaustive reports that documented events impacting education in these cities in the early 1950s. In both reports, the Defense Commission concluded that no evidence of subversive influences in the schools was apparent.

33. See Don E. Carleton, "McCarthyism was more than McCarthy: Documenting the Red Scare at the State and Local Level," *The Midwestern Archivist* 12 (1987): 13.

34. Michael Parenti argued, for example, that conservative forces and dominant elites exploited and propagated anti-communist feeling for their own political gains. He contended, "While anti-Communism may manipulate irrational images and play on irrational feelings, it itself is not a product of irrational politics. It serves a very real and rational purpose." *Inventing Reality*, 122.

35. The deliberate framing of a crisis in order to exact political control over the culture was skillfully explicated by British scholar Stuart Hall and his colleagues in *Policing the Crisis: Mugging, the State, and Law and Order* (London, 1978), viii. Using the example of how the mugging crisis in England in the 1970s was grossly exaggerated by powerful blocs in the media and the political arena, Hall convincingly documents how repressive Conservative Party law and order legislation was initiated to quell

an illusory crisis. The parallels with the United States in the 1950s are somewhat striking. The red scare was fueled by a crisis mentality that permitted conservative forces to exact control over the American culture.

36. Henry Steele Commager's remarks were reported in *Defense Bulletin* 56 (May 1954): 8.

37. Almost fanatical attacks on the NEA appeared legion. Some of the more considered, although no less aggressive, included Mortimer Smith, "The Failure of American Education," *The Freeman* 68 (December 1951): 137-139; Albert Lynd, *Quackery in the Public Schools* (Boston, 1953).

Chapter III: The NEA Establishes the Defense Commission

1. *Handbook of the National Education Association* (Washington, D.C., 1955): 254; See also Wesley, *NEA: The First Hundred Years, The Building of the Teaching Profession* (New York, 1957), 291.

2. *Addresses and Proceedings* (1942), 504.

3. Wesley, *NEA: The First Hundred Years*, 280.

4. Wesley, *NEA: The First Hundred Years*, 334.

5. Wesley, *NEA: The First Hundred Years*, 368-369.

6. Wesley, *NEA: The First Hundred Years*, 397.

7. Wesley, *NEA: The First Hundred Years*, 337.

8. Historians of the NEA agree that the formation of the Defense Commission in 1941 was a significant indication of the NEA's increasing desire to look after the interests of teachers. See, for example, Wesley, *NEA: The First Hundred Years*, 334-341; Allan M. West, *The National Education Association: The Power Base for Education* (New York, 1980), 17-20.

9. West, The *National Education Association*, 17.

10. *Addresses and Proceedings* (1941), 886.

11. The German invasion of the Soviet Union commenced on June 22, 1941. The seventy-ninth annual meeting of the NEA held in Boston began on June 29, 1941. At the time of the meeting, Russia certainly was not considered an ally of the west. Moreover, when the proposals for the creation of the Defense Commission were under consideration in the spring of 1941, the Soviet Union was regarded as a potential adversary.

12. *Addresses and Proceedings* (1941), 31.

13. *Addresses and Proceedings* (1941), 252.

14. *Addresses and Proceedings* (1941), 31.

15. *Addresses and Proceedings* (1941), 32.

16. See, for example, *Addresses and Proceedings* (1941), 31, 104-110, 868-869.

17. In 1941 alone, for example, the NEA helped to organize 50 Institutes on Professional Relations in 20 states. NEA staff members made 440 addresses to more than 125,000 people and took part in 650 conferences across the United States. The association also printed and distributed 231 million pages of educational literature and wrote more than 500,000 letters in support of education.

18. Skaife, "An Evaluation of the Program of the National Commission for the Defense of Democracy Through Education," 45-59.

19. Skaife, "An Evaluation of the Program of the National Commission for the Defense of Democracy Through Education," 53-54.

20. *Addresses and Proceedings* (1941), 767.

21. *Addresses and Proceedings* (1941), 770-771.

22. *Addresses and Proceedings* (1941), 773.

23. *Addresses and Proceedings* (1941), 767.

24. See *Addresses and Proceedings* (1941), 769-776.

25. Skaife, "An Evaluation of the Program of the National Commission for the Defense of Democracy Through Education," 42.

26. *Addresses and Proceedings* (1941), 768.

27. *Addresses and Proceedings* (1941), 768-769.

28. *Addresses and Proceedings* (1941), 778-779. Not all these purposes and activities were exclusive to the Defense Commission. Closely allied to the work of the Defense Commission, for example, were the programs of the Committee on Tenure and Academic Freedom and the Committee on Ethics of the National Education Association.

29. *Addresses and Proceedings* (1941), 828-829.

30. *Addresses and Proceedings* (1941), 828-829.

31. Throughout the history of the Defense Commission, the organization enjoyed the fruits of the labors of major educational figures such as Harold Benjamin, Richard B. Kennan, Ernest O. Melby, and William G. Carr. Although, in its first year, the Defense Commission provided full time employment to only two people, by the late 1950s, it employed a staff of 19 people. *Stewardship Report of the Defense Commission* (Washington, D.C., 1961): 6-7, box 1024, NEA Archives. Hereafter cited as Stewardship Report.

32. *Addresses and Proceedings* (1941), 769.

Chapter IV: The Defense Commission During Its Formative Years

1. *Addresses and Proceedings* (1946), 377.

2. *Addresses and Proceedings* (1947), 99.

3. The Annual Reports were written by Givens throughout his tenure as executive secretary to the NEA (1941-1952). By 1951, 42,000 copies were made available to individuals and organizations in the media, education, politics, and business.

4. *Addresses and Proceedings* (1946), 378.

5. *Addresses and Proceedings* (1946), 373.

6. See National Commission for the Defense of Democracy, "Charter for Teachers," *NEA Journal* 39 (October 1950): 526.

7. Skaife, "An Evaluation of the Program of the National Commission for the Defense of Democracy Through Education," 58.

8. *Addresses and Proceedings* (1941), 778-779.

9. For example, in addition to the four cited, between 1942 and 1948 the Defense Commission conducted unpublished investigations in Kenosha (Wisconsin); Davenport (Iowa); Moline (Illinois); Muskogee (Oklahoma); Hot Springs (Arkansas); Syracuse (New York); Shorewood (Wisconsin); Las Vegas (New Mexico); Monessen (Pennsylvania); Lebanon (New Hampshire); Cambridge (Ohio); Pampa (Texas); Buffalo (New York); and the "Holman case" in the state of Arizona.

10. Skaife, "An Evaluation of the Program of the National Commission for the Defense of Democracy Through Education," 76-78.

11. These investigations were conducted in New York City (February 1944), in Chicago, Illinois (May 1945), in McCook, Nebraska (March 1947), in North College Hill, Ohio (November 1947), in Chandler, Arizona (October, 1948), and in Grand Prairie, Texas (September 1949), *Stewardship Report*, 27.

12.   *Stewardship Report*, 27.

13.   *Addresses and Proceedings* (1945), 180-181, 256, 289.

14.   *Addresses and Proceedings* (1947), 266.

15.   See *Stewardship Report,* 9-11.

16.   For examples of towns and cities where Defense Commission investigations produced favorable results see *Defense Bulletin* 41 (December 1951): 5-7, 10-11.

17.   Skaife, "An Evaluation of the Program of the National Commission for the Defense of Democracy Through Education," 92.

18.   *Defense Bulletin* 2 (January 1942): 9.

19.   See Caute, *The Great Fear*, 267.

20.   *Addresses and Proceedings* (1941), 787.

21.   Original statement as quoted in Skaife, "An Evaluation of the Program of the National Commission for the Defense of Democracy Through Education," 17.

22.   See, for example, *Addresses and Proceedings* (1948), 380.

23.   See, for example, West, *The National Education Association*, 112, and *Defense Bulletin* 12 (February 1945): 1.

24.   West, *The National Education Association*, 113.

25.   See "The Donald DuShane Memorial Defense Fund" *NEA Journal* 39 (February 1950): 123.

26.   *Addresses and Proceedings* (1946), 376. See also, "Salaries of City School Employees, 1940-41," *NEA Research Bulletin* 19 (March 1941): 67-97.

27.   *Addresses and Proceedings* (1945), 359

28.   *Addresses and Proceedings* (1945), 83

29.   See "Salaries and Salary Schedules of City-School Employees, 1948-9," *NEA Research Bulletin* 27 (April 1949): 43-72.

30.   *Addresses and Proceedings* (1941), 32.

31.   *Addresses and Proceedings* (1948), 374.

32. See NEA Committee on Tenure and Academic Freedom, "The Freedom of the Public School Teacher" (Washington, D.C., 1951), box 1010, NEA Archives.

33. See "The Legal Status of the Public School Teacher," *NEA Research Bulletin* 25 (April 1947): 26-71.

34. *Addresses and Proceedings* (1948), 37.

35. *Addresses and Proceedings* (1945), 357.

36. *Addresses and Proceedings* (1942), 72.

37. *Defense Bulletin* 2 (January 1942): 9.

38. *Addresses and Proceedings* (1943), 331-332.

39. *Addresses and Proceedings* (1945), 361; *Defense Bulletin* 12 (February 1945): 4-5.

40. Wesley, *NEA: The First Hundred Years*, 310, 337.

41. Wesley, *NEA: The First Hundred Years,* 351.

42. William Van Til, *My Way of Looking At It: An Autobiography* (Terre Haute, Indiana, 1983), 158.

43. *Defense Bulletin* 2 (January 1942): 5-7.

44. *Defense Bulletin* 18 (September 1946): 6-7.

45. *Defense Bulletin* 18 (September 1946): 7. Fries' speech in Chicago, for example, also was favorably reported by John Evans of the *Chicago Tribune.*

46. John T. Flynn, *The Road Ahead: America's Creeping Revolution* (New York, 1949).

47. See Robert C. Morris, "Era of Anxiety: An Historical Account of the Effects of and Reactions to Right Wing Forces Affecting Education during the Years 1949-1954" (Ph.D. diss., Indiana State University, 1976), 247.

48. *Defense Bulletin* 36 (November 1950): 4.

49. See, for example, *Defense Bulletin* 18 (September 1946): 6, and *Defense Bulletin* 26 (September 1948): 7.

50. As cited in Skaife, "An Evaluation of the Program of the National Commission for the Defense of Democracy Through Education," 14.

51. See, for example, *Defense Bulletin* 2 (June 1942): 3, 9; *Defense Bulletin* 8 (June 1944): 9; and *Defense Bulletin* 33 (June 1950): 5.

52. *Defense Bulletin* 14 (December 1945): 6.

53. See, for example, *Defense Bulletin* 12 (February 1945): 11-15, and *Defense Bulletin* 24 (February 1948): 6.

54. *Defense Bulletin* 23 (January 1948): 5.

55. See, for example, *Defense Bulletin* 12 (February 1945): 15; *Defense Bulletin* 24 (February 1948): 6; *Defense Bulletin* 40 (November 1951): 6-7; and *Defense Bulletin* 48 (June 1953).

56. *Defense Bulletin* 19 (December 1946): 15.

57. *Defense Bulletin* 20 (March 1947): 6.

Chapter V: Red Scare Attackers and Their Methods

1. "Appendix A" in *Forces Affecting American Education*, ed. Van Til, 175-189, offered a detailed index of hundreds of articles concerning attacks on education published in the *New York Times* between 1949 and 1952.

2. "U.S. Schools: They Face a Crisis," special issue, *Life*, 26 (16) (1950). See also *The Transformation of the School: Progressivism in American Education 1876-1957* (New York, 1964), 343-347.

3. John Bainbridge, "Danger's Ahead in the Public Schools," *McCall's* (October 1952): n.p., article reprint, box 1026, NEA Archives. Hereafter cited as Bainbridge, "Danger's Ahead in the Public Schools."

4. *Addresses and Proceedings* (1952), 41.

5. See, for example, *Addresses and Proceedings* (1948), 174-175; *Addresses and Proceedings* (1949), 312-314; *Addresses and Proceedings* (1950), 324-326; *Addresses and Proceedings* (1951), 303-305; *Addresses and Proceedings* (1952), 338-341; *Addresses and Proceedings* (1953), 312-314; and *Addresses and Proceedings* (1954), 300-303.

6. Melby, *American Education Under Fire*, 10.

7. *Defense Bulletin* 38 (February 1951): 3.

8. See, for example, *Addresses and Proceedings* (1952), 160.

9. Bernard Iddings Bell, *Crisis in Education: A Challenge to American Complacency* (New York, 1949); Mortimer Smith, *And Madly Teach: A Layman Looks at Public School Education* (Chicago, 1949).

10. Albert Lynd, *Quackery in the Public Schools* (Boston, 1953). Texts also critical of public education in this period include Paul Woodring, *Let's Talk Sense About Our Schools* (New York, 1953) and Mortimer Smith, *The Diminished Mind* (Chicago, 1954). As the Defense Commission's bibliography suggests (see footnote 1) hundreds of articles written about educational criticism were published in this period. A selection includes Hugh Russell Fraser, "In Defense of the Critics of American Public Education," *School and Society* 74 (October 1951): 261-262; Paul Woodring, "An Open Letter to Teachers," *Harper's Magazine* 205 (July 1952): 28-32; Harry J. Fuller, "The Emperor's New Clothes, Or Prius Dementat," *The Scientific Monthly* 72 (January 1951): 32-41. By far the most impressive compilation of articles regarding criticism of education is Scott and Hill, eds, *Public Education Under Criticism*. For an excellent analysis of 25 articles written by both critics and supporters of public education in 1950 and 1951 see William W. Brickman, "Attack and Counterattack in American Education," *School and Society* 74 (October 1951): 262-269.

11. Arthur E. Bestor, *Educational Wastelands: The Retreat from Learning in Our Public Schools* (Urbana, Illinois, 1953).

12. For a discussion of Bestor's intellectual position, see Zilversmit, *Changing Schools,* 108-111; Herbert M. Kliebard, *The Struggle for the American Curriculum 1893-1958* (New York, 1986), 260-264; Cremin, *The Transformation of the School,* 343-347.

13. *Defense Bulletin* 39 (October 1951): 6-7.

14. Editorial, "Earmarks of a 'Front' Organization," *Nation's Schools* 47 (April 1951): 29-30.

15. See Robert A. Skaife, "Groups Affecting Education" in *Forces Affecting American Education*, ed. Van Til, 44.

16. See also Robert C. Morris, "The Right Wing Critics of Education: Yesterday and Today," *Educational Leadership* 35 (May 1978): 624.

17. Iversen, *The Communists and the Schools,* 245.

18. Melby, *American Education Under Fire,* 13.

19. Robert A. Skaife, "They Sow Distrust," *Nation's Schools* 47 (January 1951): 29.

20. As the Defense Commission frequently pointed out, American Patriots, Inc., appeared on the Attorney General's list as a fascist organization in both Democratic and Republican presidential administrations in the 1940s and 1950s.

21. L. M. Birkhead, director of pro-democracy organization, Friends of Democracy, sent information exposing Zoll's background to individuals who had permitted their names to be used by Zoll. Twenty of these citizens were prominent enough to be

featured in *Who's Who in America.* They included former heavy weight boxing champion Gene Tunney and Stanley High of the *Reader's Digest.* Significantly, when these individuals learned of Zoll's activities, they immediately withdrew their support from NCAE.

22. Despite the problems Zoll encountered during 1948, according to former Defense Commission Chairman, Ernest O. Melby, in 1949, Zoll netted an estimated $45,000 through the sale of his published materials and direct financial contributions. Melby, *American Education Under Fire*, 13. The source and extent of Zoll's financial support is difficult to pin down. Often, Zoll's materials were distributed in troubled communities from unknown sources. In fueling attacks on the schools in Englewood, New Jersey, however, Zoll explicitly enjoyed the financial support of Wall Street investment banker Frederick G. Cartwright. See Morse, "Who's Trying to Ruin Our Schools?" n.p.

23. Morris, "Era of Anxiety," 237-38.

24. Allen A. Zoll, "They Want Your Child," 2, as cited in Morris, "Era of Anxiety," 151.

25. National Council for American Education, "Must American Youth Be Taught That Communism and Socialism Are Superior to Americanism?" (New York, 1950): 2, as cited in Morris, "Era of Anxiety," 236.

26. Allen A. Zoll, "Progressive Education Increases Delinquency," (New York, N.D.): 11, as cited in Morris, "Era of Anxiety," 155.

27. Zoll, "Progressive Education Increases Delinquency," 15, as cited in Morris, "Era of Anxiety," 155-56.

28. See, for example, Sidney Hook, *New York Times*, Sunday book section, 30 October 1955, 6.

29. That Allen Zoll's National Council for American Education was targeted in *Defense Bulletins* 28, 35, 38, 39, 43, 46, 50, and 54 illustrated how carefully the commission attended to his actions and how seriously they perceived his threat to American schools.

30. Nelson and Roberts, *The Censors and the Schools,* 47.

31. See Verne P. Kaub, "A Critic," in Scott and Hill, eds., *Public Education Under Criticism*, 162.

32. Kaub, "A Critic," in Scott and Hill, eds., *Public Education Under Criticism*, 163

33. Kaub, "A Critic," in Scott and Hill, eds., *Public Education Under Criticism*, 162.

34. See *Defense Bulletin* 49 (March 1953): 5. Also Nelson and Roberts, *The Censors and the Schools*, 44.

35. Nelson and Roberts, *The Censors and the Schools*, 47.

36. "Danger! They're After Our Schools," n.p., pamphlet reprint, box 1025, NEA Archives. Hereafter cited as "Danger! They're After Our Schools," n.p.

37. As cited in Newsweek Club and Educational Bureaus, "New Crises for Education," (New York, 1952), 16. Hereafter cited as NCEB, "New Crises for Education."

38. Zoll's influence on American education has been well documented. See, for example, David Hulburd, *This Happened in Pasadena* (New York, 1951*)*; Iversen, *The Communists and the Schools;* Morris "Era of Anxiety"; Caute, *The Great Fear;* Kliebard, *The Struggle for the American Curriculum;* or Raywid, *The Ax-Grinders.*

39. *Defense Bulletin* 28 (January 1949): 2.

40. Iversen, *The Communists and the Schools,* 246.

41. Marjorie Murphy, *Blackboard Unions: The AFT and the NEA 1900-1980* (Ithaca, NY 1990), 182.

42. Iversen, *The Communists and the Schools,* 246.

43. The Defense Commission first noted the influence of Fries as early as 1942. See *Defense Bulletin* 2 (January 1942): 5-6. For other early indicators of Fries' activities, see also *Defense Bulletin* 8 (January 1944): 6; *Defense Bulletin* 9 (May 1944): 7; *Defense Bulletin* 14 (December 1944): 10; *Defense Bulletin* 18 (September 1946): 6-7.

44. Murphy, *Blackboard Unions*, 182.

45. Arthur D. Morse, "Who's Trying to Ruin Our Schools?" *McCall's* 78 (September 1951), n.p., article reprint, box 1025, NEA Archives. Hereafter referred to as Morse, "Who's Trying to Ruin Our Schools?" n.p.

46. *Defense Bulletin* 28 (January 1949): 5.

47. Skaife noted, for example, that the *Bulletin* "is received by many superintendents, school board members, and legislators despite the fact that they do not subscribe to it."

48. Raywid, *The Ax-Grinders*, 61.

49. *Defense Bulletin* 36 (January 1951): 4.

50. The House Select Committee on Lobbying Activities of the Eighty-First Congress, *General Interim Report* (Washington, 1950), 51.

51. See, Raywid, *The Ax-Grinders*, 59-61.

52. Raywid, *The Ax-Grinders,* 58.

53. As cited in Raywid, *The Ax-Grinders,* 58.

54. Morris, "Era of Anxiety," 251

55. John T. Flynn, *The Road Ahead* (New York, 1949), 121.

56. John T. Flynn, "Who Owns Your Child's Mind?" *The Reader's Digest* 59 (October 1951): 23-24.

57. The six were the Conference of American Small Business Organizations, the Committee for Constitutional Government, the National Economic Council, the National Council for American Education, Sons of the American Revolution, and Friends of the Public Schools. Skaife, "Groups Affecting Education," in *Forces Affecting American Education*, ed. Van Til, 52-60.

58. See, for example, Morris, "Era of Anxiety," 245; Gordon D. Hall, *The Hate Campaign Against the U. N.: One World Under Attack* (Boston, 1952), 17, box 1025, NEA Archives. Gordon D. Hall noted the active support Hart gave to the racist organization Columbians, Inc., of Atlanta.

59. See Skaife, "Groups Affecting Education," in *Forces Affecting American Education*, ed. Van Til, 55.

60. As cited in Raywid, *The Ax-Grinders*, 116.

61. Hall, *The Hate Campaign Against the U. N.*, 19.

62. As cited in Skaife, "Groups Affecting Education," in *Forces Affecting American Education*, ed. Van Til, 55.

63. Hall, *The Hate Campaign Against the U. N.*, 19.

64. Hall, *The Hate Campaign Against the U. N.*, 21.

65. For example, another notorious red scare organization was a group led by retired Army Colonel Augustin G. Rudd, the Guardians of American Education (GAE). Author of *Bending the Twig*, Rudd launched a vicious assault on progressive education and its architects. Rudd received support from many business leaders including Robert Donner, a prominent steel industrialist, who used his substantial resources to purchase 20,000 copies of the book for distribution to school board presidents and educational leaders throughout the country.

66.   See Iversen, *The Communists and the Schools*, 253; Nelson and Roberts, *The Censors and the Schools*, 45.

67.   National Society, Sons of the American Revolution, *A Bill of Grievances* (Washington, D.C., 1949): 4, as cited in Morris, "Era of Anxiety," 241.

68.   See Iversen, *The Communists and the Schools,* 254.

69.   National Society, SAR, *A Bill of Grievances*, 4, as cited in Morris, "Era of Anxiety," 242.

70.   As cited in Skaife, "Groups Affecting Education," in *Forces Affecting American Education*, ed. Van Til, 59.

71.   Skaife, "Groups Affecting Education," in *Forces Affecting American Education*, ed. Van Til, 43-86.

72.   Skaife, "Groups Affecting Education," in *Forces Affecting American Education*, ed. Van Til, 60.

73.   See *Addresses and Proceedings* (1952), 145.

74.   Defense Commission, "State of the Nation in Regard to Attacks on the Schools and Problems of Concern to Teachers." (Washington, D.C., 1955): 4-5, box 1024, NEA Archives. Hereafter cited as Defense Commission, "State of the Nation."

75.   John Dixon, "What's Wrong With U.S. History?" *The American Legion Magazine* (May 1949): 15-16.

76.   Iversen, *The Communists and the Schools,* 241.

77.   Kuhn, "Your Child is their Target," *The American Legion Magazine* (June 1952): 57.

78.   Kuhn, "Your Child is their Target," 57.

79.   *Defense Bulletin* 46 (September 1952): 1-3.

80.   According to Forster and Epstein, Chodorov complained of "the transmutation of the American character from individualist to collectivist." Arnold Forster and Benjamin R. Epstein, *Danger on the Right* (New York, 1964), 219.

81.   Forster and Epstein, *Danger on the Right*, 213. See also *Defense Bulletin* 55 (April 1954): 7.

82.   Skaife, "The Conflict Continues," *Nation's Schools* 53 (March 1954): 45.

83.   Frank Chodorov, "Educators Should be Warned by the Pasadena Revolt," *Saturday Evening Post*, 14 July 1951, 10.

84.   For an example of the Defense Commission's response to Chodorov, see *Defense Bulletin* 52 (November 1953): 6.

85.   Titles of newspapers owned by Hoiles include *Santa Anna Register* (California), *Colorado Springs Gazette* (Colorado), *Clovis News-Journal* (New Mexico), *Lima News* (Ohio), *Brownsville Herald*, *Pampa News*, *McAllen Valley Monitor*, *Odessa American*, and *Harlingen Valley Star* (Texas).

86.   See Lewis C. Fay, "'Abolish Public Schools,' says owner of newspaper chain Robert Cyrus Hoiles," article reprint, box 1026, NEA Archives. Hereafter cited as Fay, "Abolish Public Schools," n.p.

87.   Fay, "Abolish Public Schools," n.p.

88.   Fay, "Abolish Public Schools," n.p.

89.   Fay, "Abolish Public Schools," n.p. Fay's article was based on Hoiles' comments during a public debate in McAllen, Texas.

90.   Significantly, the debates attracted huge crowds. At the first meeting an estimated 5,000 residents turned out. Fay's article was originally published in *The Nation's Schools* 50 (August 1952).

91.   Skaife, "The Sound and the Fury," *Phi Delta Kappan* 24 (June 1953): 358.

92.   Fay, "Abolish Public Schools, n.p.

93.   Fay, "Abolish Public Schools," n.p.

94.   *Defense Bulletin* 52 (November 1953): 6-7.

95.   PEDE (Philadelphia), 8-9.

Chapter VI: Politics, Propaganda, and Public School Textbooks

1.   As cited in Hall, *The Hate Campaign Against the U. N.*, 8.

2.   Hall, *The Hate Campaign Against the U. N.,* 7-8.

3.   As cited in Hall, *The Hate Campaign Against the U. N.,* 9.

4.   As cited in Hall, *The Hate Campaign Against the U. N.,* 9-10.

5. Carleton, *Red Scare!* 167.

6. Kransdorf, *A Matter of Loyalty*, 39-43.

7. Kransdorf, *A Matter of Loyalty*, 41.

8. For an account of the interaction between these forces in Houston and their impact on the city's local schools see Carleton, *Red Scare!* 167-170.

9. Griffin Fariello, *Red Scare: Memories of American Inquisition* (New York, 1995), 17.

10. Fariello, *Red Scare,* 17.

11. Skaife, "An Evaluation of the Program of the National Commission for the Defense of Democracy Through Education," 25.

12. *Defense Bulletin* 27 (December 1948): 4.

13. Schrecker, *No Ivory Tower*, 180.

14. See Schrecker, *No Ivory Tower*, 180. McCarthy was appointed Chairman of the Permanent Subcommittee on Investigation of the Senate Committee on Government Operations.

15. *Defense Bulletin* 48 (January 1953): 3.

16. The impact on education of the investigating committees of Velde, McCarthy, and McCarran has been well documented. See, for example, Schrecker, *No Ivory Tower,* 180; Kransdorf, *A Matter of Loyalty,* 20-24, 28-34; Zilversmit, *Changing Schools,* 108-109; Caute, *The Great Fear,* 419-420, 441-445, 552-555; Iversen, *The Communists and the Schools,* 316-320, 336-340.

17. Caute, *The Great Fear*, 419; Iversen, *The Communists and the Schools*, 336.

18. Kransdorf, *A Matter of Loyalty*, 77.

19. Caute, *The Great Fear*, 418.

20. See Ellen Vedries, "Riding the Red Tide: The AF of T and the Los Angeles Local 430," (paper presented at the American Educational and Research Association, San Francisco, April 1995); Fariello, *Red Scare,* 459-468.

21. Vedries, "Riding the Red Tide," 19.

22. Murphy, *Blackboard Unions*, 192.

23. Schrecker, *No Ivory Tower*, 108-109.

24. Vedries, "Riding the Red Tide," 14.

25. Ravitch, *The Troubled Crusade*, 103.

26. Iversen, *The Communists and the Schools*, 321

27. Caute, *The Great Fear*, 419.

28. Ravitch, *The Troubled Crusade*, 103.

29. Schrecker, *No Ivory Tower*, 9.

30. See Schrecker, *No Ivory Tower*, 21.

31. Iversen, *The Communists and the Schools*, 343.

32. Zilversmit, *Changing Schools*, 108.

33. Defense Commission, "Proceedings of the Open Meeting," 2.

34. "Congressional Investigations Into Education," Transcript of radio broadcast hosted by Russell Tornabene, February 18, 1953, Station WRC, Washington D.C., reprint, box 1025, NEA Archives.

35. See, for example, *Defense Bulletin* 23 (January 1948): 7; *Defense Bulletin* 37 (January 1951): 6-7; *Defense Bulletin* 38 (February 1951): 5; *Defense Bulletin* 44 (May 1952): 3-4, 7; *Defense Bulletin* 47 (December 1952): 6-8; *Defense Bulletin* 48 (January 1953): 3-5; *Defense Bulletin* 51 (September 1953): and *Defense Bulletin* 57 (September 1954): 1.

36. *Defense Bulletin* 48 (January 1953): 4.

37. See Nelson and Roberts, *The Censors and the Schools*, 39

38. *Defense Bulletin* 23 (January 1948): 7.

39. *Defense Bulletin* 24 (February 1948): 6.

40. *Defense Bulletin* 26 (November 1948): 7.

41. *The Educational Reviewer*, 1, July 15, 1949, 6, as cited in Morris, "Age of Anxiety," 158-9.

42. Lucille Cardin Crain, "What Are Our Schools Teaching About Business?" *Vital Speeches of the Day* 16 (August 1950): 658.

43. Morse, "Who's Trying to Ruin Our Schools?" n.p.

44.   *Congressional Record* (August 1951). Reprint, NEA Archives, Box 1026.

45.   Skaife, "They Want Tailored Schools," 36-37.

46.   *The Educational Reviewer*, April 15, 1951, 6-7, as cited in Morris, "Era of Anxiety," 36-37.

47.   Nelson and Roberts, *The Censors and the Schools*, 43.

48.   *Defense Bulletin* 46 (September 1952): 6-7.

49.   "Reds Under Control Here, McGrath Says," *Washington Post,* January 14, 1951.

50.   U. S. Eighty-first Congress, second session, House Select Committee on Lobbying Activities. Report Number 3232: Conference of Small American Business Organizations. (Washington, D.C. 1950): 15-16.

51.   See *The Nation's Schools* 48 (July 1951): 23-27.

52.   Editorial, "Congressional Committee Doubts Reliability of CASBO," *Nation's Schools* 51 (March 1951): 30.

53.   Editorial, "Congressional Committee Doubts Reliability of CASBO," 30.

54.   See, for example, *Defense Bulletin* 37 (January 1951): 4; *Defense Bulletin* 38 (February 1951): 1.

55.   *Defense Bulletin* 37 (January 1951): 4.

56.   *Defense Bulletin* 38 (February 1951): 1.

57.   *Congressional Record* (August 1951). Reprint, box 1026, NEA Archives.

58.   Bainbridge, "Danger's Ahead in The Public Schools," n.p.

59.   See, for example, Iversen, *The Communists and the Schools*, 255, or Nelson and Roberts, *The Censors and the Schools*, 41-43.

60.   See, for example, *Defense Bulletin* 33 (June 1950): 1-2; *Defense Bulletin* 46 (September 1952): 7; *Forces Affecting American Education*, ed. Van Til, 200; Iversen, *The Communists and the Schools*, 255; Nelson and Roberts, *The Censors and the Schools*, 42-43.

61.   Iversen, *The Communists and the Schools*, 255.

62.   *Defense Bulletin* 33 (June 1950): 2.

63.   Carleton, *Red Scare!* 166.

64. These examples were detailed by Morse in "Who's Trying to Ruin Our Schools?"

65. As cited in Appendix B, "Reporting," *Forces Affecting American Education*, ed. Van Til, 200-201.

66. See Defense Bulletin 46 (September 1952): 7; Nelson and Roberts, *The Censors and the Schools*, 42-43; and Morse, "Who's Trying to Ruin Our Schools?"

67. NCEB, "New Crises for Education," 16.

68. NCEB, "New Crises for Education," 17.

69. As cited in NCEB, "New Crises for Education," 16.

70. *Defense Bulletin* 46 (September 1952): 6-7.

71. See, for example, "The Current Attacks on Public Education: A Fact Sheet," 4, January 1953, box 1025, NEA Archives.

72. "Danger! They're After Our Schools," n.p..

73. "Danger! They're After Our Schools," n.p.

74. Kenneth M. Gould, "The Scarsdale Story," *The Humanist* 4 (1952): 145-159, pamphlet reprint, box 1025, NEA Archives.

75. Carleton, *Red Scare!* 222

76. See, for example, Carleton, *Red Scare!* 223; *Defense Bulletin* 55 (April 1954): 7; Hall, *The Hate Campaign Against the UN*.

77. Hall, *The Hate Campaign Against the UN*, 25.

Chapter VII: The Activities of the Defense Commission, 1947-1954: Exposing Critics and Supporting Educators

1. See *Defense Bulletin* 35 (July 1950): 1-4.

2. "Report on the Enemy," *Defense Bulletin* 35 (July 1950): 4.

3. *Addresses and Proceedings* (1948), 148.

4. *Addresses and Proceedings* (1949), 139.

5. *Addresses and Proceedings* (1953), 275; *Addresses and Proceedings* (1954), 114.

6.   *Stewardship Report,* 6.

7.   Scott and Hill, *Public Education Under Criticism,* 7.

8.   Skaife, "An Evaluation of the Program of the National Commission for the Defense of Democracy Through Education," 149.

9.   PEDE (Denver), 19.

10. As cited in NCEB, "New Crises for Education," 14.

11. Willard Goslin, "The People and Their Schools," in *Forces Affecting American Education,* ed. Van Til, 148.

12. Skaife, "An Evaluation of the Program of the National Commission for the Defense of Democracy Through Education," 154.

13. See Skaife, "The Conflict Continues," *Nation's Schools* 53 (March 1954): 45; "They Oppose Progress," *Nation's Schools* 47 (February 1951): 31-33; "They Sow Distrust," *Nation's Schools* 47 (January 1951): 29; "They Want Tailored Schools," *Nation's Schools* 47 (May 1951): 35-37.

14. See, for example, Skaife, "The Sound and the Fury," *Phi Delta Kappan* 24 (June 1953): 358; Skaife, "Groups Affecting Education," in *Forces Affecting American Education,* ed. Van Til, 43-86; Richard Barnes Kennan, "What Are They Calling You Today?" *Childhood Education* 28 (October 1951): 53-57; Kennan, "Education—Democracy's Best Defense," *Educational Leadership* 8 (May 1951): 458; or Kennan, "No Ivory Tower For You," *NEA Journal* 40 (May 1951): 317-318.

15. Skaife, "Know the Enemy," *Connecticut Teacher* (December 1951): 68.

16. Skaife, "Know the Enemy," 69.

17. Skaife, "Know the Enemy," 70.

18. Defense Commission, "A Study of the National Commission for the Defense of Democracy Through Education," Washington, D.C., 1959, 8. Hereafter cited as Defense Commission, "Study."

19. Skaife, "The Enemies and Critics of the Schools," 7.

20. Skaife, "The Enemies and Critics of the Schools," 5-6.

21. Exposure of Zoll's organization, for example, appeared in *Defense Bulletins* 28, 35, 38, 39, 43, 46, and 50.

22. *Defense Bulletin* 28 (January 1949): 3.

23. *Defense Bulletin* 50 (May 1953): 7.

24. Examples of this occurring appeared in Sonoma, California, and Chicago, Illinois. See *Defense Bulletin* 33 (June 1950): 6-7; *Defense Bulletin* 46 (September 1952): 5.

25. As cited in Skaife, "Groups Affecting Education" in *Forces Affecting American Education*, ed. Van Til, 57.

26. Skaife, "Groups Affecting Education," in *Forces Affecting American Education*, ed. Van Til, 58-59.

27. *Defense Bulletin* 35 (July 1950): 1.

28. *Addresses and Proceedings* (1950), 326.

29. *Addresses and Proceedings* (1952), 339.

30. See *Defense Bulletin* 38 (February 1951): 2.

31. *Defense Bulletin* 56 (May 1954): 8.

32. See, for example, *Defense Bulletin* 48 (January 1953): 8.

33. See *Defense Bulletin* 40 (November 1951): 1, 7-8.

34. *Defense Bulletin* 54 (February 1954): 5-6; *Defense Bulletin* 55 (April 1954): 1-2; *Defense Bulletin* 48 (January 1953): 8.

35. See *Addresses and Proceedings* (1952), 339; *Addresses and Proceedings* (1953), 220, 315, 318.

36. Melby, *American Education Under Fire*, 10.

37. See *Defense Bulletin* 29 (April 1949): 2-8.

38. Extract from D. D. Darland, "To Some Freedom of Thought is Subversive," *Phi Delta Kappan* 30 (December 1948): 109, as cited in *Defense Bulletin* 29 (April 1949): 6.

39. For example, *Defense Bulletin* 29 (April 1949): 8 recommended 14 articles or books on academic freedom.

40. Defense Commission, "Study," 8.

41. See, for example, Defense Commission, "State of the Nation."

42. "The Three R's Hold Their Own at Mid-century," NEA Research Division, April 1951, "mimeographed 28 pages, 15 cents," as advertised in *Defense Bulletin* 39 (October 1951): 8.

43. "Danger! They're After Our Schools, n.p.

44. "Danger! They're After Our Schools, n.p.

45. See, for example, "Danger! They're After Our Schools, n.p. "The Current Attacks on Public Education: Fact Sheet," 6.

46. *Defense Bulletin* 33 (June 1950): 8.

47. For example, see Harold C. Hand, "Attacks on Public Schools Can Be Prevented," *Educator's Dispatch,* March 13, 1952 as cited in *Defense Bulletin* 43 (April 1952): 5.

48. Typical examples of articles offering constructive suggestions included Irving R. Melbo, "What Can School Board Members Do to Answer Criticism of Public Education?" *The American School Board Journal* 122 (May 1951): 27-28, 86; and W. L. Van Loan, "In Times Like These What Should Teachers Do?" *NEA Journal* 41 (January 1952): 36.

49. *Addresses and Proceedings* (1951), 16.

50. *Defense Bulletin* 36 (November 1950): 7.

51. *Addresses and Proceedings* (1949), 152.

52. See *Addresses and Proceedings* (1951), 305.

53. See, for example, *Addresses and Proceedings* (1952), 340; *Addresses and Proceedings* (1953), 314; *Addresses and Proceedings* (1954), 300-303; *Addresses and Proceedings* (1955), 308-310.

54. *Defense Bulletin* 41 (December 1951): 12.

55. *Defense Bulletin* 53 (January 1954): 8.

56. *Defense Bulletin* 53 (January 1954): 8.

57. See, for example, *Defense Bulletin* 8 (January 1944): 6; *Defense Bulletin* 28 (January 1949): 2-5; *Defense Bulletin* 33 (June 1950): 1-2; *Defense Bulletin* 38 (February 1951): 1-2.

58. See *Defense Bulletin* 14 (December 1945): 6; *Defense Bulletin* 18 (September 1946): 4; *Defense Bulletin* 33 (June 1950): 8.

59. See, for example, *Defense Bulletin* 33 (June 1950): 6-7; *Defense Bulletin* 46 (September 1952): 3-7.

60. *Defense Bulletin* 41 (December 1951): 16.

61. See, for example, *Defense Bulletin* 22 (November 1947): 11; *Defense Bulletin* 15 (January 1946): 3; *Defense Bulletin* 12 (February 1945): 12-13; *Defense Bulletin* 2 (January 1942): 9-10.

62. Committee on Tenure and Academic Freedom, "Teachers' Oaths and Related State Requirements," 5 June 1949, box 1010, NEA Archives.

63. Committee on Tenure and Academic Freedom, "Teachers' Oaths and Related State Requirements," 7, 22.

64. NEA, "1952 Report of the Committee on Tenure and Academic Freedom," 15, box 1007, NEA Archives.

65. Committee on Tenure and Academic Freedom, "Teachers' Oaths and Related State Requirements," 10.

66. Committee on Tenure and Academic Freedom, "Teachers' Oaths and Related State Requirements," 10.

67. See, for example, *Defense Bulletin* 26 (September 1948): 1-2; *Defense Bulletin* 29 (April 1949): 5-8; *Defense Bulletin* 32 (November 1949): 1-8; *Defense Bulletin* 33 (June 1950): 3-5; *Defense Bulletin* 36 (November 1950): 8; *Defense Bulletin* 44 (May 1952): 1-7.

68. Goslin, "The People and Their Schools," in *Forces Affecting American Education*, ed. Van Til, 144-145.

69. *Addresses and Proceedings* (1949), 96.

70. Committee on Tenure and Academic Freedom, "Teachers' Oaths and Related State Requirements," 3.

71. NEA, "1952 Report of the Committee on Tenure and Academic Freedom," 18.

72. NEA, "1952 Report of the Committee on Tenure and Academic Freedom," 18.

73. See NEA, "1952 Report of the Committee on Tenure and Academic Freedom," 18; *Defense Bulletin* 44 (May 1952): 3.

74. *Defense Bulletin* 44 (May 1952): 3-4.

75. Examples of individual educators who stood against loyalty legislation were highlighted in *Defense Bulletin* 33 (June 1950): 4-5.

76. As cited in *Defense Bulletin* 33 (June 1950): 4.

77. *Defense Bulletin* 44 (May 1952): 1.

78. NEA, "1952 Report of the Committee on Tenure and Academic Freedom," 16.

79. *Defense Bulletin* 44 (May 1952): 7.

80. See *Defense Bulletin* 56 (May 1954): 6.

81. *Defense Bulletin* 29 (April 1949): 5.

82. *Defense Bulletin* 29 (April 1949): 5.

83. Robert A. Skaife, "Congressional Probes Into Education," *Nation's Schools* 51 (April 1953): 48.

84. Skaife, "Congressional Probes Into Education," 49-50.

85. As cited in Skaife, "Congressional Probes Into Education," 49.

86. See, for example, *Defense Bulletin* 29 (April 1949): 5; *Defense Bulletin* 32 (November 1949): 2-8; *Defense Bulletin* 44 (May 1952): 1-7; *Defense Bulletin* 48 (January 1953): 1-3; *Defense Bulletin* 58 (November 1954): 6-7; *Addresses and Proceedings* (1953), 220.

87. *Addresses and Proceedings* (1953), 50.

88. As cited in Skaife, "Congressional Probes Into Education," 49.

89. Murphy, *Blackboard Unions*, 193.

90. *Addresses and Proceedings* (1953), 50.

91. As cited in Murphy, *Blackboard Unions*, 193.

92. See Skaife, "Congressional Probes Into Education," 49-50.

93. Murphy, *Blackboard Unions*, 195.

94. See, for example, *Defense Bulletin* 26 (September 1948): 1; *Defense Bulletin* 48 (January 1953): 1-3; *Defense Bulletin* 50 (May 1953): 5; *Defense Bulletin* 51 (September 1953): 1-4; *Defense Bulletin* 58 (November 1954): 6-7; *Defense Bulletin* 59 (January 1955): 5.

95. Skaife, "Congressional Probes Into Education," 50.

Chapter VIII: The Defense Commission's Work in the Field, 1947-1954

1. *Stewardship Report*, 12.

2. *Addresses and Proceedings* (1945), 361.

3. Defense Commission, "Study," 10.

4. Skaife, "An Evaluation of the Program of the National Commission for the Defense of Democracy Through Education," 149.

5. See Wesley, *NEA: The First Hundred Years*, 311; *Addresses and Proceedings* (1950), 325; *Defense Bulletin* 38 (February 1951): 3.

6. *Defense Bulletin* 38 (February 1951): 3.

7. *Addresses and Proceedings* (1951), 304.

8. *Addresses and Proceedings* (1952), 340.

9. PEDE (Philadelphia), 4.

10. PEDE (Philadelphia), 4.

11. PEDE (Philadelphia), 28, 31.

12. *Defense Bulletin* 56 (May 1954): 7.

13. PEDE (Philadelphia), 9.

14. PEDE (Denver), 13.

15. PEDE (Philadelphia), 8; PEDE (Denver), 21-22.

16. PEDE (Philadelphia), 30-31.

17. *Addresses and Proceedings* (1954), 303.

18. See, for example, PEDE (Philadelphia), 29-31; PEDE (Denver), 23-24; PEDE (San Francisco), 18.

19. *Addresses and Proceedings* (1950), 11-12.

20. Skaife, "Groups Affecting Education," in *Forces Affecting American Education*, ed. Van Til, 64; Bainbridge, "Danger's Ahead in the Public Schools," n.p.

21. Roy E. Larsen, "A Layman's View of the Importance of Public Education to Our Society," *The Educational Forum* 16 (May 1952): 389.

22. Larsen, "A Layman's View of the Importance of Public Education to Our Society," 394; Zilversmit, *Changing Schools*, 112-113.

23. See Skaife, "Groups Affecting Education," in *Forces Affecting American Education*, ed. Van Til, 64; Goslin, "The People and Their Schools," in *Forces Affecting American Education*, ed. Van Til, 160-166; Zilversmit, *Changing Schools*, 112.

24. *Defense Bulletin* 52 (November 1953): 1-2.

25. Skaife, "Groups Affecting Education," in *Forces Affecting American Education*, ed. Van Til, 64.

26. *Defense Bulletin* 52 (November 1953): 1-2.

27. Larsen, "A Layman's View of the Importance of Public Education to Our Society," 395

28. PEDE (Philadelphia), 11-12.

29. See Skaife, "Groups Affecting Education," in *Forces Affecting American Education*, ed. Van Til, 70-83.

30. *Defense Bulletin* 49 (March 1953): 1.

31. Harold Benjamin, "Communication Affecting Education," in *Forces Affecting American Education*, ed. Van Til, 117.

32. See William Van Til's "Research Affecting Education," in *Forces Affecting American Education*, ed. Van Til, 119-139.

33. Goslin, "The People and Their Schools," in *Forces Affecting American Education*, ed. Van Til, 174.

34. Isaac L. Kandel, "We Must Educate Our Masters," *School and Society* 76 (July 1952): 44; Harry A. Fosdick, "The Counterattack Starts in the Classroom," *School and Community* 37 (October 1951): 338-341; H. Gordon Hullfish, "The Profession and the Public Face a Common Problem," *Educational Research Bulletin* 30 (May 1951): 115.

35. Lyle W. Ashby, "Address at the Evening Session," 11, OEA-NEA Workshop.

36. *Addresses and Proceedings* (1951), 247.

37. *Addresses and Proceedings* (1952), 194.

38. *Addresses and Proceedings* (1951), 247; *Addresses and Proceedings* (1952), 283; *Addresses and Proceedings* (1954), 249.

39. *Addresses and Proceedings* (1953), 261; *Addresses and Proceedings* (1955), 39.

40. *Addresses and Proceedings* (1952), 283; *Addresses and Proceedings* (1953), 261.

41. Ashby, "Address at the Evening Session," 11, OEA-NEA Workshop

42. Skaife, "Groups Affecting Education," in *Forces Affecting American Education*, ed. Van Til, 85-86.

43. *Defense Bulletin* 39 (October 1951): 6.

44. Skaife, "Groups Affecting Education," in *Forces Affecting American Education*, ed. Van Til, 83.

45. OEA-NEA Workshop, 19.

46. See *Defense Bulletin* 61 (May 1955): 4.

47. Melby, *American Education Under Fire*, 26-35.

48. Skaife, as cited in NCEB, "New Crises for Education," 17.

49. Zilversmit, *Changing Schools*, 116.

50. Kenneth B. Henderson and Harold C. Hand, "To What Extent Is the General Public in Sympathy with the Current Attacks on the Schools?" *Progressive Education* 29 (January 1952): 110-113.

51. Robert Skaife, "Public Education at the Crossroads," PEDE (Denver), 13-14.

Chapter IX: Defense Commission Investigations

1. The investigations occurred in Grand Prairie, Texas (1949); Kelso, Washington (1950); Newport, New Hampshire (1950); The State Education Agency, Salt Lake City, Utah (1950); Twin Falls, Idaho (1950); Polson, Montana (1951); Oglesby, Illinois (1951); Pasadena, California (1951); Mars Hill, North Carolina (1951); Miami, Florida (1952), and Houston, Texas (1954).

2. National Commission for the Defense of Democracy Through Education, *Report of An Investigation of a School Controversy in Polson* (Washington D.C., April 1951), 5, box 1036, NEA Archives.

3. See Defense Commission *Report: Houston*, 18; Defense Commission *Report: Pasadena*, 3, 6.

4. The Houston controversy and the dismissal of Deputy Superintendent George Ebey received national prominence. See "Houston: That Word," *Time*, 27 July 1953, 51; "Ebey Story," *Nation*, 26 September 1953, 242; "School Man Fired as Controversial," *The Christian Century*, 17 August 1953, 885. However, while the Ebey debacle appeared significant, the Pasadena controversy, which occurred two years earlier, aroused considerably more attention. See, for example, David Hulburd, *This Happened in Pasadena*; Carey McWilliams, "The Enemy in Pasadena," *The Christian Century* 68 (January 1951): 11-13; "Quandary in Pasadena," *Time*, 27 November 1950, 85-87; "Pasadena Free-for-All," *Newsweek*, 27 November 1950, 75; James B. Conant, "The Superintendent Was the Target," *The New York Times Book Review*, 29 April 1951, 1, 27; John B. Sheerin, "What Was the Question at Pasadena?" *The Catholic World* 174 (October 1951): 1-5; Frank Chodorov, "Educators Should Be Warned by the Pasadena Revolt," *The Saturday Evening Post*, July 14, 1951, 10; "The Public School Crisis," *The Saturday Review of Literature*, 8 September 1951, and Frederick Hechlinger, "Aftermath in Pasadena," *New York Herald Tribune*, 6, 7, 8, August 1951.

5. Hulburd, *This Happened in Pasadena*, ix. See also Zilversmit, *Changing Schools*, 103 and Raywid, *The Ax-Grinders*, 162-163.

6. Defense Commission *Report: Houston*, 12-13.

7. See Carleton, *Red Scare!*, 157-160.

8. For specific examples of how each of these issues became matters of controversy, see Carleton, *Red Scare!*, 157-160, 167-168, 172-174, 221.

9. See Carleton, "McCarthyism in Local Elections," 168-177 and "McCarthyism in Houston," 163-176. In particular see Chapter 6, "Red Scare and the Schools," 154-178 and Chapter 7, "The Victim is a Symbol: The George W. Ebey Affair," 179-223 in *Red Scare!* See also Carleton, "A Crisis in Rapid Change: The Red Scare in Houston." (Ph.D. diss., University of Houston, 1978).

10. See Carleton, *Red Scare!*, 168-172, 221-222 and also Defense Commission *Report: Pasadena*, 11, 15-16, 22.

11. For explicit evidence of teacher self-censorship and caution, see Defense Commission *Report: Houston*, 23-28.

12. For example, the Defense Commission investigation of Houston reported, "There is no reason to believe there are any disloyal or communist teachers in the Houston school system." Defense Commission *Report: Houston*, 30. Similarly, no evidence of subversion was uncovered in Pasadena. Indeed, even the vehemently anti-communist *California Senate Investigating Committee* noted that there was "no clear

cut evidence of known subversives actually within the school system itself." See *California Senate Investigating Committee on Education*, 44.

13.   Zilversmit, *Changing Schools*, 103.

14.   Defense Commission *Report: Pasadena*, 9

15.   Archibald W. Anderson, "The Charges Against American Education: What is the Evidence?" *Progressive Education* 29 (January 1952): 91-105.

16.   Hulburd, *This Happened in Pasadena*, ix.

17.   Conant, "The Superintendent Was the Target," 1, 27.

18.   Chodorov, "Educators Should Be Warned by the Pasadena Revolt," 10.

19.   Sheerin, "What was the Question at Pasadena?" 1; Hugh Russell Fraser, "In Defense of the Critics of American Public Education," *School and Society* 74 (October 1951): 261.

20.   Zilversmit, Changing Schools, 103-106; John A. Beineke, *And There Were Giants in the Land: The Life of William Heard Kilpatrick*, (New York, 1998), 317-351; Ravitch, The Troubled Crusade, 107-109; and Cremin, *The Transformation of the School*, 341-342.

21.   Defense Commission *Report: Pasadena*, 3, 30.

22.   In particular, the Defense Commission questioned the timing of the school tax-election and the re-zoning program. See Defense Commission *Report: Pasadena*, 9, 12, 31, 33-35.

23.   See Hulburd, *This Happened in Pasadena*, Chapter 2.

24.   Defense Commission *Report: Pasadena*, 8.

25.   See Defense Commission *Report: Pasadena*, 11; "Danger! They're After the Schools, 6; Melby, *American Education Under Fire*, 14-15.

26.   The California State Senate Investigating Committee used Kilpatrick's visit to Pasadena as evidence of Goslin's socialist leanings. See *California State Senate Investigating Committee on Education*, 29-33, 42, box 1040, NEA Archives.

27.   John Beineke's biography of Kilpatrick unequivocally demonstrated that Kilpatrick never supported Communism and often appeared troubled by the actions of the Soviet Union. Beineke, *And There Were Giants in the Land*, 320-25, 338-39.

28.   Many historians and commentators have noted Zoll's influence in Pasadena. See, for example, Hulburd, *This Happened in Pasadena*, 87-91; Iversen, *The Communist

and the Schools, 252; Cremin, *The Transformation of the School*, 341-42; Kliebard, *The Struggle for the American Curriculum*, 258-59; Zilversmit, *Changing Schools*, 103-105.

29.   Melby, *American Education Under Fire*, 14; Defense Commission *Report: Pasadena*, 23-25.

30.   *California State Senate Investigating Committee on Education*, 35.

31.   See Defense Commission *Report: Pasadena*, 15-16, 25-26; Beineke, *And There Were Giants in the Land*, 328-330, and Hulburd, *This Happened in Pasadena*, 77, 120.

32.   John Q. Copeland, *Los Angeles Times*, "Pasadena Becomes Schools' Test Tube," May 25, 1950; "School Zones Stir Debate in Pasadena," May 26, 1950; "Pasadena Studies Camp Experiment," May 27, 1950; "Short Visit by Noted Educator Had Profound Effect on Teaching System in City Schools," May 28, 1950; "School Goal Told By Progressives," May 29, 1950, and "Teacher Drilling Key to Progressive Plan," May 30, 1950.

33.   Ex-Senator Hawkes was closely associated with extremist Merwin K. Hart of the National Economic Council. See Hall, *The Hate Campaign Against the U. N.*, 21. David Hulburd offered a detailed description of Louise Padelford in This Happened in Pasadena, 59-61. NEA officials obviously were aware of the connection between Padelford, Hawkes, and Hart. See Elsie Kroesche to Willard Givens, January 18, 1951 and Willard Givens to Elsie Kroesche, January 25, 1951, box 1040, NEA Archives.

34.   See Mrs. A. Pashgian to Robert Skaife, May 10, 1951, box 1040, NEA Archives.

35.   For an account of the way in which the investigations appeared unduly biased against Goslin, see Defense Commission *Report: Pasadena*, 19. Elsie Kroesche, who witnessed the investigation, wrote to Willard Givens, "I have been waiting to see something in print about the outrageous 'hearings' conducted here in November by the Senate intern committee on education. Two Pasadena citizens (of the school opposition group) who were also members of the state legislature, but not of the committee, also sat in. One of them even interrogated witnesses when he chose. People were asked what they thought, and what were their opinions and beliefs on various subjects. It seems as if we have the "thought police" in our very midst. In most cases only witnesses were called who seemed to point the way to certain beliefs about the schools. When others asked to be heard, or the public requested they be heard, to refute certain testimony or at least to present another viewpoint, they were refused. Some testimony was in secret [sic]." Elsie Kroesche to Willard Givens, January 18, 1951, box 1040, NEA Archives.

36.   Defense Commission *Report: Pasadena*, 19. According to John Beineke, the FBI file on William Heard Kilpatrick noted that Kilpatrick had once supported a "pro-

Communist superintendent of schools" for the position of school superintendent, New York City. The "pro-Communist superintendent" was, of course, Willard Goslin. See Beineke, *And There Were Giants in the Land*, 336.

37.   *California State Senate Investigating Committee on Education*, 44, 42. This was, of course, an explicit reference to Kilpatrick.

38.   For evidence that the public and teachers generally approved of Goslin, see Defense Commission *Report: Pasadena*, 17, 31, 37; that little curriculum changed occurred, see Melby, *American Education Under Fire*, 30, and Zilversmit, *Changing Schools*, 217; that educational standards had improved, see Van Til, *Research Affecting Education in Forces Affecting American Education*, ed. Van Til, 27-28; that no evidence of subversion existed, see *California State Senate Investigating Committee on Education*, 44.

39.   See Willard Givens to Arthur F. Corey; Givens to Willard Goslin; Givens to Herbert Clish, November 18, 1950; and Willard Givens to Harold Brooks, November 20, 1950. Givens also wrote to Worth McClure, executive secretary of American Association of School Administrators with the proposal that the Defense Commission investigate the situation in Pasadena, November 18, 1950, box 1040, NEA Archives.

40.   Skaife to Kennan, 21 November 1950, box 1040, NEA Archives.

41.   Kennan to Skaife, 13 December 1950, box 1040, NEA Archives.

42.   Givens to Howard Pillsbury, 5 December 1950, box 1040, NEA Archives.

43.   This was a problem that Skaife also encountered in his first visit to Pasadena in the summer of 1950. See Skaife to Goslin June 26, 1950, box 1040, NEA Archives.

44.   Kennan to Skaife, December 13, 1950, box 1040, NEA Archives.

45.   For example, from April 12 to April 30, 1950, Skaife received responses from dozens of NEA officials including Worth McClure, Executive Secretary of AASA, as well as Winona Montgomery, Harold Benjamin, John Davis, Virgil Rogers, and Mozelle Causey of the Defense Commission. Box 1040, NEA Archives.

46.   Ole Lilleland to Skaife, December 9, 1951, box 1040, NEA Archives. Glen Snow was the NEA's Assistant Secretary for Lay Relations, NEA president during 1948, and a former member of the Defense Commission.

47.   George A. Bowman to Pillsbury, July 18, 1951, box 1040, NEA Archives.

48.   Defense Commission *Report: Pasadena*, 3.

49.   See, for example, Alfred Ludlow to Skaife, January 17, 1951; Dorothea Fry to Skaife, February 5, 1951; Robert Gilchrist to Skaife, July 11, 1951, box 1040, NEA, Archives.

50. Defense Commission *Report: Pasadena*, 39.

51. See Purcell to Skaife, July 10, 1951; See also Purcell to Skaife, July 15, 1951, September 13, 1951, and September 19, 1951, box 1040, NEA Archives.

52. Skaife, "Groups Affecting Education," in *Forces Affecting American Education*, ed. Van Til, 73.

53. See requests from Superintendent Goslin, Alfred Ludlow, president of the Pasadena Education Association, and Lionel De Silva of the California Teachers' Association, box 1040, NEA Archives.

54. Skaife to Goslin, June 26, 1950.

55. See Skaife to Kennan, November 21, 1950, box 1040, NEA Archives.

56. See Skaife to Pillsbury, February 8, 1951, box 1040, NEA Archives.

57. A big difference existed, for example, between the tone and substance of the final report and Skaife's observations in much of his correspondence. Skaife clearly was troubled by the highly destructive impact of red scare rhetoric and propaganda. See, for example, Skaife to Kennan, (November 21, 1950), Skaife to Fry, (February 1, 1951) Skaife to Ludlow (January 25, 1951), box 1040, NEA Archives.

58. Defense Commission, "Study," 5.

59. On February 8, 1951, Skaife wrote to Pillsbury that "some of the 'rolling of heads' which teachers said would be forthcoming under the new superintendent has already come to pass." On May 3, 1951, Skaife wrote to the President of the Pasadena Education Association, "I was quite shocked and sorry to hear of the death of Blair Nixon [former personnel director]. Apparently the strain of what he has been going through was too much for him, and I imagine also that all of you have felt a very heavy strain." Skaife to Ludlow, May 3, 1951, box 1040, NEA Archives.

Chapter X: The Defense Commission Versus the Educational Red Scare

1. Van Til, *My Way of Looking At It*, 164.

2. *Addresses and Proceedings* (1954), 301.

3. See Schrecker, *No Ivory Tower*, 241.

4. Schrecker, *No Ivory Tower*, 339.

5. Beineke, *And There Were Giants in the Land*, 339; See also Carleton, "McCarthyism Was More Than McCarthy," 18.

6. Caute, *The Great Fear*, 406.

7. For the cases of Eisenberg and Bettington, see Kransdorf, *A Matter of Loyalty*, 48-63.

8. Hutchins made these remarks in an article entitled "Are Our Teachers Afraid to Teach?" published in *Look* on March 9, 1954. The Defense Commission printed excerpts of the article in *Defense Bulletin* 55 (April 1954): 2.

9. See, for example, Iversen, *The Communists and the Schools*, 332-358; Caute, *The Great Fear*, 403-430, and 431-445; Raywid, *The Ax-Grinders*, 158-160, *Defense Bulletin* 44 (May 1952): 5-7, Defense Bulletin 55 (April 1954): 2-3, and *Defense Commission*, "State of the Nation," 2-8.

10. Defense Commission *Report: Houston*, 38.

11. Defense Commission *Report: Houston*, 27.

12. Bainbridge, "Danger's Ahead in the Public Schools," n.p.

13. Caute, *The Great Fear*, 441.

14. For example, William Van Til observed, "The U. S. Office of Education in 1949 found the core curriculum [a centerpiece of progressive education practice] to be characteristic of only 3.5 per cent of junior and senior high schools queried." Van Til, "Research Affecting Education," in *Forces Affecting American Education*," ed. Van Til, 122. See also Zilversmit, *Changing Schools*, 119.

15. See Wesley, *NEA: The First Hundred Years*, 203.

16. Iversen, *The Communists and the Schools*, 246.

17. See Wesley, *NEA: The First Hundred Years*, 203, and Zilversmit, *Changing Schools*, 110.

18. *Addresses and Proceedings* (1949), 323.

19. Attention to the "three R's" or the "fundamentals" was very pronounced in the red scare period. See NEA Resolution 3, "Mid-Century Fundamentals," *Addresses and Proceedings* (1952), 160; NEA Resolution 5, "Mid-Century Fundamentals," *Addresses and Proceedings* (1953), 153; NEA Resolution 8, "Fundamentals of Instruction," *Addresses and Proceedings* (1954), 126.

20. See Murphy, *Blackboard Unions*, 182, and Iversen, *The Communists and the Schools*, 367.

21. For the explicit relationship between educational policy and practice and school funding, see Raywid, *The Ax-Grinders*, 157, 160; Murphy, *Blackboard Unions*, 182, and Zilversmit, *Changing Schools*, 118-120.

22. Examples of how the red scare affected school curriculum abound. See, for example, Kransdorf, *A Matter of Loyalty*, 33-34; Carleton, *Red Scare!* 172; *Forces Affecting American Education*, ed. Van Til, 202-203, and Raywid, *The Ax-Grinders*, 159.

23. Author William F. Buckley, Jr., for example, characterized the belief of many on the political right that "academic freedom" was a dangerous concept because it offered security to those teachers who wanted to "teach Socialism or urge Communism." "Academic Freedom Lauded, Called Hoax," *Worcester Daily Telegram*, November 22, 1952, newspaper reprint, box 1025, NEA Archives.

24. *Defense Bulletin* 55 (April 1954): 2.

25. Defense Commission, "State of the Nation," 5.

26. See Defense Commission *Report: Houston*, 44.

27. These subjects were identified as controversial in California by classroom teacher Frances Eisenberg. See Kransdorf, *A Matter of Loyalty*, 94.

28. For details of other communities, see, for example, Kransdorf, *A Matter of Loyalty*, 93-94; Raywid, *The Ax-Grinders*, 158-160, and Iversen, *The Communists and the Schools*, 259-260, 344-345.

29. Morse, "Who's Trying to Ruin Our Schools?" n.p.

30. *Addresses and Proceedings* (1952), 160.

31. Spaulding, "Textbooks Under Fire," PEDE (Philadelphia), 19.

32. Carleton, *Red Scare!* 173. See also Raywid, *The Ax-Grinders*, 160.

33. See *Addresses and Proceedings* (1949), 94-102.

34. The NEA adopted Hook's position. See, for example, the reasoning of John K. Norton, chairman of the NEA's Educational Policies Commission, *Addresses and Proceedings* (1949), 97.

35. Sidney Hook, "Should Communists Be Allowed to Teach?" *New York Times Magazine*, 27 February 1949, 7, 22-29, and Alexander Meiklejohn, "Should Communists Be Allowed to Teach?" *New York Times Magazine*, 27 March 1949, 10, 64-66.

36. *Addresses and Proceedings* (1949), 157.

37. The Educational Policies Commission was established jointly by the NEA and the American Association of School Administrators. See *Addresses and Proceedings* (1949), 94.

38. The resolution was accepted by a vote of 2,995 to 5.

39. *Addresses and Proceedings* (1949), 99.

40. *Addresses and Proceedings* (1949), 96.

41. *Addresses and Proceedings* (1949), 97.

42. *Addresses and Proceedings* (1953), 49.

43. *Addresses and Proceedings* (1949), 100.

44. *Addresses and Proceedings* (1949), 95.

45. *Addresses and Proceedings* (1949), 96.

46. See "Groups Affecting Education" in *Forces Affecting American Education*, ed. Van Til, 84.

47. Melby, *American Education Under Fire*, 32.

48. *Addresses and Proceedings* (1949), 157.

49. *Addresses and Proceedings* (1949), 119.

50. *Addresses and Proceedings* (1951), 324.

51. *Addresses and Proceedings* (1953), 14.

52. *Addresses and Proceedings* (1953), 33.

53. Carr was NEA executive secretary between 1953 and 1961.

54. *Addresses and Proceedings* (1953), 33.

55. *Addresses and Proceedings* (1951), 304.

56. See, for example, the opinions of teachers on the influence of the American Legion in Defense Commission, "State of the Nation," 4-5.

57. The article that most incensed NEA leaders was Irene Corbally Kuhn, "Your Child is Their Target," *The American Legion Magazine* (June 1952): 18.

58. See Wesley, *NEA: The First Hundred Years*, 316-320.

59. *Addresses and Proceedings* (1951), 57.

60. See *Addresses and Proceedings* (1950), 118-119; *Defense Bulletin* 33 (June 1950): 2-3, and *Defense Bulletin* 42 (March 1952): 3.

61. See, for example, *Addresses and Proceedings* (1950), 120 and *Addresses and Proceedings* (1952), 234.

62. *Addresses and Proceedings* (1950), 120.

63. For example, the NEA "endorsed and widely distributed" the Counter-Subversive Manual, published by the Americanism Commission and Counter-Subversive Activities Committee of the American Legion. *Addresses and Proceedings* (1955), 296.

64. West, *The National Education Association*, 68.

65. Murphy, *Blackboard Unions*, 182.

66. Murphy, *Blackboard Unions*, 183. The early wave of strikes that afflicted education in the 1940s was extensively reported in the December 1946 issue of the Defense Bulletin. See also "The St. Paul Story," *American Teacher* 31 (February 1947): 8-9; "Struck Buffalo," *Newsweek*, March 3, 1947, 22; "Teachers Strike," *Newsweek*, March 8, 1948, 80; "Teacher Strikes," *School and Society* 65 (April 1947): 277, and "A Teachers' Strike, " *American School Board Journal* 113 (October 1946): 54.

67. Murphy, *Blackboard Unions*, 183.

68. *Defense Bulletin* 19 (December 1946): 3.

69. *Defense Bulletin* 41 (December 1951): 7.

70. See *Addresses and Proceedings* (1950), 320.

71. See, for example, *Addresses and Proceedings* (1953), 159.

72. Zilversmit, *Changing Schools*, 108.

73. *Stewardship Report*, 25.

74. For the AFT's stance in this period, see, for example, Murphy, *Blackboard Unions*, 184-195; Kransdorf, *A Matter of Loyalty*, 24-26; Iversen, *The Communists and the Schools*, 208-222, and Schrecker, *No Ivory Tower*, 74-78.

75. For a comprehensive study of the insipid response of professional educational associations and their journals, see Morris, "Era of Anxiety," 259-320.

76. For further details of Myers' career in education, see *Addresses and Proceedings* (1948), 110.

77. See also Melby, "Dishonest and Unjustified," *NEA Journal* 40 (October 1951): 441

78. Wesley, *NEA: The First Hundred Years*, 349.

79. *Stewardship Report*, 14.

80. *Addresses and Proceedings*, (1949), 13.

81. See *Addresses and Proceedings*, (1941), 772-775.

82. The rapid growth in NEA membership compared favorably with that of the AFT. For example, in 1940 NEA membership was 203,000. In 1950, it soared to 454,000, and, in 1960, it reached 714,000. In contrast, the AFT rose gradually from 30,000 in 1940 to 41,000 in 1950, then to 59,000 in 1960. Murphy, *Blackboard Unions*, 277.

83. Wesley, *NEA: The First Hundred Years*, 314.

84. William S. Gray and William J. Iverson, "What Should be the Profession's Attitude Toward Lay Criticism of the Schools?" *The Elementary School Journal* 53 (September 1952): 2-6.

85. Scott and Hill eds., *Public Education Under Criticism*, 7.

86. Fine, as cited in *Forces Affecting American Education*, ed. Van Til, 193.

87. *Addresses and Proceedings* (1952), 338.

88. Defense Commission, "Study," 5.

89. Skaife, "Groups Affecting Education," in *Forces Affecting American Education*, ed. Van Til, 40.

90. Wesley, *NEA: The First Hundred Years,* 337.

91. *Defense Bulletin* 41 (December 1951): 1-2. These three purposes frequently were repeated in Defense Commission publications and *Defense Bulletins*.

Selected Bibliography

Books, Proceedings, Reports

Aronson, James. *The Press and the Cold War*. Indianapolis: Bobbs-Merrill, 1970.

Bayley, Edwin R. *Joe McCarthy and the Press*. Madison: University of Wisconsin Press, 1981.

Beineke, John A. *And There were Giants in the Land: The Life of William Heard Kilpatrick*. New York: Peter Lang, 1998.

Bell, Bernard Iddings. *Crisis in Education: A Challenge to American Complacency*. New York: McGraw-Hill, 1949.

Bell, Daniel, ed. *The New American Right*. New York: Criterion Books, 1955.

———, ed. *The Radical Right*. New York: Doubleday Anchor, 1964.

Benjamin, Harold [J. A. Peddiwell, pseud.]. *The Saber-Tooth Curriculum*. New York: McGraw-Hill, 1939.

Bestor, Arthur E. *Educational Wastelands: The Retreat from Learning in Our Public Schools*. Urbana, Illinois: University of Illinois, 1953.

———. *The Restoration of Learning*. New York: Alfred A. Knopf, 1955.

Brameld, Theodore, ed. *The Battle for Free Schools*. Boston: Beacon, 1951.

Carleton, Donald E. *Red Scare! Right Wing Hysteria, Fifties Fanaticism, and Their Legacy in Texas*. Austin: Texas Monthly Press, 1985.

Caute, David. *The Great Fear: The Anti-Communist Purge Under Truman and Eisenhower*. New York: Simon and Schuster, 1978.

Ceplair, Larry, and Steven Englund. *The Inquisition in Hollywood*. Garden City, NY: Doubleday, 1980.

Chodorov, Frank. *One is a Crowd*. New York: Devin-Adair Company, 1952.

Cochran, Bert. *Labor and Communism*. Princeton: Princeton University Press, 1977.

Cohen, Robert. *When the Old Left Was Young: Student Radicals and America's First Mass Student Movement, 1929-1941.* New York: Oxford University Press, 1993.

Cook, Fred J. *The Nightmare Decade: The Life and Times of Senator Joe McCarthy.* New York: Random House, 1971.

Counts, George S. *Dare The Schools Build A New Social Order?* New York: John Day, 1932.

Cremin, Lawrence A. *The Transformation of the School.* New York: Alfred A. Knopf, 1961.

Crosby, Donald F. *God, Church, and Flag: Senator Joseph R. McCarthy and the Catholic Church, 1950-1957.* Chapel Hill: University of North Carolina Press, 1978.

Diggins, John Patrick. *The American Left in the Twentieth Century.* New York: Harcourt, Brace, Jovanovich, 1973.

————. *The Proud Decades: America in War and Peace 1941-1960.* New York: Norton, 1988.

Draper, Theodore. *The Roots of American Communism.* New York: Viking Press, 1957.

Drucker, Peter. *The New Society: The Anatomy of an Industrial Order.* New York: Harper and Row, 1950.

Eaton, William E. *The American Federation of Teachers 1916-1961.* Carbondale, Illinois: Southern Illinois University Press, 1975.

Ehrenreich, Barbara. *Fear of Falling: The Inner Life of the Middle Class.* New York: Pantheon Books, 1989.

Fariello, Griffin. *Red Scare: Memories of American Inquisition.* New York: Norton, 1995.

Fine, Benjamin. *Our Children Are Cheated: The Crisis in American Education.* New York: Henry Holt, 1947.

Flynn, John T. *The Road Ahead: America's Creeping Revolution.* New York: Devin-Adair Co., 1949.

Forster, Arnold, and Epstein, Benjamin R. *Danger on the Right.* New York: Random House, 1964.

Franklin, Barry M. *Building the American Community: The School Curriculum and the Search for Social Control.* Philadelphia: The Falmer Press, 1986.

Fried, Richard M. *Men Against McCarthy.* New York: Columbia University Press, 1976.

———. *Nightmare in Red: The McCarthy Era in Perspective.* New York: Oxford University Press, 1990.

Galbraith, John Kenneth. *American Capitalism: The Concept of Countervailing Power.* Boston: Houghton Mifflin, 1952.

———. *The Affluent Society.* New York: The New American Library, Inc., 1958.

Gellhorn, Walter, ed. *The States and Subversion.* Ithaca, New York: Cornell University Press, 1952.

Goldman, Eric. *The Crucial Decade: America 1945-1955.* New York: Knopf, 1956.

Goulden, Joseph. *The Best Years: 1945-1950.* New York: Atheneum, 1976.

Griffith, Robert. *Politics of Fear: Joseph McCarthy and the Senate.* Lexington, Kentucky: University of Kentucky Press, 1970.

Griffith, Robert, and Athan Theoharis, eds. *The Specter: Original Essays on the Cold War and the Origins of McCarthyism.* New York: Franklin Watts Incorporated, 1974.

Halberstam, David. *The Fifties.* New York: Villard Books, 1993.

Hall, Gordon D. *The Hate Campaign Against the U. N.: One World Under Attack.* Boston: Beacon Press, 1952.

Hall, Stuart, and others. *Policing the Crisis: Mugging, the State, and Law and Order.* London: Macmillan, 1978.

Hodgson, Godfrey. *America in Our Time.* New York: First Vintage Books, 1978.

Hofstadter, Richard. *The Paranoid Style in American Politics and Other Essays.* London: Jonathan Cape, 1966.

House Select Committee on Lobbying Activities, Hearings, Part V Committee for Constitutional Government, Eighty-First Congress, 1950.

——— on Lobbying Activities, General Interim Report, Eighty-First Congress, 1950.

——— on Lobbying Activities, House Select Committee on Lobbying Activities. Report Number 3232: Conference of Small Business Organizations, Eighty-First Congress, 1950.

Hulburd, David. *This Happened in Pasadena.* New York: Macmillan, 1951.

Hutchins, Robert M. *The Conflict in Education in a Democratic Society.* New York: Harper and Brothers, 1953.

Iversen, Robert. *The Communists and the Schools*. New York: Harcourt, Brace, 1959.

Jones, Kitty, and Robert L. Olivier. *Progressive Education Is REDucation*. Boston: Meador, 1956.

Kaub, Verne P. *Communist — Socialist Propaganda in American Schools*. Boston: Meador, Co., 1953.

Keeran, Roger. *The Communist Party and the Auto Workers Union*. Urbana: University of Illinois Press, 1980.

Kellner, Douglas. *Television and the Crisis of Democracy*. Boulder, Colorado: Westview Press, 1990.

Kliebard, Herbert M. *The Struggle for the American Curriculum 1893-1958*. New York: Routledge, 1986.

Kransdorf, Martha. *A Matter of Loyalty: The Los Angeles School Board vs Frances Eisenberg*. San Francisco: Caddo Gap Press, 1994.

Lazarsfeld, Paul F., and Thielens, Wagner Jr., *The Academic Mind: Social Scientists in a Time of Crisis*. Glencoe: Free Press, 1958.

Leuchtenburg, William E. *A Troubled Feast*. New York: Bobbs-Merrill Company, 1979.

Levenstein, Harvey A. *Communism, Anti-Communism, and the CIO*. Westport, Conn.: Greenwood Press, 1981.

Lynd, Albert. *Quackery in the Public Schools*. Boston: Little, Brown, and Company, 1953.

MacDonald, J. Fred. *Television and the Red Menace: The Video Road to Vietnam*. New York: Praeger, 1985.

Markowitz, Ruth Jackson. *My Daughter, The Teacher: Jewish Teachers in the New York City Schools*. New Brunswick, NJ.: Rutgers University Press, 1993.

Matusow, Allen J., ed. *Joseph McCarthy*. Englewood Cliffs, New Jersey: Prentice Hall, 1970.

McAuliffe, Mary S. *Crisis on the Left: Cold War Politics and American Liberals*. Amherst: University of Massachusetts Press, 1978.

Melby, Ernest O. *American Education Under Fire: The Story of the Three-R Fight*. New York: Anti-Defamation League of B'nai B'rith, 1951.

―――. *The Education of Free Men*. Pittsburgh: The University of Pittsburgh Press, 1955.

Melby, Ernest O., and Morton Puner. *Freedom and Public Education.* New York: Praeger, 1953.

Murphy, Marjorie. *Blackboard Unions: The AFT and the NEA 1900-1980.* Ithaca, New York: Cornell University Press, 1990.

National Education Association of the United States. *Journal of Proceedings and Addresses of the Annual Meeting.* Washington, D.C.: NEA, 1941-1955.

————. *Handbook of the National Education Association.* Washington, D.C.: NEA, 1955.

Navasky, Victor. *Naming Names.* New York: Viking Press, 1980.

Nelson, Jack E., and Gene Roberts, Jr. *The Censors and the Schools.* Boston: Little, Brown, and Company, 1963.

Oakley, J. Ronald. *God's Country: America in the Fifties.* New York: Dembner Books, 1986.

O'Reilly, Kenneth. *Hoover and the Un-Americans.* Philadelphia: Temple University, 1983.

Oshinsky, David. *A Conspiracy So Immense.* New York: Free Press, 1983.

Parenti, Michael. *The Anti-Communist Impulse.* New York: Random House, 1969.

————. *Inventing Reality: The Politics of News Media.* New York: St. Martin's Press, 1993.

Ravitch, Diane. *The Troubled Crusade: American Education 1945-1980.* New York: Basic Books, 1983.

Raywid, Mary Ann. *The Ax-Grinders.* New York: The Macmillan Company, 1962.

Reeves, Thomas C. *McCarthyism.* Hinsdale, Illinois: The Dryden Press, 1973.

————. *The Life and Times of Joe McCarthy: A Biography.* New York: Stein and Day, 1982.

Rogin, Paul Michael. *The Intellectuals and McCarthy: The Radical Specter.* Cambridge, Massachusetts: The M. I. T. Press, 1967.

Rovere, Richard H. *Senator Joe McCarthy.* New York: Harcourt, Brace, and Co., 1959.

Sanders, Jane. *Cold War on the Campus.* Seattle: University of Washington Press, 1979.

Schlesinger, Arthur M., Jr. *The Vital Center: Politics of Freedom.* Boston: Houghton Mifflin Company, 1949.

Schrecker, Ellen W. *No Ivory Tower: McCarthyism and the Universities.* New York: Oxford University Press, 1986.

Scott, C. Winfield, and Clyde M. Hill, eds. *Public Education Under Criticism.* New York: Prentice Hall, 1954.

Smith, Mortimer. *And Madly Teach: A Layman Looks at Public School Education.* Chicago: Henry Regnery Company, 1949.

―――. *The Diminished Mind.* Chicago: Henry Regnery Company, 1954.

Spring, Joel H. *Education and the Rise of the Corporate State.* Boston: Beacon Press, 1972.

Steinberg, Peter L. *The Great "Red Menace": United States Prosecution of American Communists, 1947-1952.* Westport, Conn.: Greenwood Press, 1984.

Stouffer, Samuel A. *Communism, Conformity, and Civil Liberties.* Garden City, New York: Doubleday, 1955.

Thayer, V. T. *American Education Under Fire.* New York: Harper and Brothers Publishers, 1944.

―――. *Public Education and Its Critics.* New York: Macmillan, 1954.

Theoharis, Athan. *Seeds of Repression: Harry S. Truman and the Origins of McCarthyism.* Chicago: Quadrangle, 1971.

―――. *Spying on Americans.* Philadelphia: Temple University Press, 1981.

Tyack, David B. *The One Best System: A History of American Urban Education.* Cambridge, Massachusetts: Harvard University Press, 1974.

Van Til, William, ed. *Forces Affecting American Education.* Association for Supervision and Curriculum Development, 1953 Yearbook. Washington, D.C.: National Education Association, 1953.

―――. *My Way of Looking At It: An Autobiography.* Terre Haute, Indiana: Lake Lure Press, 1983.

Wesley, Edgar B. *NEA: The First Hundred Years, The Building of the Teaching Profession.* New York: Harper and Brothers, 1957.

West, Allan M. *The National Education Association: The Power Base for Education.* New York: Free Press, 1980.

Woodring, Paul. *Let's Talk Sense About Our Schools.* New York: McGraw-Hill, 1953.

Zilversmit, Arthur. *Changing Schools: Progressive Education Theory and Practice, 1930-1960.* Chicago: The University of Chicago Press, 1993.

Zinn, Howard. *Post War America 1945-1971.* Indianapolis: Bobbs-Merrill, 1973.

———. *A People's History of the United States.* New York: Harper and Row, 1980.

Articles

Allen, Raymond B. "Communists Should Not Teach in American Colleges." *Educational Forum* 13 (May 1949): 443-441.

Anderson, Archibald W. "The Charges Against American Education: What is the Evidence?" *Progressive Education* 29 (January 1952): 91-105.

———. "The Cloak of Respectability." *Progressive Education* 29 (January 1952): 69-70, 79-80.

Armstrong, O. K. "Treason in the Textbooks." *American Legion Magazine* (September 1940): 8-9, 51, 70-72.

Axtelle, George E. "Should Communists Teach in American Universities?" *Educational Forum* 13 (May 1949): 425-433.

Bainbridge, John. "Danger's Ahead in the Public Schools." *McCall's* (October 1952): 56-61.

Benjamin, Harold. "Report on the Enemy." *Virginia Journal of Education* 44 (September 1950): 23-24.

Berninghausen, David K. "A Policy to Preseve Free Public Education." *Harvard Educational Review* 21 (Summer 1951): 138-154.

Bestor, Arthur. "'Life-adjustment' education: A Critique." *Bulletin of the American Association of University Professors* 38 (1952): 413-441.

———. "Anti-Intellectualism in the Schools." *New Republic*, January 19, 1953, 11-13.

Brickman, William W. "Attack and Counterattack in American Education." *School and Society* 74 (October 1951): 262-269.

Brown, JoAnne. "A is for Atom, B is for Bomb! Civil Defense in American Education 1948-1963." *Journal of American History* 75 (June 1988): 68-90.

Buchanan, Frank. "Lobbying and its Influence on the Public Schools." *The Nation's Schools* 48 (July 1951): 23-27.

Burton, William H. "Get the Facts: Both Ours and the Other Fellows!" *Progressive Education* 29 (January 1952): 89.

Carleton, Donald E. "McCarthyism in Local Elections: The Houston School Board Election of 1952." *Houston Review* 3 (Winter 1981): 169.

———. "McCarthyism Was More Than McCarthy: Documenting the Red Scare at the State and Local Level." *The Midwestern Archivist* 12 (1987): 13-19.

———. "McCarthyism in Houston: The George Ebey Affair." *Southwestern Historical Quarterly* 80 (October 1986): 174-176.

Case, Gilbert E. "Quackery in the Public Schools: An Answer." *The Atlantic Monthly* 185 (June 1950): 57-60.

Caswell, Hollis L. "The Great Reappraisal of Public Education." *Teachers College Record* 54 (October 1952): 12-22.

Chodorov, Frank. "Educators Should be Warned by the Pasadena Revolt." *Saturday Evening Post,* July 14, 1951, 10.

Commager, Henry Steele. "Our Schools Have Kept Us Free." *Life*, October 16, 1950.

Conant, James B. "The Superintendent Was the Target." *The New York Times Book Review*, April 29, 1951, 1, 27.

Cousins, Norman. "The Public School Critics." *The Saturday Review of Literature* 34 (September 1951): 1.

Crain, Lucille Cardin. "What Are Our Schools Teaching About Business?" *Vital Speeches of the Day* 16 (August 1950): 657-660.

Cremin, Lawrence A. "The Curriculum Maker and his Critics: A Persistent American Problem." *Teachers College Record* 54 (February 1953): 234-245.

Crockett, Ann L. "Lollipops vs. Learning: A High School Teacher Speaks Out." *Saturday Evening Post*, March 16, 1940, 29, 105-106.

Crosby, Otis A. "The Nation Reaches a Verdict in the Case of the People vs. the Schools." *Nation's Schools* 47 (January 1951): 34-37.

Darland, D. D. "To Some Freedom of Thought is Subversive." *Phi Delta Kappan* 30 (December 1948): 109.

Dixon, John. "What's Wrong With U.S. History?" *The American Legion Magazine* (May 1949): 15-16.

"The Donald DuShane Memorial Defense Fund." *NEA Journal* 39 (February 1950): 123.

Editorial. "Congressional Committee Doubts Reliability of CASBO." *Nation's Schools* 51 (March 1951): 30.

Editorial. "Earmarks of a 'Front' Organization." *Nation's Schools* 47 (April 1951): 29-30.

Editorial. "P. E. Gets Kicked Around." *Nation's Schools* 49 (February 1952): 33-34.

Editorial. "Who Speaks for the Legion?" *Nation's Schools* 50 (August 1952): 28.

Eklund, John. "We Must Fight Back." *The American Federationist* 59 (January 1952): 14-15.

Fay, Lewis C. "Abolish Public Schools." *Nation's Schools* 50 (August 1952): 31-36.

Flynn, John T. "Who Owns Your Child's Mind?" *The Reader's Digest* 59 (October 1951): 23-28.

Fosdick, Harry A. "The Counterattack Starts in the Classroom." *School and Community* 37 (October 1951): 338-341.

Fraser, Hugh Russell. "In Defense of the Critics of American Public Education." *School and Society* 74 (October 1951): 261-262.

Fuller, Harry J. "The Emperor's New Clothes, Or Prius Dementat." *The Scientific Monthly* 72 (January 1951): 32-41.

Gould, Kenneth M. "The Scarsdale Story." *The Humanist* 4 (1952): 145-159.

Gray, William S., and William J. Iverson, "What Should be the Profession's Attitude Toward Lay Criticism of the Schools?" *The Elementary School Journal* 53 (September 1952): 2-6.

Hand, Harold C. "A Scholar's Documentation." *Educational Theory* 4 (January 1954): 27-48.

Harding, Lowry W. "How Well Are the Schools Now Teaching the Basic Skills?" *Progressive Education* 29 (January 1952): 7-14, 32.

Henderson, Kenneth B., and Harold C. Hand. "To What Extent Is the General Public in Sympathy with the Current Attacks on the Schools?" *Progressive Education* 29 (January 1952): 110-113.

Henry, George H. "Alas! The Poor Superintendent." *Harper's Magazine* 193 (November 1946): 434-441.

Hook, Sidney. "Should Communists Be Allowed to Teach?" *New York Times Magazine*, February 27, 1949, 7, 22-29.

————. "What Shall We Do About Communist Teachers?" *Saturday Evening Post*, September 10, 1949, 43;

Hullfish, H. Gordon. "The Profession and the Public Face a Common Problem." *Educational Research Bulletin* 30 (May 1951): 115.

Kaplan, Louis. "The Attacks on Modern Education." *Phi Delta Kappan* 32 (January 1951): 223-226.

Kandel, Isaac, L. "The Challenge of Pasadena." *School and Society* 72 (December 1950): 72.

————. "The Defense of American Schools." *School and Society* 74 (August 1951): 123-124.

————. "To Meet the Attacks on the Schools." *School and Society* 75 (May 1952): 299.

————. "We Must Educate Our Masters." *School and Society* 76 (July 1952): 44.

Kaub, Verne. "A Critic." *Saturday Review of Literature* 35 (April 1952): 16-17, 57.

Kennan, Richard Barnes. "Education — Democracy's Best Defense." *Educational Leadership* 8 (May 1951): 458-461.

————. "No Ivory Tower For You." *NEA Journal* 40 (May 1951): 317-318.

————. "What Are They Calling You Today?" *Childhood Education* 28 (October 1951): 53-57.

Kuhn, Irene Corbally. "Your Child is Their Target." *The American Legion Magazine* (June 1952): 18-19, 53-60.

Larsen, Roy E. "A Layman's View of the Importance of Public Education to Our Society." *The Educational Forum* 16 (May 1952): 389-397.

"The Legal Status of the Public School Teacher." *NEA Research Bulletin* 25 (April 1947): 26-71.

Long, Stuart. "Thunder on the Right." *The Reporter* 3 (June 1950): 11-13.

Lynd, Albert. "Quackery in the Public Schools." *Atlantic Monthly* 185 (March 1950): 33-38.

———. "Who Wants Progressive Education?" *Atlantic Monthly* 191 (April 1953): 29-34.

McCloskey, Gordon. "Meeting Attacks on Public Education." *Progressive Education* 29 (January 1952): 119-122.

McWilliams, Carey. "The Enemy in Pasadena." *The Christian Century* 68 (January 1951): 11-13.

Meiklejohn, Alexander. "Should Communists Be Allowed to Teach?" *New York Times Magazine*, March 27, 1949, 10, 64-66.

Melbo, Irving R. "What Can School Board Members Do to Answer Criticism of Public Education?" *The American School Board Journal* 122 (May 1951): 27-28, 86.

Melby, Ernest O. "Dishonest and Unjustified." *NEA Journal* 40 (October 1951): 441-442.

———. "Leadership in an Age of Anxiety." *Phi Delta Kappan* 24 (June 1953): 381-386.

Meyer, Agnes. "The Hub of the Wheel." *NEA Journal* 41 (May 1952): 277.

Morris, Robert C. "Thunder of the Right: Past and Present." *Education* 99 (Winter 1978): 167-171.

———. "The Right Wing Critics of Education: Yesterday and Today." *Educational Leadership* 35 (May 1978): 624-629.

Morse, Arthur D. "Who's Trying to Ruin Our Schools?" *McCall's* 78 (September 1951): 102, 108-109.

National Commission for the Defense of Democracy Through Education. "Charter for Teachers." *NEA Journal* 39 (October 1950): 526.

———. "The Public School and the American Heritage." *Harvard Educational Review* 21 (Summer 1951): 137.

Pesognelli, Mary Ann. "The Erosion of Freedom." *NEA Journal* 40 (May 1951): 321-322.

Rice, Arthur H. "Teachers Mobilize to Strike Back at Organized Attacks on Public Education at the NEA Convention." *Nation's Schools* 48 (August 1951): 70.

"Salaries and Salary Schedules of City-School Employees, 1948-49." *NEA Research Bulletin* 27 (April 1949): 43-72.

"Salaries of City School Employees, 1940-41." *NEA Research Bulletin* 19 (March 1941): 67-97.

"School Board vs. Communism in Schools." *American School Board Journal* 126 (June 1953): 54.

Schrecker, Ellen W. "Academic Freedom and the Cold War." *Antioch Review* 38 (Summer 1980): 313-327.

———. "Archival Sources for the Study of McCarthyism." *Journal of American History* 75 (June 1988): 197-207.

———. "The McCarthy Era Blacklisting of School Teachers, College Professors and other Public Employees." *Journal of American History* 81 (June 1994): 360-61.

Sheerin, John B. "What Was the Question at Pasadena?" *The Catholic World* 174 (October 1951): 1-5

Skaife, Robert A. "They Sow Distrust." *Nation's Schools* 47 (January 1951): 27-30.

———. "They Oppose Progress." *Nation's Schools* 47 (February 1951): 31-33.

———. "They Want Tailored Schools." *Nation's Schools* 47 (May 1951): 35-37.

———. "Know the Enemy." *Connecticut Teacher* (December 1951): 68-71.

———. "Congressional Probes Into Education." *Nation's Schools* 51 (April 1953): 48-50.

———. "The Sound and the Fury." *Phi Delta Kappan* 24 (June 1953): 358.

———. "The Conflict Continues." *Nation's Schools* 53 (March 1954): 45.

Smith, Mortimer B. "Who Criticizes Public Schools?" *Christian Century* 48 (June 1951): 736-738.

———. "The Failure of American Education." *The Freeman* 68 (December 1951): 137-139.

Spaulding, William B. "Academic Freedom." *Progressive Education* 28 (February 1951): 111-117.

"The St. Paul Story." *American Teacher* 31 (February 1947): 8-9.

"Teacher Personnel Procedures: Employment Conditions in Service." *NEA Research Bulletin* 20 (March 1942): 83-116.

"Teacher Personnel Procedures: Selection and Appointment." *NEA Research Bulletin* 20 (March 1942): 50-79.

"A Teachers' Strike." *American School Board Journal* 113 (October 1946): 54.

"Teacher Strikes." *School and Society* 65 (April 1947): 277.

Trow, William Clark. "Professional Education and the Disciplines: An Open Letter to Professor Bestor." *Scientific Monthly* 76 (March 1953): 149-152.

———. "Academic Utopia?" *Educational Theory* 4 (January 1954): 1-11.

Van Loan, W. L. "In Times Like These What Should Teachers Do?" *NEA Journal* 41 (January 1952): 35-36.

"What U. S. Thinks About Its Schools — Roper Survey Finds Both Complacency and Dissatisfaction." *Life*, October 16, 1950, 11-18.

Woodring, Paul. "An Open Letter to Teachers." *Harper's Magazine* 205 (July 1952): 28-32.

Unpublished Sources

Carleton, Donald E. "A Crisis in Rapid Change: The Red Scare in Houston." Ph.D. diss., University of Houston, 1978.

Marden, David L. "The Cold War and American Education." Ph.D. diss., University of Kansas, 1975.

Morris, Robert C. "Era of Anxiety: An Historical Account of the Effects of and Reactions to Right Wing Forces Affecting Education during the Years 1949-1954." Ph.D. diss., Indiana State University, 1976.

Skaife, Robert A. "An Evaluation of the Program of the National Commission for the Defense of Democracy Through Education." Ph.D. diss., University of Maryland, 1951.

Vedries, Ellen C. "Riding the Red Tide: The AF of T and Los Angeles Local 430." Unpublished paper presented at the annual meeting of the American Educational Research Association, San Francisco, April 1995.

Manuscript Collection

National Education Association Archives. Located in Springfield, Virginia. Accessed via the National Education Association Headquarters, 16th and M Streets, N.W., Washington, D.C.

Index

Democrat, 14, 23, 28-33, 40- 92, 96, 109, 118, 127-131, 148, 149, 185, 188
Denmark, 28
Denver (Co), 6, 104, 142, 143, 150
Department of Classroom Teachers, 108
Detroit (MI), 77, 95, 135, 182, 185
Dewey, John, 59, 64, 76, 148
Dies Committee, 28
Dies, Martin, 86
Dilworth, Nelson, 74, 169, 170
Dixon, John, 76
Dodd, Bella, 18, 89
Dondero, George A., 54
Douglas (Justice), 129
Drucker, Peter, 11
du Pont, Lammot, 73
"Duck and Cover," 17
Durkin, Martin, 13
DuShane, Donald, 2, 28, 34-37, 45, 46, 53, 197
DuShane Memorial Defense Fund, 46

Eastman Kodak, 72
Ebey, George, 162, 163, 181, 182
Economic Council Letter, 72
Education Forum, The, 148
Education or Indoctrination, 70
Educational Guardian, 64, 65
Educational Leadership, 197
Educational Policies Commission, 127, 187, 189
Educational Reviewer, 93, 94, 95, 96, 97, 98, 99
Educational Wastelands, 59
Educator-Lay Conferences, 49, 50, 109, 139, 140, 159, 177, 199, 203
Ehrenreich, Barbara, 11
Eisenberg, Frances, 19, 88, 181
Eisenhower, Dwight D., 11, 13, 14, 187
Elizabeth (NJ), 37
Ellison, Lucile, 148

Emmert, W. L., 159
Employers Association of Chicago, 53
Engelman, Finis E., 131
Englewood (NJ), 4, 65, 101, 185
Essex, Martin, 128
Eugene (OR), 4
Europe, 12, 18, 28, 32

Fay, Lewis C., 79, 80
FBI, 16, 76, 86, 89
Federal Aid to Education, 3, 21, 69, 71, 72, 75, 122, 124, 161
Feinberg Law, 129
Female Teachers, 48
Ferndale (MI) 149
Fifth Amendment, 87, 90
Fine, Benjamin, 100, 201
Florida, 66, 79, 99, 134, 159
Flynn, John T., 53, 70, 71, 77, 81, 99
Forces Affecting American Education, 9, 71, 127, 149
Fosdick, Harry, 151
Foundation for Economic Freedom, 112
France, 19, 28, 88, 181
Frank, Kate, 37, 45
Frankfurter, Felix, 62
Fraser, Hugh Russell, 166
Freedman, Benjamin, 73
Freedom Club of Chicago, 112
Freedom Newspapers Inc., 79
Freuhauf Trailer Company, 54
Friends of the Public Schools, 52, 68, 69, 98, 179, 196
Fries, General Amos A., 52, 68, 77, 179, 196, 199
Fuchs, Klaus, 7

Gailbraith, John Kenneth 12
Gallup Poll, 1, 6
Gannett, Frank, 69
Gardiner (ME), 42
General Motors Corporation, 13, 72